SHREWSBURY

Millennium Essays

CHARTA MISSIONARIA ANGLIA

Published in 1826 with the *Ordo* for
Divine Office.   + indicates Mission
Centres and * indicates Seminaries.
The contrast between Shropshire/
Cheshire/North Wales and their
neighbouring counties is notable.

Northumberland

Cumberland

Durham

Westmoreland

York

I. Man

Lancashire

I. Anglesea

Flint

Derby

Cheshire

Nottingham

Carnarvon

Montgomery

Salop

Stafford

Leicester

Warwick

Cardigan

Radnor

Worcester

Pembroke

Hereford

Carmarthen

Brecknock

Glocester

Oxford

Monmouth

SHREWSBURY

Millennium Essays

for a Catholic Diocese

◆ ◆ ◆

edited by John P. Marmion

DOWNSIDE ABBEY

Dedicated in Thanksgiving for the Millennium of
Our Saviour's Birth and for the Jubilee of the
Foundation of the Diocese,
this volume is presented to

The Right Reverend Brian Michael Noble
Tenth Bishop of Shrewsbury

with gratitude for the blessing and encouragement which he
has given to the project from its inception.

Downside Abbey Books
Stratton on the Fosse
Bath, England, BA3 4RH

British Library Cataloguing in Publication Data:
A catalogue record of this book is available from
the British Library.

ISBN 1-898663-13-0

Typeset at Downside Abbey, Bath
Printed by Hobbs the Printers, Totton, Hampshire SO40 3WX

CONTENTS

LIST OF ILLUSTRATIONS

The Protestant Reformation of the sixteenth century brought to an end the unity of the medieval *Ecclesia Anglicana* with the Church Universal. Although the new church order was gradually accepted by a majority of the population, there never lacked a faithful remnant who gave their allegiance in matters spiritual to the See of Rome and, over the years of hostility and persecution which followed, this small community developed a distinctive and cohesive identity of its own. In the years prior to the nineteenth century it was served by some 6000 individual priests, 'as proud to be English Catholics as they were to be Roman Catholics', many of whom suffered imprisonment and even martyrdom for their courage, and these in turn were guided and ruled, first by a single 'arch-priest' and later by regional 'vicars apostolic' — missionary bishops who kept a low public profile as they travelled almost continuously in the service of their priests and their poor, scattered flocks.

The passage of time and the influence of a variety of factors, not least the European Enlightenment, the French Revolution and the politics of Ireland, led to a more tolerant attitude towards English Catholics and a number of Relief Acts were passed by Parliament culminating in virtually full Catholic 'Emancipation', or freedom from restriction, in 1829. During the first half of the nineteenth century, the Catholic population in England, and especially in the North West, grew rapidly, mainly because of the influx of famine-stricken Irish workers for employment in the ever-expanding industries. At the same time the 'Oxford Movement' and the conversion of several prominent Anglicans, notably the future Cardinals Newman and Manning, gave the bishops both at home and in Rome sufficient confidence in the future to propose the restoration of a national hierarchy of diocesan bishops and this was brought about on 29th September 1850. Thirteen new dioceses covering England and Wales were established that day by the Apostolic Letter *Universalis Ecclesiae* of Pope Plus IX and among these was Shrewsbury.

This new Diocese of Shrewsbury was unique in being formed from parts of three of the old apostolic vicariates and viii

was arguably the most varied in character, encompassing, in addition to the whole of Shropshire and Cheshire, the six northern counties of Wales. However, in 1895 a Vicariate of Wales (not to be confused with the old Welsh District) was formed and, after two somewhat unsatisfactory years, this became the Diocese of Menevia. Thus it is that the stable basis of the Diocese of Shrewsbury has ever been the counties of Shropshire and Cheshire of which the latter came to have the larger proportion of Catholic residents, prompting a move of the administrative centre to Birkenhead in 1882.

It is the story of this diocese, and the desire to mark its one hundred and fiftieth anniversary, which has inspired the essays which make up the book. It is not a systematic history, but a reflection upon various aspects of life and development in the diocese over the years.

The editor and publisher join in thanking the contributors for making available the fruit of their research. Our thanks also go out to the Bishop of Shrewsbury, The Rt Revd Brian Noble, and to the Trustees and officials who have so generously supported us with both encouragement and practical assistance.

Special thanks is due to those whose copyright material has been included in this work, in particular: the Editors of *Recusant History* and of *Cheshire History* for permission to use or re-work articles which have appeared in their journals and to Canon Francis Pullen, Administrator of Shrewsbury Cathedral, for permission to use the drawing of the cathedral by Ken Whelan and for the extended loan of archival material relating to the history of the cathedral and of the diocese.

INTRODUCTION

RECUSANT ROOTS: FROM DISSOLUTION TO RESURRECTION

J.P. Marmion

The aim of this introductory essay is to take a brief glance over the three or more centuries before the establishment of the Diocese to set the scene for 1850. The Diocese at its inception covered the old boundaries of Cheshire, Shropshire, and a generous share of North Wales. It is proposed to restrict attention to the two counties. Some themes can be introduced which other essays in this book will carry forward. It is not at present possible to write a full history of recusancy in the two counties, but there is a good introduction to the Elizabethan period in Cheshire by K.R. Wark, and William Price did a doctoral thesis (unpublished) on Shropshire recusancy. There was an article resulting from this, 'Three Priests at Plowden in the Eighteenth Century', in the *Diocesan Year Book*, and in *Recusant History*.[1]

This article will look at the scene on the eve of the Reformation, then the dissolution of the religious houses; Catholic Recusancy in Cheshire and Shropshire, with a glance at some relics of this past. Then attention turns to recusant devotions of the past, and the significance of this tradition,

then Catholic Emancipation and finally the return of the
religious.

The Eve of the Reformation

There is some suggestion of Celtic missionaries in the Wirral
peninsula, and there was a large Celtic monastery at
Bangor-is-y-coed. Many of these monks were massacred at
the battle of Chester about 615. But all the foundations
which really covered Cheshire and Shropshire were made
after the Conquest. There were nearly one hundred if you
include monastic granges, cells (such as Hilbre), centres for
the Knights Templar and the Knights Hospitaller, hospitals,
secular colleges and schools.[2] The Black Monks,
(Benedictines) were to be found at Birkenhead Priory and St
Werburgh's Abbey, Chester, in Shrewsbury and Much
Wenlock. Cistercians had been at Combermere and then at
the great Vale Royal Abbey and at Buildwas. These were the
White Monks. The Augustinian Canons were at Norton
Priory in the north and Lilleshall and Haughmond to the
south. There had once been Premonstratensians at
Warburton, but in 1271 they moved to Cockersand.
Dominicans were at both Chester and Shrewsbury, and
likewise the Franciscans who in addition were in Bridgenorth.
Carmelite Friars were in Chester and Ludlow while the Austin
Friars were in Ludlow, Shrewsbury and Woodhouse. The
nuns were Benedictine in Chester and Augustinian in
Brewood. It was never more than a day's walk from one
religious house to another. A monk of Wenlock had been a
widely read author of a vision of hell, and John Mirk, a canon
of Lilleshall about 1405 had collected 74 sermons together
with a refutation of contemporary errors of the Lollards, now
known as *Mirk's Festial*. His other work *Instructions to Parish
Priests* covered an outline of material on faith and tradition,
the commandments and the sacraments. The life of the
monasteries flowed out into the counties, and influenced the
devotions in church and chapel. By the time of Henry VIII
there was a thousand years of religious tradition which

permeated society, influenced the life of the gilds and was part and parcel of every day life. H.O.Evenett has noted that in most ages the state of the religious orders provides a good test of the state of religion elsewhere. Certainly on the eve of the Reformation they provided the flavour of the Christian life in the land. From the time of Augustine and Bede down to the early days of Henry VIII they set a style for singing in church, praying and the background to many devotions. The spirituality of the land was monastic in its origin and much of its expression.

The Dissolution of the Monasteries

The Bishop of Rochester, the saintly John Fisher, warned his fellow clerics in Convocation that 'the fort is betrayed even by those who should have defended it'. They compromised weakly with the King, no doubt thinking that matters would soon right themselves. The monasteries began to fall one by one. St Werburgh's Chester had never been one of the richer houses and when in 1536 Parliament vested all monastic possessions in the Crown, Cromwell arranged for some of the revenues to revert so that it could become a cathedral. The Prior of the monastery was to be the Dean of the new cathedral, but he died within a month of appointment. The sub-dean was not a former monk but a Grey-friar, and he lived on until 1574 to see further changes.[3] The lesser houses were the first to be taken: Birkenhead Priory in 1536, the abbeys in 1538 like Lilleshall, Chester in 1537 but Shrewsbury only in 1540. By then virtually all the monastic and religious houses had ceased, and some of the hospitals like Battlefield and Bridgenorth too, not to mention the secular colleges at Bridgenorth, Burford, Newport, Pontesbury and Tong. This is not an exhaustive list but a suggestion as to how the spiritual landscape was changing dramatically. The Act of 1536 for the suppression of the lesser monasteries was unusual in having a preamble full of propaganda to justify the pillage of these houses and the taking of their property; they were places of 'carnal and abominable living' and, it was incautiously suggested, a contrast to the 'great solemn Monasteries of this Realm wherein (thanks be to God) Religion is right well kept and observed'. However four years later this telling phrase was forgotten when royal avarice plundered the greater religious houses as well. No excuse was really offered when it came to the chantries, hospitals and schools. On occasions when popular opinion was heard about all this, like the 'Pilgrimage of Grace', the restitution of the religious houses was part of the demands of the people.[4]

While there was some restoration under Mary Tudor in London, there does not seem to have been a revival of any religious house in either Cheshire or Shropshire. The one exception to this would seem to be the establishment of the Knights Hospitaller in Halston, Shropshire which was refounded.[5] There is probably an interesting history here to be explored. With the Act of Uniformity of 1559, however, religious life in England was again to cease. The Marian Hierarchy was not for compromise. Bishop Scott of Chester spoke out strongly twice in Parliament against the Bill. He noted of the old Hierarchy that most, before they died, were penitent and 'those who do still live have openly revoked the same'. The Marian Hierarchy were all deprived between May and November in 1559. Scott refused the oath in June and was for a while in the Fleet prison. He escaped to the Continent in 1563 to die in Louvain in October 1564.[6]

The Reaction of the Clergy in 1559

What about the priests and religious? In Cheshire most seem to have remained at their posts with whatever misgivings they had. Some are known to have gone missing and some turn up again later as recusant priests. Most probably followed *The Book of Common Prayer* but some will have reverted to the old Mass on the side. An example of this sort of reaction may be seen in John Chapman (not from Cheshire) once a parson in Dorset who left his parish 'without resignation or making anyone privy of his parish that he would depart'; but he turned up at the English College in Rheims, came back to England and was captured in 1582. Haigh, in his study of Lancashire, has suggested that most of the clergy were reluctant to change again, and were 'cryptopapists', possibly adapting the Anglican service to Catholic tastes. Wark, in his study of Cheshire, is able to identify some of the Marian priests who went missing.

There is a long-standing debate about the numbers involved.[7] Fuller, an eminent historian, suggested a maximum of 180 across the whole country. Henry Gee thought over 200. Elton and Powicke prefer a total of 300. Norbert Birt thought a much higher figure was correct, reckoning that between 370 and 600 of the Northern Province alone departed, which would suggest a thousand over the country. C.W.Field has looked at the Province of Canterbury and lists 430 as ejected and another 200 as having resigned.[8] The influence of the Marian clergy is important. With the Act of Establishment in place in 1559, it was 1574 before any 'seminary priests' arrived in England, and another decade before they were here in any number. The Jesuits did not arrive until 1580 and while authors have written of a Jesuit invasion, this is either a compliment to the reputation of the Jesuits or a monument to the enduring influence of Foxe and his *Book of Martyrs*. Professor Patrick McGrath and his colleagues found the Marian clergy significant for the establishment of recusancy.[9]

Wark is able to offer in an appendix a list of forty priests in Elizabethan days who either came from Cheshire or worked for a time in the county. He mentions Richard Bannister as an 'old priest' which, in the documents of the time, meant a Marian priest; John Bushell, former chantry priest of Bunbury; John Culpage (or Coppage), an old priest; Richard Hatton, a Marian priest who was deprived; Thomas Houghton, from Wrenbury; John Maddocks, another old priest; John Morwen (or Murren), who disappeared; Richard Sutton, an old priest and prisoner in Chester Castle and William Worthington, an old priest.[10] Cheshire men need to be distinguished from those in Lancashire, where recusancy was to prove much stronger. An early Bishop of Chester described Lancashire as 'a sink of popery'!

To survey the period up to 1800, the number of recusant priests ordained in the sixteenth century is Cheshire 11, Shropshire 9; with an increase in the seventeenth century to Cheshire 24, Shropshire 39; and decreasing in the eighteenth century to Cheshire 14 and Shropshire 22. This gives a strong lead to Shropshire with 70 against 49 from Cheshire. In terms of 'religious' the list includes a Dominican and a Franciscan, four Benedictines and fourteen Jesuits for Cheshire; the rest being seculars. In Shropshire apart from one Carmelite Friar the rest who were not seculars were a dozen Benedictines, fourteen Jesuits and a single Carthusian. These figures raise interesting questions as to which families produced these vocations, who sheltered the priests when they were working in the two counties and where they were educated.[11]

Recusant Homes and Families

The names of recusant families like the Plowdens and the Stanleys are well known and deserve to be studied in some detail. But other families too were loyal to the old faith and many of these have yet to be researched. In some known cases in the country, male members became 'church-going papists' because of the crippling fines for recusancy, while the female members supported the hunted priests and kept the faith alive. Wark has an interesting account of Lady Egerton, who had a Catholic chaplain who managed to remain nameless, and Lady Warburton, at Congleton, who was keeping an old (ie: Marian) priest who calls himself Watkenes (*sic*) but the document claims is really Wyllyam Worthyngton.[12] If a lot of the picture here is hidden, the story of the colleges and monasteries abroad is much more clear.

Recusancy Abroad

A Lancashire priest, William Allen, later a Cardinal, founded a college at Douai for the Catholic exiles which was initially intended to train a group of priests for the next change in religion in England. But, though this was the intention in 1568, when the first group of four priests were ordained in 1573 they chose to come to England and accept the risk of working under cover. Four came in the following year, seven in 1575, eighteen in 1576, fifteen in 1577, twenty in 1578, twenty the following year and twenty nine in 1580. The number of secular priests coming to England before the arrival of the first two Jesuits in 1580 was about one hundred.[13] A whole series of colleges abroad followed, one in Rome, based on an ancient Anglo-Saxon hospice for English pilgrims, others in Paris, Lisbon, Valladolid, Seville, Madrid and San Lucar.

There were eventually English Benedictine monasteries at Douai, Dieulouard, Paris and Lamspring. The first three are now respectively at Downside, Ampleforth and Douai (Berkshire). The English Jesuits had colleges at St Omers, Bruges, Liège and Louvain, now represented by Stonyhurst. The Franciscan Friars were eventually established at Douai, and the Dominicans at Bornhem-Louvain. The English Carmelites were at Tongres, and the Carthusians at Nieuport; they now have a Charterhouse at Parkminster.[14]

Convents Abroad

Turning to the nuns, the real heroine must be Sister Catherine Parker, one of the Bridgettines of Syon. When Henry VIII suppressed their monastery in 1539 she led a group of monks and nuns into exile at Antwerp; in 1554 they returned to Syon at the invitation of Cardinal Pole, only to face exile again in 1559. They went to Termonde and other places, but found further opposition to their community. Finally in 1594 twenty nine nuns set sail, on Good Friday, for Portugal and found a more secure haven. Some returned at the French invasion in 1809, but it was only in 1861 that the entire community came back. In 1915 they celebrated the 500th foundation of their order. More recently they moved from Chudleigh to South Brent in Devon.[15]

Among the nuns there were Benedictines in six different locations; Carmelites in eight or nine; Austin Canonesses in three; Bridgetines also in three places; Franciscans in eight, Dominican Sisters at Vilvorde and Brussels, and Mary Ward's nuns in about eight.[16] And there were the Canonesses of the Holy Sepulchre at Liège. This is a long list, but it speaks of the continuity of English religious life, and as the houses abroad did not feel the same constraints of secrecy as did the recusants in England during the penal days, there is the possibility of finding out more about the families which supported all these religious foundations.

At the present time recusancy studies have made more progress with some of the colleges and monasteries, and from these it is possible to glean who came from Cheshire and Shropshire. So Jesuit and Benedictine sources give us names such as Bruerton, Clough, Elliott, Foxe, Harmer, Howe, Jukes, Leech, Middlemore, Pendril, Percy and Plowden as Jesuits from the counties; and Bolas, Bradshaw, Crowther, Elliott, Foster, Lacon, Northall, Preston, Sandford and Woolfe as Benedictines, with Pickering a Carmelite and Sandford a Carthusian.[17]

It is also possible to find the locations where some of the Benedictines worked, such as Comberford (Staffordshire) Hawarden (Flint), Long Compton and Weston in Warwickshire, and Orleton and Rotherwas in Herefordshire. The Jesuit 'residences' were very strong in Lancashire, but eventually included Hooton Hall, with the Benedictines in touch with the Stanleys at Alderley. There also occurs in the papers a Stanley nun,[18] and an abbess Chomondeley, and although it is difficult to trace them back to Cheshire, the names are county ones. The number of colleges and monasteries abroad is a pointer to the general strength of recusancy at home. But the surviving documentary evidence leaves the picture clouded. How else can we gain some glimpses?

Fragments of Recusancy

There is some evidence of the secret hiding places in Cheshire and Shropshire which are monumental testimony of an unusual kind to underground Catholicism. In 1934 Alan Fea wrote *Secret Chambers and Hiding-Places,* to be followed in 1934 by Granville Squiers', *Secret Hiding-Places.* This latter was a more substantial work, but recently a professional historian has been writing articles on the subject in various county magazines and in *Recusant History.* And by 1989 Michael Hodgetts had brought out his *Secret Hiding Places* which is now the standard work of reference.[19] In Cheshire there are, or have been, hides at Little Moreton Hall, Congleton, Puddington, Poole Hall, Thurstaston Hall, Hooton Hall, Audlem, Gawsworth Old Hall, Bramhall Hall, Lyme Park and Poole Hall. In Shropshire, Hodgetts lists Benthall Hall, Boscobel House, Salter's Hall, Newport, Wem, The Ditches, Wilderhope Manor, Greet Court, Madeley Court, Oswestry Park Hall and Plowden Hall; but he considers that the hide in Pitchford Hall (the finest black and white house in the county) was more likely to be a Royalist refuge, though Mary Ottley was certainly a recusant in 1635-1636. The existence of these hides takes us a little further than some of the manuscript evidence. It might be an indicator of a background for Margaret Ward of Congleton, who eventually worked in London, and rescued a Father Watson from prison, but was herself arrested and though offered her life if she would renounce her religion, died at Tyburn on the 30th August 1585.[20]

Another relic is the Penal Cross, mentioned in the *Diocesan Year Book,* and given to Father Pownell before the war, possibly by one of the Plowdens.[21] There is also in the Chester Record Office the Latin play, *Sanctus Tewdricus, sive Pastor Bonus,* which was the subject of the opening paper of the 1998 Diocesan History Day. It clearly comes from one of the colleges abroad, and in the margins carries the names Charles Peters, Daniel Gifford, Nicholas Tempest, Richard and Frank Simons, William Parr and Richard Smith. Many of them are well known recusant names from Lancashire, though the Giffards were on the borders of Shropshire and Staffordshire.[22]

Wark offers the sort of scenario which could indicate how such a play came into unfriendly hands. A group of people were arrested leaving Chester or the neighbourhood for Ireland in 1595. One of this party was George Huxley, husbandman of Bunbury, by whose direction his son, George, 'pretended to go to Spain to some popish university there, and so to become a Seminary priest contrary to his duty to God and true religion and his allegiance to her Majesty, with lewed determination'. With him was Thomas Cause from Drayton in Shropshire. The escort to the lads was called Stevenson. He had escaped from the Northgate gaol in Chester in 1592.[23] Huxley was a determined lad and got over to Ireland and then abroad a couple of years later, was ordained and returned to England. For the centuries up to the French Revolution there was a quiet stream of boys going abroad to the colleges, and possibly even bringing incriminating material back with them like *Sanctus Tewdricus*.

Various documentary sources, including a spy's report, give a picture of Thomas Holford, born at Aston in 1541, and later schoolmaster in Hereford to the Scudamore family before being ordained at Rheims.[24] By 1853 he was back working as a priest in Cheshire, and a couple of years later arrested in Nantwich. He is a colourful figure:

> . . . a tall, black fat strong man, the crown of his head bald, his beard marquezated. His apparel was a black cloak laid on with murrey lace, open at the shoulders, a straw coloured fustion doublet laid on with red lace, the buttons red, cut and laid with red taffeta doublet, ash coloured hose laid on with byllmit lace, cut and laid under with black taffeta. A little black hat lined with velvet in the brims, a falling band and yellow knitted sockes.

PUDDINGTON HALL
where the Massey family sheltered St John Plessington

While a prisoner in Chester Castle he is known to have said Mass on three occasions, and converted the gaoler's wife and daughter, Joan and Anne Browne. He later escaped, to be captured again in London and martyred in August 1588.

Another group of recusants who fell into unfriendly hands in 1601 were Leake, a suspected priest, and three companions, Bartholomew Brooksbie, a gentleman of Frisby on the Weak (Leicestershire), his son Gregory, and their servant Matthew Green. They were incriminated by a quantity of Catholic literature found in their possession. *A Method to Meditate on the Psalter of Our Blessed Lady*, the *Palestra Hominis Catholice*, a *Modus Orandi Deo*, a Roman Breviary, a Sum [should be *summa*] of Cases of Conscience, and a Roman *Catechism*.[25] This arrest raises the whole question of recusant literature.

Recusant Literature

Since the publication in 1956 of *A Catalogue of Catholic Books in English Printed Abroad or Secretly in England 1558-1640* by A.F.Allison and D.M.Rogers (which added six or seven hundred titles to the Pollard-Redgrave *Short Title Catalogue*), much work has been done on recusant literature and some of it reprinted. Clancy took the work forward with *English Catholic Books, 1641-1700*, (Loyola University Press 1974) and a team of Blom, Korsen and Scott with their *English Catholic Books 1701-1800* has enabled us to span the centuries. About one third of this literature is concerned with spirituality. It includes the sort of works for which Bartholomew Brooksbie was arrested. What was the official attitudes to these publications by the courts here in England?

In 1595 Jane Davye and her husband Edward of St Bridget's, Chester, were charged for 'kepinge of popishe reliques such as a superaltare and popishe books'.[26] In 1578 John Whitehead had been prosecuted for using a Latin primer. During the reign of Edward VI primers were among the books ordered to be burned; possession of them was illegal. And in 1571 Archbishop Grindal's instructions to the laity contained the warning that 'no person or persons whatsoever shall pray upon any popish Latin or English primer'.[27]

The Primer was a devotional work current among the educated laity in the later Middle Ages. Its nucleus was normally the Office of the Blessed Virgin Mary, modelled on the monastic offices and supplemented with the seven Penitential and fifteen Gradual psalms, a litany and an Office for the Dead. There were, from an early date, editions both in Latin and in the vernacular and there had been printed editions from 1494. The spirituality was both Catholic and monastic and did not meet with approval from the Reformed Churches. However, in 1599 the Tridentine *Officium Beatae Mariae Virginis* was translated into English and became a most popular book of devotions for the English recusants, both at home and abroad. A monograph on the subject by Blom is able to identify 42 editions of the primer between 1599 and 1796 and an additional 83 editions of a *Manual of Prayers* (related to the primer) from 1583 to 1800. Later editions were expanded with devotions coming from St Ignatius Loyola and St Francis de Sales, among others. But the basic tradition is both monastic and medieval.[28]

The titles which were made available include the works of Margery Kempe; some of St Augustine, especially his *Confessions*; Boethius' *De consolatione Philosophiae*, which had been in monastic libraries continuously since the sixth century and which Caxton had printed in Chaucer's translation in 1478.[29] There was Lanspergius's *Epistle . . . of Jesus Christ to the Soule*; Heigham's selection from St Bonaventure as *The Life of Our Lord*; from St Albert the Great one work offered *The Paradise of the Soul* and also *A Treatise. . . of Union with God*. H.Hawkins offered *Certaine selected epistles of S.Hierome*. The Franciscans provided *The Rule of our holy Mother S.Clare* and *The Rule and Testament of the Seraphical Father S.Francis*. The prayers of St Bridgit were available and three of the works thought to be those of Walter Hilton: *The*

Scale of Perfection, The Cloud of Unknowing, The Epistle of Privy Counsel. There was a good selection of the lives of the saints, St Catherine of Siena, *The admirable life of Saint Wenefride*, St Thomas of Canterbury, St Patrick, St Bridgit (of Ireland) and St Columba. A number of the works of St Bonaventure, the *Soliloquium, Meditationes Vitae Christi, Incendium Amoris,* and the *Stimulus Divinum Amoris: that is the Goade of Divine Love.*[30] And in very much the same monastic tradition came the *Spiritual Exercises* of Dame Gertrude More, a Benedictine nun and descendant of St Thomas More, who died in the monastery in Cambrai in 1623, with a reputation for sanctity.[31] Her name raises that of Dom Augustine Baker, a noted writer and spiritual director in the same Benedictine tradition.[32] In addition to all the writings from the past, the new masters of the spiritual life were eventually made available in English editions by the recusants, especially St Francis de Sales, St Vincent de Paul and some of the works of Teresa of Avila and John of the Cross. This was a large and rich tradition, much used in the colleges, monasteries and convents abroad, but also being smuggled back into various homes throughout the shires. It is of course impossible to state which works came into Cheshire and Shropshire, but it is certain that some did.[33]

In 1639 an Irishman, Darby Bantre, was arrested at Euston for begging. He was found to have in his knapsack rosary beads, and five books called the *Officium Beatae Virginis Mariae.* All were confiscated. In 1641 the House of Lords ordered a number of confiscated Primers to be burnt by the Sheriff of London at Smithfield. And there were reports of more works getting through, with Sir Kenelm Digby named as 'a great merchant in these commodities'.[34] Clearly the official opposition to all this literature was because it represented the piety of the past and not religion as now established. Significantly much that was in these works, especially in the Psalter and the Primer, was taken up by the late eighteenth-century Catholic authors, notably Bishop Challoner,[35] and passed into prayerbooks like his *Garden of the Soul* and Gahan's *The Catholic Piety*, and the *Loretto Manual, compiled for the Young Ladies educated by the Religious of the Institute of the B.V.M.* Gahan includes the golden litany commemorating 'Our Lord's Passion and Death' and concluding briefly with 'His Resurrection and Ascension'.

One result of this tradition was a notable difference in culture between English Catholics, basically medieval and monastic, and Anglicans based on the *Book of Common Prayer*, the Bible and perhaps Foxe's *Book of Martyrs*. The historian of culture, Christopher Dawson, was of the opinion that the cultural difference was more significant than the doctrinal. This may be an insight of ecumenical importance. For the moment it is enough to note the body of spiritual literature which helped to nourish the English recusants. The volume in this tradition immediately to hand is the Rheims New Testament of 1582.[36]

Catholic Emancipation

John Milner, who was destined to be a bishop of the Midland District, and so to be responsible for Shropshire, was born in London in 1752, but educated at Edgbaston and Sedgley Park (Staffordshire).[37] The age of major persecution was past, but fines and harrassments continued. In 1767 the March edition of the *Universal Museum* reported:

> Another Mass House was discovered in Hog Lane, near the Seven Dials . . . John Baptist Malony, a Papist priest, was taken up for exercising his function in Kent Street contrary to law . . . He was convicted at Croydon, August 23, and sentenced to perpetual imprisonment.

And in 1770, Sir William Stanley of Horton, Baronet, was indicted for refusing to part with his four coach-horses to a Church dignitary, who had tendered him a £20 note; but was acquitted on the grounds of its not being 'a legal tender'.

In 1778, Edmund Burke presented a petition to the King, signed by the Duke of Norfolk, the Earl of Shrewsbury and others, which led to a Bill in Parliament for the repeal of

certain disabilities and penalties against Catholics. This
would seem to have led directly to the outbreak of bigotry
which culminated in the 'Gordon Riots' of 1780. The
Protestant Association requested Lord North to move in
Parliament for the repeal of these concessions to Catholics.

By this time John Milner was a priest in Winchester and
gave the funeral discourse of Bishop Challoner. Within a
decade he was a Fellow of the Society of Antiquaries (March
1790) and much involved in the debates within the Catholic
community. Some were willing that the Government should
have a veto on episcopal appointments in exchange for
concessions and further relaxation of the penal laws. Milner
strongly favoured their total repeal without any concessions
by the Catholic body. While the First Relief Act of 1778 had
led to the Gordon Riots, other relief bills led to deep divisions
among Catholics themselves, with Milner featuring as a very
strong proponent of his own opinion. He wrote a history of
Winchester in 1798 and by 1803 he was Vicar Apostolic of
the Midland District, living in Giffard House at
Wolverhampton and ministering to the Catholics in
Shropshire. He saw the Relief Bill of 1813. As an author he
is known especially for his *The End of Religious Controversy*
(among about seventy publications) but it should be noted
that he also continued the devotional tradition with a
selection of meditations from St Teresa and devotions on the
theme of the Sacred Heart, as well as an account of a cure at
Holywell. He died at the age of seventy three in the April of
1826. His portrait in oils given by J.Gillow to Bishop
Moriarty hangs in the Diocesan Archive Offices.[38]

Not only were the laws against Catholics disappearing,
but the land was changing with canals and railways, and the
first trickles of Irish immigrants. Long before the terrible
potato famines, Irish migrant labourers were visiting parts of
the future diocese to help with the harvests on a seasonal
basis. A paper by C.J.Boyle will look in detail at the arrival of
the Irish in Birkenhead, while another by Sister Mary
Campion will give an account of the first of the nuns to come,
which represents a part of the return of the religious. The

clergy of 1850 are in need of a detailed study, and Dr Peter Philips will look at our first bishop. We will also detail something of the growth of the schools of the Diocese as they became a major preoccupation in the pastoral structure of the new communities. The devotional life of the nineteenth century deserves documentation as the watershed of the Second Vatican Council now almost serves to hide the pieties of a previous age. Diocesan History Days have begun to look at some of the artistic treasures of the past, such as the stained-glass work of Sister Margaret Rope, and the large question of how such a poor community could expand, build schools and churches, and also meet all its needs, demands a study of the finances of the last century. Many other themes naturally suggest themselves, and it is hoped through Diocesan History Days to continue to build up the picture of the faith of our fathers.

Thanks are due to those who have made possible the progress so far. With the Archives in new premises, it may be feasable to encourage post-graduate students to develop some of the themes which remain to be studied in depth. Parishes have been asked to produce a good history for the Millennium; It is also important that we study some of the recusant families scattered throughout the two counties who provided shelter for the hunted priests, continuity for the supporters of the ancient faith and ultimately a platform for the nineteenth- and twentieth-century development of the Diocese of Shrewsbury.

NOTES

Much of this essay is developed from a paper given to the Cheshire History Society in the autumn of 1997, and a revised and reduced edition of that was published in *Cheshire History* 38, 1998-99. I am grateful to the editor for his agreement to use the material here.
1. K.R.Wark, *Elizabethan Recusancy in Cheshire* Chetham Society 1971 and William Price 'Three Priests at Plowden' in *Shrewsbury Diocesan Year Book*, 1970 and 'Three Jesuits at Plowden Hall in Shropshire in the Eighteenth Century' in *Recusant History* X p. 164. Also his 'Catholicism in Shropshire, 1570 to 1970' in *Shrewsbury*

Diocesan Year Book, 1972. Marie Rowlands '"The Several Parishes which I did help" The Mission at Linley Shropshire,1693-1734' in *Midland Catholic History* 4 (1995) pp 14-22. M.D.G. Wanklyn 'Recusancy in Seventeenth Century Shropshire, with particular reference to the parish of Madeley' *Worcestershire Recusant*, 43, June 1984. E.Maurice Abbott, 'History of Acton Burnell' in *Shrewsbury Diocesan Year Book* 1971 and 1972.

2.   David Knowles & R.Neville Hadcock, *Medieval Religious Houses. England and Wales,* 1953. The figure was estimated by using the index and listing all references to buildings with any monastic/religious connection in both Cheshire and Shropshire. A simpler picture can be gained by using the two O.S. maps of Monastic Britain.

3.   For the Chester monastery, David Knowles, *The Religious Orders in England,* III pp.392 & 473 together with R.V.H.Burne, *The Monks of Chester*, 1962 and *Chester Cathedral* 1958.

4.   For some details of the Pilgrimage of Grace and the participants' thoughts on the religious houses, see Philip Hughes, *The Reformation in England* I, 'The King's Proceedings', 1954 p.312. Cobbett noticed the excuse given for the despoliation of the lesser houses contradicted the action later taken against the great houses. William Cobbett, *A History of the Protestant Reformation in England and Ireland,* 1847, pp.96-98 and especially p.99. The robbing of the chantries is studied by Professor J.J.Scarisbrick in a paper 'Henry VIII and the Dissolution of the Secular Colleges' in *Law and Government under the Tudors,* edited by Claire Cross & others, 1988,. Philip Hughes had a study of the Pilgrimage of Grace in *The Clergy Review,* XII, 4 Oct.1936.

5.   For Halston see the note in Knowles & Hadcock op cit p.243.

6.   Philip Hughes, *Reformation in England,* III pp.25, 245, 422.

7. C.W.Field, *The Province of Canterbury and the Elizabethan Settlement of Religion,* 1972 p.i, and Godfrey Anstruther, O.P., *The Seminary Priests, Vol.I, Elizabethan,* 1968, p.72.

8.   Field, op.cit. pp.iv-v. and 325-330.

9.   Patrick McGrath, *Papists and Puritans under Elizabeth I,* 1967 and various articles in *Recusant History:* 17;2. 'The Marian Priests under Elizabeth I', & 20;4 'Imprisonment of Catholics under Elizabeth I'.

10. Wark, op.cit. p. 49 & 53.

11. The four volumes of Anstruther provide a reference system for the English post-Reformation secular clergy, and Dominic Aidan Bellenger O.S.B. has provided an invaluable index to this and to the

religious clergy in his *English and Welsh Priests 1558-1800: A Working List,* 1984.

12. Wark op.cit. p.49 & 53.

13. McGrath, *Papist & Puritan under Elizabeth I,* 1967, p.111.

14. For the colleges and religious houses abroad the first work of importance is Peter Guilday, *The English Catholic Refugees on the Continent 1558-1795,* Vol.1 *The English Colleges and Convents in the Catholic Low Countries, 1558-1795.* Alas there was no Volume II. But in 1963 Professor A.C.F.Beales published *Education under Penalty,* and in *Recusant History* 7;6 'A Biographical Catalogue of Catholic Schoolmasters in England.' *St.Gregory's College, Seville 1592-1829,* edited by Martin Murphy, is volume 73 in the Catholic Record Society series (1992). This series includes some of the *Douay Diaries* (10.&11) *Annals of the English College, Seville* (14), *The English College at Madrid* (29), *The English College at Valladolid* (30), *Liber Ruber of the English College,Rome* (37) ,and a further instalment of the same (40), *Responsa Scholarum, English College, Rome* (54-55), *St Omers and Bruges Colleges, A Biographical Dictionary* (69) and *The Lisbon College Register 1628-1829* (72). Michael Williams has published histories of the English College in Rome and Valladolid and articles in *Recusant History* 20;2 & 20;4. Ampleforth, Stonyhurst and Downside have published various histories of their time abroad, especially David Lunn's *The English Benedictines 1540-1688,* 1980. The result is that the female religious houses are the area in most need of further study. A start has been made in *Recusant History* 18;1 'The Chronicles of the English Poor Clares of Rouen' by Foster and in 21;4 'The English Augustinian Convent of Our Lady of Syon, Paris' by A.Allison, also in the same edition, Mason writes on recusant nuns.

15. John Rory Fletcher wrote in 1933 *The Story of the English Bridgettines of Syon Abbey*; there is some coverage in the three volumes of Philip Hughes, *The Reformation in England* and more recently Roger Ellis, Syon Abbey: *The Spirituality of the English Bridgettines,* 1984.

16. For Mary Ward's nuns (IBVM) see Maria Theodolinde Winkler, *Maria Ward und das Institut der Englischen Fräulein in Bayern,* München, 1926, and Henriette Peters, *Mary Ward A World in Contemplation,* translated Helen Butterworth, 1994

17. Names from the index provided by Bellenger (c.f. note 11), with Catholic Record Society volumes 70, Holt, *English Jesuits 1650-1829,* and 74, & 75 McCoog, *English & Welsh Jesuits 1555-1650.* Also David Lunn's *The English Benedictines.*

18. Catholic Record Society, 62 p.147-8 for Sister Ignatius Stanley.

19. His articles include in *Recusant History* 16;2 'A Topographical Index of Hiding Places' and the same title II in *Recusant History* 24;1. Also in 11, 12, 13, and 14, articles on various houses.

20. Margaret Ward occurs in John Stow's *Annals*, see Philip Caraman, *The Other Face. Catholic Life under Elizabeth I, 1960*, p.250. She was one of the forty martyrs of England and Wales canonized in October 1970. There is a pamphlet life of her.

21. *Shrewsbury Diocesan Year Book* 1997, pp.131-32

22. Chester Record Office, the Crewe Cooper Collection, DCC 13 *Sanctus Tewdricus, sive Pastor Bonus;* an illuminated title page by Henry Matthew Chamberling, and some music by Beveridge. Dr.Nigel Griffin has promised to edit this text, after giving a paper on the background and the contents.

23. Wark op.cit. p.112, with a reference to *Mayors' Books (Chester), 1592-6,* 11 August, 1595, and S.P.,12,253,22.

24. Wark op.cit. p.60-62 and Anstruther *op.cit,* Vol.I pp.170-72.

25. Wark op.cit. p.125; the *Sum of Cases of Conscience* is actually recorded as *the third called the same (?) of Cases of Conscience.* In scholastic texts of the time, a *summa* was often part of the title indicating a summary.

26. Wark, op.cit. p.116. For the legal restrictions 3 & 4 Ed. VI cap 10. I owe this reference to the work of J.M.Blom, *The Post-Tridentine English Primer*, Catholic Record Society (Monograph Series), 1982, p.35.

27. Also from Blom (above) who refers to Philip Caraman, *The Other Face*, 1969, p.35

28. The monograph of Blom may usefully be used in conjunction with the important article of David Rogers 'The English Recusants: Some Mediaeval Literary Links' in *Recusant History* 23;4 Oct 1997.

29. Rogers, *art.cit,* p.493.

30. Dr Rogers notes some doubt about the authenticity of some of the works translated and attributed to St Bonaventure; ibid., p.495

31. For Dame Gertrude More there is an article in *Recusant History* 13;3 and *The Writings of Dame Gertrude More*, revised and edited by Dom Benedict Weld-Blundell O.S.B. 1910.

32. For Augustine Baker there is some coverage in Lunn's *The English Benedictines 1540-1688* and (David Rogers) *The Benedictines and the Book,* published by the Bodlean Library in 1980, and *The Benedictines in Britain,* published by the British Library in the same year. Augustine Baker was a convert lawyer who became a monk (later of St Laurence's) and spiritual director to the nuns, among whom was Dame Gertrude More. He was in touch with Robert Cotton (whose manuscripts were to provide a nucleus for the

British Library), and was obtaining both manuscripts and printed books for the nuns "in English containing contemplation, saints' lives or other devotions" (*sic*). Eventually the longer version of the work of Mother Julian of Norwich finished up in the monasteries abroad, quite probably through this contact. It is a clear example of the continuity of the devotions of the past surviving through recusant interest.

33. The recusant publications, which Dr Rogers studies in his article, represent the major part of Catholic English recusant literature, with controversial works running a clear second. The dates at which the works of post reformation French and Spanish spirituality came into use in England would perhaps illustrate something of the influence of the colleges abroad.

34. The reference is from Blom, *op.cit* pp. 40-41.

35. Challoner was studied at length in two volumes by E.H.Burton, *The Life and Times of Bishop Challoner, 1691-1781*, 1909. Since then there have been many important articles. A catalogue of his works, issued by John Bevan in 1981, offered many early editions of his works, indicating their enduring popularity. Apart from many works of devotion, Challoner was also responsible for transmitting the catechetical text. J.P.Marmion, 'The Penny Catechism: a long lasting text' in *Paradigm: The Textbook Colloquium*, 26 Oct 1998.

36. The value of the Rheims New Testament is considered in an important article by Ward Allen, 'Contributions of the Rheims New Testament to King James's Translators', pp.51-65, with two other articles by Edward C.Jacobs and Scott Ward.in *Le Lexique Chrétien Permanences et avatars*, Vol 2, 1993, edited by Germain Marc'hadour.

37. Milner is well covered in Anstruther, *The Seminary Priests, Vol.4: 1716-1800*, (1977) pp.191-92. And see Peter B.Nockles, 'The Difficulties of Protestantism: Bishop Milner, John Fletcher and the Catholic Apologetic against the Church of England in the Era from the First Relief Act to Emancipation 1778-1830' in *Recusant History* 24;2, Oct 1998. The reference to Malony and Stanley comes from Cobbett. *The Shrewsbury Diocesan Year Book*, 1964, also carries an article on Bishop Milner and Shropshire.

38. This could be the Gillow of the five volumes of *Biographical Dictionary of English Catholics*, 1885 ff. and reprinted since.

I

THE RETURN OF
WOMEN RELIGIOUS

Mary Campion McCarren, f.c.J.

The invitation

When, in 1849, Dr Brown, Vicar Apostolic, suggested that Madame d'Houet, foundress of the Sisters Faithful Companions of Jesus, transfer part of the school she had established in Great George's Square, Liverpool, to a site across the Mersey, he had several dreams in mind.

Clearly it would ensure the return of female religious life to the Wirral for the first time since the Reformation. Furthermore, since he specifically asked her to open a first class boarding school he was providing an opportunity for the education of Catholic girls, or Young Ladies as they were always called according to the accepted social norms of the times,[1] without their having to travel abroad. In the Catholic Directory of 1842[2] we read of an earlier foundation made at Gumley House, Isleworth. Under the heading 'Advantages of Continental Education Combined with Residence in England' the notice speaks of the choice facing Catholic parents. Those wishing to give their daughters 'the best and most religious education' had been obliged to send them to the Continent. Those not wishing to be so separated from their children had been obliged to choose between schools not of their religion or to have them 'but nominally accomplished at

home in modern languages'. From Jane Austen's novels it is
clear that accomplishments were of prime importance; so this
stress on foreign languages is not unexpected nor is the ability
to converse with others. Those 'doomed' to be educated at
home,

> . . . when they went abroad, from the ear not having been
> accustomed to the constant sound of the languages they had
> learned, the children have too often been discovered scarcely
> capable of taking part in the commonest conversation on the
> most indifferent subjects.
>   The great desideratum then has been, to give to the child in
> England all the advantages she would possess in a foreign
> country, by surrounding her with those who were themselves
> foreigners. The only plan by which this could be made to
> succeed, was by transferring, as it were, an entire establishment
> from abroad, and setting it down within this country . . .
> making all within the walls French or Italian, while all without
> was English — conveying here not merely the language and the
> manners, but the holy and pure religion of which these ladies
> are the humble and devoted handmaids. The child is here
> educated as if she were separated by the sea and hundreds of
> miles from London, while, now that railways are extended all
> over England, she is within a few hours' journey of her parents.
> The mother is relieved from all the agony, pain and doubt that
> a long distance from her offspring inevitably brings with it; and
> the child has all the advantages that, under other
> circumstances, it must inevitably purchase by travelling a long
> journey from home.[3]

Mother Frances Gibson, later Provincial in England, whose
forebears included two 18th century Vicars Apostolic, used to
say: *All my ancestors were brought up at the Bar (Convent, York)
but I was sent to Lingdale because it was nearer my home in
Manchester'.* St Mary's (Micklegate) Bar Convent, York had
since 1685 been offering this kind of Catholic education.

And there was a third reason for Dr. Brown wanting
Madame d'Houet to make a foundation in Birkenhead. The
Faithful Companions of Jesus had gone to Liverpool in 1844
at the request of Father Parker of St Patrick's, to take care of

the Parish School in the face of great poverty, sickness and overcrowding. Dr Brown knew that it would not be long before the Sisters sought ways of undertaking similar work from their new convent and the schools would become the gateway to the homes. Educating girls who would be the Catholic wives and mothers of the next generation was of prime importance at all levels of society.

Lingdale House

Lingdale House, variously said to be situated in Oxton, Claughton or Birkenhead, was leased in 1849. It is described as being

> An elegant house with 6 acres of gardens; terraces, lawns, groves and flower beds . . . a forest of pine trees as far as Bidston Road on one side and Palm Grove on the other.

Many wealthy families had suffered set-backs in 1847 when the docks went bankrupt and Lingdale had passed into the hands of creditors. It took the Society almost a year to conduct negotiations through lawyers and friends 'including a Protestant'. (The awareness of who was Catholic and who was Protestant runs like a *leitmotif* through all the documentation of this period and owes much to the general climate of the times). The Society lawyer, Mr John Yates of Liverpool was instructed to discover whether Lingdale was for sale without saying that he had been asked to do this. The negotiations were complicated by the fact that there were two so called proprietors. In 1837, John, Earl of Shrewsbury had leased the estate to William Ravenscroft for 99 years and in 1846 sold the property to a Mr Potter subject to the same lease. It was eventually taken by the Society on a 14 year lease with an expectation of renewal or even outright purchase.

The lease was signed on September 14th 1849[4] and the following month on October 10th twelve Sisters and twenty-four pupils transferred from Great George's Square to

Lingdale House, the first school of its type in this part of the country. Writing in his diary for 1851 about the beginning of the Diocese, Bishop Brown noted: 'The only community of nuns was at Lingdale House near Birkenhead'. Mother Clotilde Dupont, Superior first of Lingdale and then of Upton, wrote that in the beginning

> we were not altogether welcome here — several times our house was threatened. Gradually this animosity has ceased and now we receive all that is amiable from those who initially were the most ill-disposed to us, Ministers and others.

She does not give examples of what they had lived through but from the *Birkenhead Advertiser's*[5] report of an address by the Revd P.L. Sandberg we get something of the atmosphere abroad in the area.

> We live in dangerous times, in times when the inspiration of God's word is questioned. Did you ever see ladies in Birkenhead wearing a very peculiar dress, in long black cloaks and long black veils and so forth?[6] . . . if the Protestants were not busy, those ladies were (Hear, hear). I can assure the Meeting that those ladies crept into Birkenhead stealthily and were doing a work, not the work of God, I am sorry to say, but a work proving that, if Protestants would not labour, the enemy labours (Hear hear.) and scatters the seed which will germinate into the destruction of souls far and wide in Birkenhead, as it has throughout the whole land[7].

In the mid-nineteenth century, Catholicism, convent life and foreigners were all highly suspect. The early 1850s were marked by a growing public campaign to secure state inspection of convents, both Anglican and Roman, on the grounds that

> factories, prisons, mines, workhouses and madhouses had to be open to public scrutiny so why not convents too?[8]

Fifty years later Protestant members of the Night Classes at Upton 'questioned our Mothers about the dungeon and the punishments which they thought existed in the Convent'.[9]

Curriculum

In keeping with the rationale published in the *Catholic Directory* (as well as reflecting the composition of the Society itself) the first community of twelve included French, English, Italian and German Sisters. The Curriculum reflected both contemporary movements in the Catholic Church in England and contemporary educational goals.

> The French, English, Italian and German Languages are taught by natives. The French language is chiefly spoken, and as the ladies of the house are principally of that nation, it may not improperly be called a French establishment. . . . the use of the Globes, Botany, History, Writing, Arithmetic, useful and ornamental needlework. . . . The fees £28 p.a. Music, Drawing and Dancing extra. A vacation is allowed at Midsummer but no extra charge is made for young ladies who remain at the establishment during that period.[10]

The mention of 'needlework both useful and ornamental' is significant in the light of Rock's *Church of Our Fathers* (1849-1854).[11]

> Let us hope that such of our Catholic ladies as have the time, the talents and the means, may soon begin to follow that good example set them by their high-born Anglo-Saxon, their Norman and their later English sisters in the faith. Then, indeed, the never-ending working of fire-screens and slippers will sometimes, at least, give way to a stole, or maniple, or the figured orphrey for a cope or a chasuble ...

The useful and ornamental needlework furnished many a gift to the early Bishops of Shrewsbury and Menevia. A rochet and stole in April 1852 for Bishop J. Brown and another in 1855 elicits the following somewhat fulsome thanks:

> It forms another link in that pleasing bond of gratitude with which my most sincere and affectionate regards towards my dear children at Lingdale are bound together.

The Gothic Revival aside, needlework was from the start used at Lingdale as a means of arousing social conscience. Thirty-five years after the opening of Lingdale, the YWCA attributes its founding in Birkenhead to

> the ever increasing numbers [of] young girls seeking employment in shops, and domestic service. This inflow of a growing female population stimulated the socially conscious members of our Society to seek means of providing spiritual and practical support for them[12]

At Lingdale, and later at Chester, Holt Hill and Upton, the pupils made and distributed garments to those in need and in time dozens of garments were contributed for the Catholic Needlework Guild.

The Devotional Life

The school year itself, was essentially the liturgical year with great emphasis being placed on the celebration not only of the major feasts but also on the round of patronal feasts. Devotions flourished and they too bore the marks of continental influence. Processions abounded; recitation of the Rosary and Litanies was prominent; March was the month of St Joseph, May of Our Lady; June the Sacred Heart, July the Precious Blood; October the Rosary, November the Holy Souls, whilst the crowning feast of the year was that of the Immaculate Conception on December 8th.

Down the years, the local bishops and their guests emphasised the links between the local community and Rome. Cardinal Wiseman was one such visitor to Lingdale in 1859. The welcome accorded him is a forerunner of what became the great feast of the secular year — Prize Day — when the pupils were able to show what they had learned and, of equal importance, show that they could comport themselves creditably in public. On this occasion 'six pupils in white dresses played on two pianos a piece for 12 hands'. In the School Room they presented their compliments in English,

French and Italian and the visit ended, two hours later, when everyone sang together Wiseman's hymn in honour of the Pope.[13]

Retreats

There was another religious practice which the foundress was anxious to inaugurate at Lingdale. As a young widow (her husband died before the birth of their son) Marie Madeleine had availed of opportunities for retreat and spiritual direction and knew the value she had found in those exercises. Bishop Brown considered

> the possession of such an Establishment as yours is one of the greatest blessings of the Diocese; and I beg most tenderly to assure you that it shall always form the object of my most special regard.[14]

When she spoke to him and to the Bishops of Liverpool and Menevia of her desire to offer retreats for ladies this was a new venture in England and they encouraged her. They advised that the retreats be offered during the summer holidays for the upper class, 'for ladies of the world'. The Revd Mr Lennon,[15] who was her constant and devoted friend, helped greatly with the project. When July 2nd 1851 arrived there were 20 retreatants (including 11 former pupils). The Retreat Master was George Spencer (Father Ignatius, C.P.) one of the famous pre-Oxford Movement converts. These summer retreats, which were continued after the move from Lingdale to Upton Hall, also stimulated social consciences.

A Poor School and a Parish

The Sisters had gone to Liverpool for the Poor School (the legal term for the parish elementary school since they were attended, where they existed, without payment of fee) and then founded a boarding school. At Lingdale the foundress came for the boarding school but immediately founded a Poor

School.   Bishop Brown's Diary notes that the 'Faithful Companions of Jesus derived their support from a Boarding School and also maintained a Poor School for the benefit of the neighbourhood'.[16] The foundress believed that God blessed the one in proportion to the zeal with which the Sisters worked in the other.

The nineteenth century had begun with a spectacular boom for Birkenhead, but by 1847 bank crashes and railway bankruptcies meant that investors were ruined and the workers suffered great hardship.   The problems were compounded by the immigration of Irish workers after the Great Famine, for the increased numbers seeking work led to local dock troubles.   The 1841 Birkenhead Census shows that the population was 8,223, of whom 5,471 had been born outside Cheshire and the well planned town had 'given way to much inferior property being flung up'[17] to accommodate the great demand.   In a Dickensian world, thronged with real people in real need, the Sisters cared compassionately for those whose lives they touched and if the vocational training given to those in the Poor Schools fitted them and placed them as servants, they were at least enabled to make their way in life.   It may seem to us that the conditions in which they were educated left much to be desired from the beginning and were, eventually, overcrowded, but the enterprise had far reaching results.

Hand in hand with the material poverty went deprivation of religious support.   Many immigrants, removed from the influence of their homes, drifted into non-observance; others found that what employment they could find necessitated either hiding their religion altogether or working at Mass time; others found that their poverty was so great that they could not face going to church so poorly clad.

At Lingdale, outhouses were converted for the purpose of a school and the initial hope was that twenty children might be found.   But soon there were a hundred, and from that Poor School sprang a quasi-parish.   The nuns were instructing the children and the chaplain, The Revd R. McCarte, began to gather the parents for the same purpose.   The fact that the convent had a chaplain meant that the community could share this advantage with the people of the neighbourhood. Bishop Brown had assured the Foundress that he would be happy if she could obtain a French chaplain . He urged the great wants of England and pointed out to her that he had no seminary and was obliged to obtain priests where he could.[18]

With the Bishop's approval, in December 1850 Mr McCarte rented a simple room at Gilbrook for Sunday Mass and confessions.[19] All First Communions at the North End of the town, (March 1851 - November 1857)[20] were made at Lingdale[21]. In 1857 this Poor School was transferred from Lingdale to Our Lady's, Price Street, and two FCJs continued to serve there. On good days there were between 140-160 children and spiritual instruction was given by the Revd Patrick Power.

Birkenhead

In 1852, happy with what was being achieved at Lingdale, Bishop James Brown asked that the FCJs would take charge of the schools in Birkenhead, and at the same time open a second class boarding school and a first class day school. The Foundress recognised the need that there was for all these works since on both sides of the Mersey the middle class was growing both in numbers and significance. Bishop Brown's diary records:

> 1852: During this year a filiation from Lingdale House was established in Birkenhead. The poor schools of the town were placed under the care of the Sisters, and an immediate increase in the numbers attending the School, as well as a marked improvement amongst them was most consoling and edifying.

The following year, 1853, he asked for a foundation in Chester, a parish school and a boarding school, and in January 1854 four Sisters left Birkenhead for Chester. In both places, in addition to teaching the children, the Sisters also trained pupil teachers so ensuring a multiplier effect.

The first Birkenhead house was rented in Hampden Street. The community moved in during January 1852 and the first pupils arrived the following week. They moved from there to Hamilton Square in 1854 and finally, in 1856, bought what was then known as Tranmere Hall, later Holt Hill. In Spring 1857 the new community and some forty pupils made the move. By 1858 there were fifty in the boarding school and twenty five in the day school. Already novices had come from the school membership. Life there followed very much the pattern established at Lingdale.

Day Schools, Night Schools, Sunday Schools

By 1858 there were 240 in the parish day school and a Night School, with some sixty members, had been started for those who had had no previous opportunity to gain even a basic education. In addition religious instruction was given every evening for adults, with attendance varying between 300 and 400. When Cardinal Wiseman visited in 1859 he was greeted by 400 children together with 200 adults who regularly attended.

Sunday Schools were a feature of parish life. Some 300 children who during the week either remained at home looking after younger children or were out selling things in the street came to Mass under the guidance of two of the Sisters and in the afternoon came again for Religious Instruction and what are called 'little exercises of piety which one tries to make as attractive as possible'. At 6 o'clock on Sunday evenings, they were replaced by about one hundred young girls, many of whom were in domestic service, who, unable to attend Mass in the morning, came for Instruction and to receive words of encouragement for the week ahead. From the school room, they went to the church where Benediction ended the day.

The Lancashire Vicariate *Status Missionis 1847*[22] lays great stress on parish Confraternities and, where there are none established, there are notations indicating that the matter will be looked into. Birkenhead had none; Chester had two. The

Living Rosary would seem to have been established in many places in 1843 and certainly it became a very vibrant and vital devotion. By 1858, the Sodality of Our Lady had been introduced into Birkenhead and there were some forty enrolled.

The Conversion of England

The first generation of FCJs saw themselves as missionary women and the climate of the times was very much directed to 'the conversion of England'. The Sisters encouraged both the Children of Mary and the children in the schools to play their part in the enterprise. The list of converts is likened to that of Notre Dame des Victoires in Paris, in fact the local clergy often referred to the school as '*Notre Dame des Victoires de Birkenhead*'. The school was indeed a gateway to the homes. A *Hail Mary* was said in school every hour for the conversion of the town, especially for a certain street known as *the hell of Birkenhead*. The local clergy urged the Sisters to foster adult education and instruction classes were announced in church. Some women came spontaneously and eagerly, others were led by their children 'by their pinnies, with an air of triumph'. The classes ended with the recitation of the rosary — again for the conversion of sinners. The first comers brought others; they told their neighbours and friends and conversions became almost everyday occurrences. The women then started asking for prayers for their husbands, a list was started of names of those whose conversion was desired and the list put in an envelope in the hands of Our Lady's statue. There were novenas, there was talk at home and gradually husbands and sons began to be brought to the priests. It is recorded that the priests were willing to welcome anyone at any hour sent to them from the nuns

The priests started going from house to house, all the time tapping back into the school room for the children's prayers and those of the deeply committed women of the evening classes. Two years later the pastor names another street as the object of combined prayer, Oak Street now being completely accounted for![23]

Initially attention was focused on Irish immigrants, who, as the Annalist says 'had forgotten not their religion, but the practice of their religious duties'. In the second wave, it was non-Catholics being converted, either by example or by marriage. And again the mothers played a big part in all this. Once the mother was received, the whole family often followed. In the boarding and day schools too, there was a steady flow of converts among both children and parents. Mother Catherine Connolly, who had charge of St Werburgh's School, was considered by the rector to have a special grace for helping converts[24]

Chester

Less than five years after taking up residence at Lingdale House Madame d'Houet accepted another invitation from Bishop Brown to make a foundation in the Diocese, this time in Chester. The initial plan had been to build a church to meet the needs of the increasing numbers of Catholics. The idea came to nothing and the property which had been bought, was now bought by the Sisters since it was seen as suitable for a boarding school. From Dee House, as from Lingdale and Holt Hill the Sisters would teach girls and infants in the parish school. On January 29th 1854 four Sisters arrived.

There were many similarities. Chester, like Liverpool and Birkenhead, had received large numbers of immigrants driven from Ireland by the famines. And as for 'young ladies' there seems to have been nothing for them in Chester since 1828. Bishop Brown and Canon Carberry, the Parish Priest, looked to the FCJs to help educate both classes.

Once again the first Superior was French, Reverend Mother Marie de Bussy, who afterwards became the third General Superior. She was succeeded in 1855 by Mother Josephine Stritch, an Italian, who in her turn was succeeded 23 years later by Mother Aloysia Russell, Superior from 1878 to 1887. It is to her that we are indebted for the submission to the Slaughter Manuscript (1892) in the Shrewsbury Diocesan Archives.

Chester had nothing to equal the Stockport and Birkenhead[25] Riots, but Mother Aloysia's account contains interesting details of the religious atmosphere into which the Sisters came.

> Between the Convent ground and the Dee stands the Protestant Bishop's palace... the old part of the building was, when the nuns came to Chester, occupied by Chancellor Raikes who died soon after their arrival. It was said that he died of a broken heart on account of their coming so near him. Chester being essentially a Protestant City its inhabitants naturally looked with horror on the fact of Catholic nuns coming amongst them and for a while were not very friendly. However when they found that they had neither horns nor cloven feet as some foolishly fancied, they came quietly round'.

Arrangements were soon under way to open a parish school. A coach house and hayloft in the grounds were pressed into service. The girls and infants were in the hayloft; the boys in the coach house under the care of a master. In 1858 the boys moved to a newly built school in Queen Street and a new building was erected for the girls at Dee House, the *top room was for the girls, the lower room for the infants with a gallery running from end to end*.

To defray the cost of building the Poor School, the Sisters held a series of bazaars. The first raised £200; the second £178 and what is recorded as 'The Liverpool Bazaar' £175.6.6d. There were also donations from well-wishers. Both the Diocesan and FCJ Archives have incomplete copies of the financial agreement entered into:

AGREEMENT A.M.D.G

The Community of the Faithful Companions of Jesus at Dee House Chester intending to erect a school for poor girls and infants upon a portion of their land, it is hereby agreed at the time of the said erection between the Bishop of Shrewsbury and the General Superior of the above mentioned community, Madame Josephine Louise Petit, that, if at any future time the said building should be required for the use or purpose of the community, or if the premises including the said building should be sold, the following sum should be paid by the community to the Bishop for the time being as a compensation for certain moneys derived from charitable sources which have been expended in the building.

    1. £100 paid by the Bishop himself
    2. granted by the Poor School Committee
    (No amount entered)
    3. One third of the amount realised by a Bazaar
    held for the purpose amounting to (also left blank)
    4. Any private donation given expressly for the
                           purpose

The above arrangement is made in accordance with the decree of the II Pro. Council of Westminster.[26]

October 13 /60   *+ J. Brown*

Unlike the foundations at Lingdale and Birkenhead, that at Chester never had a second, or third, home. But like the others extensions were pu up and on February 2nd 1867, Father Mulvaney, acting Parish Priest, laid the foundation stone for 'a new wing comprising chapel, study-room and dormitory for the boarders. . . . The new chapel was solemnly opened on 23rd October 1867 by Bishop Brown, in the presence of a large number of priests, and dedicated to the Sacred Heart of Jesus'.

The gardens at Lingdale and Holt Hill had been among the reasons given for those houses being so suitable for the purpose the Foundress had in mind. In 1843 a Royal Commission had reported that Liverpool, Manchester, Birmingham and Leeds had no public park. Mortimer writing in 1847[27] after the establishment of Birkenhead Park, speaks of the value and importance of parks 'not only in a physical but in a moral point of view'. Natural beauty was something Madame d'Houet had sought wherever possible and knew how therapeutic its enjoyment could be for women and girls whose lives were otherwise spent in the depressing surroundings of factories, mills and laundries. Visits to the Convent garden was a regular feature of First Communion Days long after the Elementary Schools had moved away from Dee House.

Conclusion

So within five years the Society of Sisters Faithful Companions of Jesus had come into the Wirral, been present at the establishment of the Diocese of Shrewsbury and made three foundations with an outreach into parish education and pastoral care.

In 1863 they had to leave Lingdale House because of legal controversy. Between 1803 and 1854 many leases had been granted by three successive Earls of Shrewsbury under various Acts of Parliament. On the death of Bertram, the 17th Earl, in 1856, the next Earl, a protestant cousin who lived in Ireland, disputed the validity of the leases and it was ruled that those contracted between 1803 and 1843 were invalid. Madame d'Houet gave up all hope of being able to buy the property and in 1863 the Sisters left Lingdale for Upton Hall.

NOTES

1. The Church too followed the usage. Dr Brown, V.A., in his Diary records '22/10/1848 confirmed a numerous multitude of females in Church of St Ignatius (Preston); 30/5/1849: confirmed the young Ladies at the Convent in Gt. George's Square'. (Lancs. R.O. RCLv Box 56).
2. Page 118ff.
3. *The Laity's Directory* advertisement in 1850, speaking of the foundation at Lingdale, commented that: 'the distance from Liverpool is very convenient; the Woodside steamboats cross the river every 10 minutes and at the ferry every convenience may be had by either omnibus or car'.
4. *The Liverpool Mercury* for 7.8.1849 announced that 'it is stated that Lingdale House, Oxton Hill, lately occupied by Mr M. Freeman, has been purchased by Roman Catholic Sisters of

Charity'. An interesting observation, even if only because of its many errors.

5. April 1864. I am indebted to Mr C. Boyle who drew my attention to this passage.

6. As late as 1918 it was being said in Rome 'there are two things which characterise the FCJs — their ugly dress and their very beautiful spirit!' (Cardinal Gasquet's Secretary to General Superior Philomena Higgins).

7. Words spoken 35 years after Catholic Emancipation; 14 after the Restoration of the Hierarchy.

8. G.F.A. Best, 'Popular Protestantism in Victorian Britain' in R.Robson (ed.), *Ideas and Institutions of Victorian Britain* (1967, p.128); Quoted M. McClelland: 'In Search of the Hull Mercy Nuns', Paper presented at CAS Conference 1995 and printed in *Catholic Archives*, 1996.

9. Upton Hall Annals, 1898.

10. This practice continued well into the twentieth century. Boarding schools were as much a home as a school. Listed by Gore 1864, Claughton had 8 boarding schools, Oxton 3 and Tranmere 13.

11. J.A. Hilton's North West Catholic History Society, *Selection* (1992).

12. *A History of the Birkenhead YWCA 1883 - 1983*.

13. Presumably: *Full in the Panting Heart of Rome*.

14. Letter, 6 August 1851.

15. Rector of Liscard 1843-68.

16. The financial link between the two undertakings is clearly expressed in 1895. 'If we are obliged through lack of resources, to give up this school, sixty poor little Catholics will have to go to a Protestant school or even, what is worse, a Board School, where no Religion is taught, may be established in the village of Upton. We have begun a collection under the special protection of St Anthony, and we ask the prayers of the society, for the success of the undertaking, as well as for an increase in the number of boarders, which will enable us more easily to meet the outlay attendant on the alterations in the Poor School and thus continue to keep the Faith in our little village of Upton, and the surrounding country'. (*Upton Annals*).

17. Birkenhead R.0. YHD 1/1 LXII J.E.Allison: Early Claughton and its Neighbours MSS.

18. 22/6/1852.

19. Dallow records that whilst the Revd Mr McCarte said Mass at Gilbrook, confessions of females were always heard at Lingdale. This is perhaps akin to Bishop Goss's pronouncement, of March 28th 1856, that not to separate the sexes in the free seats of the churches is 'a great evil and contrary to the spirit of the church'.

20. Mr.McCarte left in February 1857. It should be noted that the title 'Father' was not normally used for secular priests until encouraged by Manning in the latter part of the nineteenth century.

21. A number of the North Wirral parishes have the FCJs in their ancestry. There was Mr McCarte's Gilbrook parish; in 1862 Canon Lennon bought 14 Chapel Street to serve as presbytery at Seacombe; Upton (1863), from which in 1923 Moreton and Leasowe were separated. In 1940 Our Lady of Pity was opened at Greasby. For four years it was served from Upton when Father William Corcoran, Parish Priest of Upton bought a site in Mill Lane and erected on it an old army hut which had served since 1919 as a church in Heswall. The first Mass in this new chapel, dedicated to Our Lady of Pity, was said on 5 August 1940. Sunday Mass was said by Father Corcoran who used to walk from Upton until the Revd J.A. Murphy (later Archbishop of Cardiff) became the first resident priest.

22. Lancs. R.O. RCLv Box 56.

23. St Laurence's Notice Book, 24 May 1936, announces that: 'After the May procession in church, the procession will proceed into Beckwith St., Watson St., Oak St. Oak St. has been specially chosen because the little girl who is to crown Our Lady resides there and because Oak St. will soon disappear as the houses are to be demolished. Oak St. has played a worthy part in the development of St Laurence's parish. . . '. To which the Editor has added: 'This was not just a slum clearance; it was the violent rupture of a close network of deep relationships between friends and relatives. We are paying the price now'.

24. M. Mary Hey was her Assistant; M. Margaret Stokes, Head of Infants and M. Mary Hannon, Assistant.

25. 1852 and 1862 respectively.

26. The fullest version of this statement is in FCJ A2506/1.

27. W.W. Mortimer: *The Hundred of Wirral*, 1847.

II

SHREWSBURY

A CATHOLIC COMMUNITY

Peter Phillips

Shrewsbury, like many towns of eighteenth century England, bears witness to the slow emergence of an urban Catholic community. The fact that its first Catholic chapel could be built as early as 1776, two years before the first Relief Act, and thus laying the community open to serious reprisals, is an indication of the easing of relations between the Catholic and his neighbours. It was not until 1791 that the building of chapels was permitted, but after 1778 most of the penal restraints were removed from the statute book. This, too, is a reflection of the growing toleration rather than its cause, although it was prompted immediately by the need to recruit Catholic highlanders into the army. The '45 could now be forgotten and the Catholic tended to be regarded as a somewhat quaint, though harmless, figure. This was a time of transition from from country to town and perhaps the Catholic community, unencumbered by the social restraints of the establishment from which it had been excluded for so long, was to gain particularly from the change. The Catholic Brook family of Madeley Court, for example, felt free to turn its attention to industry, opening the first iron forge in Coalbrookdale, the cradle of the Industrial Revolution.

Social patterns, nevertheless, change slowly. Far into the century Catholic life was centred on the extended family of the local gentry.   There were virtually no independent chapels. Most priests were still chaplains to recusant gentry, travelling form house to house in order to minister to the needs of their scattered flock.   One such 'riding circuit', centred on the eighteenth century Acton Burnell, stretched as far afield as Much Wenlock, Plowden and out to Welshpool. In fact the Catholic population of Shropshire was always well scattered. The Lichfield diocesan returns of 1676 indicate a mere handful of Catholics: eight within the bounds of the town parishes of Shrewsbury itself, out of a population of a little over 3,000.[1] A generous estimate of the Catholics in the whole county at the beginning of the eighteenth century might reach up to few more than 1,000.[2] By the end of the century numbers could have been rather lower: the Returns made by the Vicar Apostolic to the Congregation of Propaganda Fidei record a mere 480 Catholics in Shropshire, although these are acknowledged as being incomplete.[3] Around Shrewsbury were several Catholic enclaves. Plowden, standing in the discreet shade of the Long Mynd, maintained a series of Jesuit chaplains. The Smythes of Acton Burnell had close contact with Benedictines. The Brooks and Wolfes of Madeley, the Cloughs of Myndtown, near Bishop's Castle, and their kinsmen, the Beringtons of Moat Hall, outside Pontesbury, all supported secular missioners.

The Berington family has its town house in Saint Alkmund's Square, Shrewsbury, for long the focus of Catholic life in the town.   Both Cloughs and Beringtons were associated with the house. In fact as early as 1622 we hear of a search made for a priest named Clough.[4]   In the early eighteenth century a Mrs Clough, widow of Richard Clough of Myndtown, was living in the house with her brother Philip Berington. Both Philip Berington, who died in 1735, aged 55, and a kinsman, William, were noted as medical practitioners.   Like Dr Vavasour who, in an earlier generation, formed the centre of the Catholic community in York which claimed Margaret Clitherow as a member, they might well have found medicine a useful means of contact. In 1745 we find William Berington acting as executor, with one Richard Wolley, of Mary Peakman.[5] She could well have been a member of the household for she leaves £20, together with her bed and the furniture of her room, to Berington himself, and a bequest to another member of the family. Her mark on the will is witnessed by Elizabeth and Mary Clough and John Hornyold of Blackmore Park, most probably Mary Clough's father. Five years later, in a letter dated January 1750, William Berington explains that the bequest was meant for the upkeep of a priest:

> The money due upon this note was left for me in trust for Mr Jakeman's use during his living in this country and serving the congregation, and to his successors for ever on condition of remembering her in the proper manner.[6]

This priest was Francis Jakeman of Staffordshire, born a non-Catholic in March 1698 and entering the Church at the age of twelve.[7] Both he and his father are referred to in the list of Catholics and Non-Jurors compiled by Cosin after the Stuart Rising of 1715.[8] Jakeman studied at St. Omers, going to Rome in 1721. Here he completed his training for the priesthood and was ordained sub-deacon by the Pope, Benedict XIII, in March 1725. A few months later he was a priest. On his return to England in the early summer of 1728 he took up an appointment at Madeley Court. A few years later, probably by September 1731, he made his home in Shrewsbury and spent the rest of his priestly life there until illness forced him to retire to Longbirch, the home of the Vicars Apostolic, in Staffordshire. Here he died at the age of eighty, towards to end of March 1778. He certainly remained in Shrewsbury until after 1769, when he made his will. Like Mary Peakman, he could well have been a member of the Berington household but life could not have been easy. Mary Peakman's bequest would have helped somewhat;

before this he relied on the Beringtons for support. John Talbot Stonor, Vicar Apostolic of the Midland District, wrote of his situation in October 1740:

> I had a letter last post from Mr Jakeman who tells me that on the death of his patron 'twill be impossible for him to continue at Shrewsbury, without an addition of at least six pounds a year: if he can, even with that. I think by all means he ought to be kept there.[9]

In fact William Berington died in 1766 aged merely 56,[10] and two years afterwards the house in St. Alkmund's Square was sold. Mary Clough still lived in Shrewsbury: perhaps she provided a home for the priest. She acted as executrix to Jakeman and it was to her that he left the residue of his property, after several small bequests and £500 in Old South Sea Annuities, the interest to be given to the person who does duty in Shrewsbury. Age and infirmity were beginning to take their toll and Jakeman clearly needed assistance. In 1775, Anthony Clough came to visit his mother and was paid twelve guineas to supply in Shrewsbury.[11] He was chaplain to the Gifford family at Chillington, the estate which included Longbirch. He, too, became executor to Jakeman, in a codicil to the will, dated February 23rd 1777.

Some years earlier another priest was associated with Shrewsbury. This was Joseph Valentine, who was born in Rome on March 5th 1713, trained there and, after ordination, settled with the Giffard family of The Hay, near Madeley. He came to Shrewsbury, most probably on the death of John Giffard in 1759 and lived there until his own death on February 21st 1761. Whether he lived in Berington House is hard to tell: perhaps the priest already had a small house, or cottage, of his own. In 1775 John Manning did duty in Shrewsbury, whether as resident priest, or merely a passing visitor. It is his name which marks the opening of the baptismal register for the Shrewsbury mission, recording his baptising of Petronilla Death on December 11th that year.

Urban Community and First Chapel

The impression of Catholicism in Shrewsbury is of a small, house-based community, but this is not altogether accurate, as the Papists' Return of 1767 shows. In this year each Anglican vicar had to draw up a list of all the Catholics living in his parish, giving their names, ages occupations and the number of years they had resided in the parish. Unfortunately the Return for St Alkmund's parish is missing, or was perhaps never completed, and, with the Berington household there, one might expect to find a small group of Catholics, including Mary Clough and Jakeman himself. It cannot be certain that the other parishes made complete returns, but they list 32 Catholics:

Parish		Occupation	Age	Residence
St Mary's	Miss Alcock	companion to Mrs Holt	30	
	Joseph Laurence	Inn-holder	50	
		(NB his wife and children all Protestants)		
	-- Coffee	Plasterer	50	
	Widow Dod	Inn-keeper	48	
St Julian's	Widow Hill		40	6
	Cicily,	wife of George Bray	60	30
	Catherine Halsall	Cottager	65	19
	Rose,	wife of Fowler Lloyd	45	1
St Chad's	Mary Ann, widow of Wm Sandford, Apothecary			
	(two sons and one daughter, eldest 9)		40	12
	Ann Weaver	her Servant	18	1
	Thomas Mansell Staymaker		30	30
	His wife		30	20
	Elizabeth Ballard		50	20
	Margaret Walker her Servant		30	20
	Jane, wife of Wm Pillsbury Staymaker		50	14
	Thomas Pritchard Watchcase-maker		50	50
	His wife		50	30
	Mary Green		48	
	Magdalen Green		46	15
	Michael Kavannah Glover		47	20
	Two daughters	elder	19	
	Jane, wife of Geo. Jones Bargemaster		56	7
	Anne, wife of Jn Asterley Grocer		37	12
	Edward Tobin Glover		60	30

Jane, wife of Thos Boliver Smith		56	6mths
Edward Ruff		25	1
Henry Ruff		21	2
Benjamin Fenn	Inn-holder	60	21

Return of the Catholics in Shrewsbury 1767[12]

Using such small statistics, it is hard to give an accurate analysis of the sort of community it must have been. It is noteworthy, however, that the list points to a large proportion of women and very few children, although several family names mentioned in the list recur in the baptismal registers of the next generation. The community appears middle-aged and for the most part individuals seem to have moved into the town from elsewhere: there are dramatically few Shrewsbury-born Catholics. At the same time it is significant that most belong to the class of small traders and craftsmen; including three inn-keepers, a high percentage in such a tiny group. There must have been opportunity fir Catholics to make a comfortable living in what had become a busy County town. Local nobility and lesser gentry built town houses here. There were the Hunt Balls, the Shrewsbury Races and the Infirmary. The Shrewsbury season was comparable to the London ones. In fact Francis Pritchard, who could well have been the son of Thomas Pritchard, the Watchmaker, was able to leave £2,000 to support the mission, provided that a guinea a year be given to the Infirmary, in a bequest dated 1807.

With the death of William Berington and the presence of a small, but growing, community of Catholics in Shrewsbury, it was becoming evident that an independent chapel was necessary for the town. This project was initiated by Sir Edward Smythe of Acton Burnell, one of the best known Catholic laymen of the period. The Smythe family originated in Eshe in County Durham, and it was their property at Ushaw which eventually provided a new home for the students from the English College, Douai, forced to flee in the face of the French Revolution. The Smythe family, though after 1781 living generally at Wootten Wawan, Warwickshire, had long maintained property in Shropshire, supporting a continuous succession of Benedictine chaplains at Acton Burnell from 1748 until this present century. Acton Burnell was to provide a temporary home for two returning Benedictine communities, driven like the seminarists from the shores of France. In 1793 the community of St Laurence, Dieulouard, came to Shropshire before moving north and eventually settling at Ampleforth and two years later, after a spell of imprisonment in France, the monks of St Gregory's, Douai, arrived, staying at Acton Burnell until their removal to Downside in 1814.

In 1785 Sir Edward Smythe's niece, Maria, already twice widowed, married the Prince of Wales, though in secret in a London drawing-room before a bribed clergyman.[13] The king treated the marriage as null and arranged for his son to marry the Protestant Caroline of Brunswick. After this second marriage failed, the Prince lived with Maria Fitzherbert in secret for some years, Rome having declared the marriage, though clandestine, to be valid. This event more than ever hardened George III's heart against accepting emancipation for Catholics and at the same time won over Catholics a little further to the Hanoverian succession. The priest and historian, John Kirk, who himself came from Ruckley, just outside Acton Burnell, and could well have known her, is at pains to uphold her honour in the affair:

> Mrs Fitzherbert's long and intimate and mysterious connection, after the death of her husband, with George IV, while Prince of Wales, rendered her the topic of general conversation, more than perhaps any other female of her time; but by her friends and relations, and by all those who have ever enjoyed the honour of her acquaintance, she has always been regarded with the most unqualified sentiments of approbation and esteem.[14]

Sir Edward Smythe had been involved with the concerns of the small Catholic community in Shrewsbury for some few years. In 1774 his name occurs on a memorandum relating to a bequest of £500 towards the upkeep of a priest for the congregation at Shrewsbury left by Thomas Bell of Atcham, who died in the preceding year.[15] A series of rough accounts are still preserved amongst the Smythe papers at the County Record Office, which document the building of the first small chapel and priest's house, which stood at the beginning of Town Walls, just past Belmont Bank. The site is now marked by a pair of late-Victorian semi-detached houses but originally the chapel was set back discreetly from the roadway, shielded from view by the priest's house. During the course of 1776, Sir Edward raised funds from amongst the Catholic gentry.[16] The list provides an interesting note on the social patterns which bound the small community together. Smythe himself gave £50, matched by a further £50 from two of the Vicars Apostolic: Hornyold of the Midland District and Talbot of the London District. Other gifts came from farther afield and included generous gifts from the Earl Fingal, Lady Stourton, Lord Langdale, Mrs Townley, Thomas Giffard and Lord Shrewsbury. The collection raised £269 12s, to which was added £164, raised by the sale of Old South Sea Annuities. Meanwhile, at the end of March, Samuel Scoltock had been commissioned to buy a house and garden. During the summer the old house was pulled down and the new building started. The total work came to £390 5s and the bill was finally cleared by the last day of October. There is no reason to believe that the first mass was not celebrated within a few weeks, although it was not until the following July that Sir Edward presented a Missal to the Chapel. This still rests in the sacristy of the Cathedral, the inscription reading:

> This Missal was given by Sir Edward Smythe, Bart., for the use of the Shrewsbury Chapel, July 18th 1777. Pray for him and all his family.

The first priest to be associated permanently with this new chapel was James Corne. He was born on 20th August, 1745 in Betley, not far from Newcastle-under-Lyne, Staffordshire.

The Diary of the 'Blue Nuns' in Paris[17] records that his father had been a Protestant but became a Catholic upon reading Challoner's *Think Well On't*, an apologetic work, which he had picked up out of a marl pit. As a result of his conversion, he threw open his home in January 1762 to welcome Challoner's small boarding school, run by the Revd William Errington. The following year, on Lady Day 1763, the twelve or thirteen boys removed in a covered wagon to Sedgley Park, Wolverhampton. At this time James was already at Douai, entering the first year, aged 11, on November 3rd 1756. The Prefect of Studies' Book[18] records his progress through the College. It seems that life at Douai affected his health, for his studies were interrupted by periods in England. For a time, also, he stayed with his uncle, Charles Corne, who lived in Paris as chaplain to the 'Blue Nuns'. The elder Corne must have been a colourful figure and had a wealth of stories to tell his nephew. Like his brother, Charles had grown up a Protestant, settling in Chester as a distiller. Their mother's family, the Butlers of Great Eccleston, had long supported the Stuart cause and Charles himself threw in his lot with Bonnie Prince Charlie and the '45. After the defeat at Culloden, Charles Corne fled to Ireland and, on becoming a Catholic, left for France to train as a priest, settling eventually with the nuns in Paris. He never returned to work in England.

James Corne stayed with his uncle for some time, returning to Douai in August 1768. By October 1771, after a further spell in England, he became a minor professor in charge of High Figures, the third form. A few months later he was ordained sub-deacon in Arras. By the following Spring he had been ordained deacon in Cambrai and soon later he left Douai for Paris *en route* for England and priestly ordination. For the first few years of his priestly ministry he worked as spiritual director at Sedgley Park, before moving to take charge of the mission in Shrewsbury. Exactly when he moved presents us with something of an enigma. Kirk, who know Corne well, asserts that he did not move to Shrewsbury until 1783. The baptismal registers of the mission, however, indicate that he officiated at a baptism early in November

1776. Whether he remained in Shrewsbury from this date is hard to tell but it could well have been the case. Certainly Bishop Talbot's confirmation lists record James Corne as resident in the mission in early April 1782. There seems to be no evidence pointing to any other priest serving the small community of Catholics in Shrewsbury at this time. Perhaps for a short period the new priest's house on Town Walls was indeed without a resident priest and duties were carried out by the Benedictines of Acton Burnell, but the is no indication of this.

Corne remained in Shrewsbury until his death in 1817. He seems to have been a well-read, gentle priest, who won the hearts of all, both Protestants and Catholics alike. The note in Tichborne Blount's Diary, as he left Douai for the English mission records 'a man of excellent talents, great application and edifying conduct'.[19]   It is echoed in the comment preserved in Owen and Blakeway's *History of Shrewsbury* after his death:

> His peculiarly mild, unassuming and Christian-like manners obtained him the respect and esteem of all ranks and persuasions.[20]

Corne, in fact, epitomises the spirit of the late eighteenth century intellectual renaissance among Catholics, concerned to nurture the values of tolerance and reason inherited from the Enlightenment.

This is the tradition reflected in the historical work of John Kirk, who numbered Corne among his friends and especially in the many published works of John Lingard, the priest and historian. Indeed Lingard, too, must have been a visitor to Shrewsbury: we find his name mentioned in the baptismal register of the mission in July 1812. These men were concerned to stress the English quality of the Catholic community, preserving its strong tradition of lay involvement in religious affairs and seeking to maintain a certain independence from Rome. In some urban communities, such as can be found in Wigan, or Liverpool, some moves were

made towards constitutional parish government, with affairs
in the hands of a committee of lay-people.[21] As a model for
church administration, however, this seemed to be short
lived.

The issue became painful and acrimonious, casting a
shadow of division in the Catholic community.[22] The more
extreme representatives if this tradition, such as the
theologian Joseph Berington, supported to a greater or lesser
extent by a group of Staffordshire clergy, were challenged by
the intemperate language of the opposing party, increasingly
dominated by the figure of John Milner, who became Vicar
Apostolic of the Midland District in 1803. Milner, hammer
of Berington and the Staffordshire clergy, epitomises the new
character of English Catholicism. Born in 1752 and educated
at Sedgley Park and Douai, he took charge of the Catholic
mission in Winchester, where he was ordained bishop in
1803. His first act on moving north might be considered
symbolic: he transferred his residence from the old country
home of the Vicars Apostolic, Longbirch, in rural
Staffordshire, to Giffard House in the heart of the fast-
growing industrial Wolverhampton. His life-work was
marked by a struggle to free the Church from the oversight of
landed interest, which had nurtured the Catholic community
through the rigours of penal days, and at the same time to
preserve its independence from control by the newly
emerging middle class. He opted for a model of the Catholic
community fully under the control of the clergy. In spite of
the reservations we might have, it must be admitted that this
was also an option for the poor. Right through the
nineteenth century, the Catholic clergy remained a voice for
the working class. As a result of the vision of men such as
Milner, the Catholic community was the only denomination
that may be regarded as retaining strong ties with the urban
poor.[23]

Many Catholics were unhappy with both extremes of the
argument. Sir Edward Smythe, for example, representing
landed interest, while happy with lay involvement, was
particularly ill at ease with those whom he considered to be

propagating 'diabolical . . . republican and levelling principles'.[24] Corne, advocating tolerance as ever, was a non-participant in the feuding. When the Staffordshire clergy tried to clear the air by publicizing their beliefs in *A Short and Plain Statement of Facts,* issued at the beginning of December 1798, we find Corne anxiously writing to Kirk, one of the signatories, ten days later:

> The (bishops) might have been satisfied with the explanation given and I am sorry to see the disturbance still kept up. If any measures shall be proposed that are likely to silence the clamour and restore peace and harmony, you may depend on my willingness to concur in them.[25]

Even a man as outspoken as Milner himself evidently warmed to Corne: contrasting him with John Corne, his brother, Milner commented, 'James Corne was all soul; John all body'.[26] In the thick of the dispute in 1798 we find Corne's name put forward as a suitable candidate to fill the vacant Midland Vicariate, although in the event it remained unfilled until 1800, when Gregory Stapleton, first President of St Edmund's, Ware, was appointed as a 'stop-gap'.

Corne's worries over property tax in 1803 prompted a letter to John Roe, which gives us a glimpse of the financial situation of a small independent mission at this time.[27] The collection from such a small congregation was minimal and Corne relied mainly on the small endowments left to the mission as Mass offerings. Most of the money for the District seems to have been in the hands of the London bankers, Wright and Company, much of it invested in Old South Sea Annuities. This brought in a small, but adequate interest. As we have seen, Mary Peakman, Philip Berington, Jakeman, Thomas Bell of Atcham, Francis Pritchard, had all left money to support the priest. To this was added money for other Masses from the Common Purse, the general funds at the disposal of the priests of the Midland District. All this amounted to £49 a year. Corne himself had a small annuity from private sources which meant that his yearly income amounted to about £100. Sometimes the terms of a will might affect a priest's salary. Berington's trust, for example, stipulates that 'none but a secular priest can be entitled to the produce of this Fund'.[28]   When Louis Le Maitre assumed control of the mission, being a monk he could not fulfil this requirement and the Berington Masses were celebrated by John Kirk.[29] Corne could have managed to live simply within the constraints of this slender budget, but it would not have been easy. Nevertheless, many Anglican clergy had similarly low incomes at this time: in 1827 over half the livings had an income of £50 a year or less though, in this case in order to make ends meet, many of the clergy were compelled to hold more than one benefice and pastoral care necessarily suffered.[30]

Out of this income in the last period of his life, with his health beginning to give way, Corne had to provide for assistance. Amongst the bequests made in his will is a gift of £150 to Elizabeth Butler 'for her careful attendance on me in my long illness'.[31] Miss Butler could well have been a cousin: his grand-mother had been an Elizabeth Butler, as we have already noted. Out of this money, also, Corne had to provide for priestly help in periods of illness. John Kirk, writing after a visit to Acton Burnell to celebrate the funeral of his mother, mentions that Corne had been unable to celebrate Mass for some months owing to his 'being in a serious situation from an abscess in the Jaw' resulting from a decayed tooth.[32] Perhaps again Anthony Clough had helped out in the mission as he had done in 1775. Certainly Corne was anxious that he appreciated that the £5 forwarded to Clough at this time had come from Shrewsbury.

Shadow of the French Revolution

Soon, however, events which were to send shock waves throughout Europe resulted in more permanent help being available in Shrewsbury. Corne's concern regarding the property tax reflected the need to finance a war which had broken out between Britain and France in the wake of the

French Revolution. This had already driven the English
Benedictines to make a temporary home in Acton Burnell.
Troubled times drove many others to seek refuge on English
shores and for the first time Catholics were seen to be victims
of a despotism of the mob more terrible than the absolutism
of the old Catholic monarchies. English Protestantism
warmed somewhat towards the plight of the Catholics. 1791
saw the passing of a Second Relief Act which at last
legitimated Catholic Chapels, provided that worship did not
proceed behind closed doors - a shadow of ancient fears.
Many houses were thrown open to the French refugees. In
fact more than 5,000 clergy and many lay-people fled to
England before the Terror that bore down on France. Many
made little contribution to English Catholic life, living on
small Government pensions in hope of a speedy return across
the channel. Some, however, made what contribution they
could to the small Catholic communities, enriching the
pattern of local affairs.

   This was the case in Shrewsbury. The Forresters of
Dothill Park, near Wellington, opened their house as a refuge
for emigre clergy. It was here that the two brothers, Stephan
and Louis Le Maitre first came. The Shrewsbury baptismal
registers show that both provided assistance to Mr Corne,
although Louis most probably was more involved with the
Mission at Dothill Park from 1811 -1818.[33] Earlier than this,
in 1809, we find the latter celebrating a baptism in
Shrewsbury. As Corne's health began to fail, they must have
taken a more prominent part in the affairs of the mission and,
on his death, on 4th December 1817, appear to have taken
over the administration of the community. About Stephan
we know virtually nothing: he died in 1818 after slipping on a
piece of glass in Pride Hill, Shrewsbury. Louis was a
Benedictine monk, originally coming from the observant
house of Saint-Vaast at Arras which has close associations
with the community of St. Gregory at Douai.[34] Certainly his
association with the Gregorians is borne out by two letters,
preserved in the archives at Downside. They give some
indication of the exiles' attempts to find new direction. One,

a letter written by Le Maitre himself in February 1808 to
Dom Anselm Lorymer about some French texts which had
been ordered, suggests that he might well have been running
a small French class at this time.[35]   The other letter is from
Soeur Maur, a French Trappistine whose community
eventually settled at Stapehill in Dorset.   She is writing to her
confidant and spiritual director, Dom Hilaire Le Weugue,
another monk from Saint-Vaast who lived at Acton Burnell as
a boarder for the last few years.   It was her hope that Le
Maitre and a companion of his at Dothill Park, Leveaux,
might find happiness with the group of French Cistercians,
led by Dom Augustin de Lestrange, which had settled at
Lulworth.[36]   It was not to be: Leveaux, a Maurist, joined Le
Weugue at Acton Burnell and Le Maitre ended his days in
Shrewsbury.   He outlived his brother by four years, dying at
the age of 65 in June 1822.   He had been looked after, in the
small priest's house, by his sister, or possibly cousin, Maria
Rosa Le Maitre, whose name occurs frequently in the
baptismal register at this time.   In fact they share the same
grave, still to be found in Old St Chad's churchyard.

A small group of emigres eventually settled in
Shrewsbury.   Owen and Blakeway record the death of Maria
Anna de Bremond de la Feuillade in 1803.[37]   Her husband
apparently became a dancing master.   They further record
that this woman's epitaph had been written by Peter Francis
Peltier, or Pelletier, whom they describe as a former Canon of
Arras Cathedral before his exile to Shrewsbury, where he
made a living by teaching French.   In fact this could well be
the same priest whose death was noted in *The Laity's
Directory*, 1808, as having died the previous January.   Here he
is described as a former member of the Congregation of the
Oratory and professor of the College du Mars.

In September 1794, Pelletier had been godfather to the
son of another emigre, William Bourlay, a former dancing
master from Angers, who had been befriended by Sir
Frederick Corbett of Sundorne Castle and brought to
Shropshire.   Bourlay made his home in St John's Hill,
Shrewsbury, and ran a dancing academy in the Town Hall,

holding other classes as far afield as Wellington, Church Stretton and Pontesbury. Shortly before Christmas 1791 he was arranging an Annual Ball to be held in the Theatre and was running a regular Wednesday fencing class. We have already mentioned the thriving social round of late eighteenth century Shrewsbury: Bourlay's talents must have been in great demand, for he seems to have had considerable success. By 1796 he published a pamphlet, *The Pupil's Assistant in Dancing, or, The Master's Advice to his Scholars*, Three years later he was again advertising classes in fencing for two hours, twice weekly:

> no period of History furnishes a more just Criterion for impressing the rising generation with the obvious Powers of Self-Defence.[38]

Bourlay himself died, aged 57, in April 1817 but his son, William Vestris Bourlay, continued the academy most successfully, publishing his *Companion to the Ballroom* in 1820 and defending his dancing pedigree against libel from another school in 1833. The family remains in Shrewsbury to this day.

The tension that such a group of refugees must have caused in a small provincial county town, such as Shrewsbury, is well illustrated by an appeal made by William Bourlay in the local paper, 12th August 1795. He offered a reward of five guineas to anyone aiding the conviction of a person spreading rumours that he refused to drink the health of the King in the Fox Inn - a report 'not more false than malicious'.[39]

The times were not easy. At the turn of the century Bourlay was host to his nephew from Antwerp, Philippe Delahault, who had come to England to perfect his English with a view to setting up business. Delahault's letters after his return to the Continent provide an interesting commentary on the course of the war between England and France:

the Frenchmen speak more of war than they do in England. They say that they are going to breakfast this summer and drink port wine.[40]

Boats were already standing by at Dunkirk and troops in Holland prepared for the invasion. The scare soon receded. Another letter, written on 5th April 1803 (noted also in the French style, 15 Germinal an II) records the preparation afoot for Napoleon's visit to Brussels and Antwerp. In Brussels 60,000 francs were laid out for a carriage of splendid proportions; gowns of Brussels lace were being made ready for Bonaparte's wife; the merchants were preparing a pavilion for a grand supper at which the nobility would form a guard of honour with new gold bedecked uniforms. Antwerp went to no less trouble. The hall that was to house a supper for three or four hundred, at five guineas a head, was decorated with great murals depicting Bonaparte's victories. All along the route, through towns and villages, vagrants, the population of the work houses and the *filles publiques* seem to have been bundled off to the colonies — 'islands that have never been inhabited by Europeans before'[41] — though we might accept this as something of an exaggeration born out of the enthusiasm of the day!

We hear no more of Delahault but the war was long and painful. French prisoners of war came to Hawkstone and Bonaparte's brother, Lucian, was for a time under house arrest at Mawley Hall, near Ludlow. His son, Louis Napoleon, was baptised there on January 5th 1813. Two years later Napoleon was finally defeated at Waterloo. In the Catholic mission at Shrewsbury, someone preserved the report of the battle from *The Times*. It was the end of an age. Nevertheless the French Revolution left its scars. The cry of revolution brought to an untimely end many hopes for long overdue social and religious reform in Britain. Within the Catholic community the party which had worked for a more democratic church, with only fairly loose ties with Rome, was in eclipse. For nearly everyone the aspirations of the Age of Reason had only one outcome — revolution. Many saw

Edmund Burke as the prophet of a new security rooted in a traditional English conservatism.

Consolidation

Bishop Milner can be found celebrating the sacrament of Confirmation in Shrewsbury in 1808, in 1817, and again in 1822. Perhaps he resided in the Mission for a few weeks in the autumn of 1822; his name certainly occurs in the baptismal register for September 1822. After the death of Louis Le Maitre in June 1822, the chapel seems to have been left without a permanent priest. George Howe, missioner at Newport, appears to have done duty in the summer of that year, filling in as best he could. *The Laity's Directory* of 1824 records that in the previous year the Mission was in the care of two priests, Augustine Harrison and Benedict Wassel. These were both Benedictines from Acton Burnell. Wassel was the younger, having been educated at Acton Burnell and solemnly professed as a monk in June 1808.[42] He died in retirement after a long career on the mission, in July 1871. Harrison was also ordained priest in England but must have been one of the last monks of the community to be professed at Douai; he was one of the group of monks who had escaped to Acton Burnell in 1793.[43] By January 1824, Samuel Jones had taken over the oversight of the mission. He had been educated at Oscott and must have been a man in the mould of Milner himself, publishing an epitome of Milner's *End of Controversy* with the title *Rule of Faith*. This little work of apologetics was published in Shrewsbury by Charles Hulbert in the summer of 1831. In fact on Milner's death in 1826, Samuel Jones received a small bequest of £20.

The congregation numbered about 60 each Sunday at Mass but must have been steadily growing at this time as the Catholic community itself was gaining in self-confidence. The baptismal registers for the first half of the nineteenth century record a slow but steady increase of baptisms from a mere 6 in 1821 to 22 in 1831, 26 in 1841 and 39 in 1851. Figures relating to Easter communicants indicate 33 in 1823.

By 1833 the number had risen to 111 and within the next ten years had grown to 244.[44] Even from the early part of the century, the registers suggest that a gradual stream of Irish immigrants was swelling the numbers of worshippers. Many of these represent families of Irish labourers journeying towards the Midlands in search of work. In February 1824 a local Justice of the Peace, Justice Smith, was heard to remark, concerning the work on the new turnpike road through Shrewsbury north to Holyhead:

> What were they going to do all this for? For the Irish he supposed. We should we do it, we get nothing by them![45]

A wealth of social comment lies behind the phrase. In fact, however, this new road from London to Holyhead, and the increasing ease of coach travel was indeed to change the face of Shrewsbury in more ways than one. The Shrewsbury Season at least had become a thing of the past: those who could afford such entertainment preferred now to travel up to London.

In view of the growth in numbers, one of Samuel Jones first tasks was to enlarge the tiny chapel. The chapel, now to contain a congregation of nearly 250, was re-opened on October 4th 1826: a somewhat indifferent sketch has been preserved in a scrapbook, now in the Local Studies Library in Shrewsbury.[46] Henry Pidgeon was present at the ceremony and gives a detailed description of the newly appointed building.[47] A passage to the west of the chapel was incorporated into the building and a spacious gallery erected by reducing the priest's house and bringing the front of the chapel itself about ten feet nearer the road. The discretion which had been in order when the chapel had first been established, before the abolition of penal restraints, was no longer necessary. Now the building of stone and stucco was fronted by a porch which overlooked the street. This was surmounted by a plain cross. The whole building was strictly classical in style with not a hint of the Gothic.

The inside of the building had also been redecorated and re-ordered. Pidgeon speaks approvingly of the elegance of its interior decorations and the taste displayed in the decoration of the ceiling. The work had been completed by John Carline, a member of the local family of sculptors and architects responsible for much fine work in the Shrewsbury area. The firm of Carline and Tilley had build the Welsh Bridge in 1791 and rebuilt St Alkmund's a few years later. Pidgeon notes that the previous Altar Piece had been a large square of tooled leather, gilt and chequered. At each angle of this were flaming cherubs and a blazing star with cross and a heart pierced with nails at the centre. The new altar, however, was somewhat more elaborate. It was approached by steps and had on it a copy of Da Vinci's Last Supper executed by Corbett, a local artist. The tabernacle had gilt pilasters and above, Carline had placed a crucifix with bas relief figure surmounted with a semicircular inscription, 'Thus God so loved the world'. The Communion rails ran straight across the Sanctuary from wall to wall of the building and the body of the chapel was simply divided by one central aisle.

The re-opening of the chapel was celebrated with High Mass, presided over by Thomas Walsh, the new Vicar Apostolic for the Midland district. Prayers were said in Latin and English and the Revd J. Abbot came from Oscott to preach. It seems to have been a long service, beginning at 10.00 a.m. and continuing until nearly 1.00. Again Pidgeon is an appreciative observer, commenting favourably on the excellent music and singing, and noting that the congregation, though a respectable size, did not fill the chapel. There was a larger attendance at the afternoon service, at which the bishop himself preached 'seated on his throne with a gilt crozier in his left hand'. His sermon, possibly with a view to calming the local opposition to the growing Catholic community in Shrewsbury, was an exhortation to patience in the face of calumny. He insisted that the Catholic religion forbade the worship of false idols and emphasised that no power on earth, even for millions of pounds, could pardon someone for telling an untruth. All these comments smack of a refutation of common gossip and the accusation of equivocation so often directed at Catholics. Pidgeon carefully records what was said:

> The conditions bestowed upon you are that you should give alms to the poor not money for the Pope... Never seek to advance your religion by reviling that of your enemies. When a neighbour is in distress seek not to enquire of what is his religion but immediately fly to his relief. Be strictly just in all your dealings - yet it is from the sacredness of an oath that prevents you from sitting in Parliament.[48]

Already we can sense a change of attitude in the air. On the one hand the quiet tolerance of the eighteenth century has given way to a strong surge of anti-Catholic feeling; and at the same time there is talk of giving Catholics the vote.

Towards Emancipation

Some weeks later, on December 10th, Mr Jones was clearly echoing the bishop's words. His Sunday sermon was preached as an appeal for the Salop Infirmary, raising £7 for the hospital. That Sunday, the congregation was about 70. But the hostility to Catholicism which must have inspired Bishops Walsh's exhortation to patience, was also clearly evident in Shrewsbury at this time. On November 5th, that great celebration of anti-Catholic feeling, the local Wesleyan minister, Mr Marsden, gave a flaming sermon against the Pope and the absurdities of the Roman Catholic religion'.[49] In March 1827, a vast petition was sent from Shrewsbury to Parliament as part of a national campaign to scotch plans for emancipation: 1,526 signatures went to the House of Lords, 1,583 to the Commons. Pidgeon himself, as always, proved to be a sympathetic observer. Whatever his own opinion might have been, he records the extreme bias of the petition:

> had a public meeting been called the above petition would have had a better effect on the inhabitants - children were allowed to

sign the present one and many names were put down *in absentia*.[50]

As was to be expected, the Catholic question was lost this year but as ever generated dramatic interest. Pidgeon records the news. It was a close thing: 272 voting for emancipation, 276 against. With 552 Members present in the House it was 'the greatest number ever known'. The local Shrewsbury M.P., Panton Corbett, voted against the Catholic lobby.

If Catholic Emancipation had been simply a matter of popular feeling, it might well not have been introduced for many years. It was in fact a matter of political necessity. When the Tory Government steered it through Parliament in April 1829 they did so in an attempt to quell serious unrest in Ireland. In England, apart from the ill-feeling generated against Catholics, the Catholic community remained for the most part untroubled; after all in what was still an un-reformed Parliament few possessed the vote anyway. The Bill passed through its various stages amidst further petitions: in February 1829, 2,000 names form Shrewsbury were added to another 5,000 from the rest of the county in protest against attempts to extend the Catholic franchise in any way. The chief political result of the Act was that it signalled the end of the long Tory ascendancy. The first piece of Parliamentary reform weakened the government and, at least indirectly, made way for the great Whig administration which heralded the Reform Act of 1832.

This must have been a time for the Catholic community to explore where it stood in relation to the establishment. In the days of Berington and the Staffordshire clergy, many felt that Catholics had more in common with the body of Dissenters. Indeed Berington engaged in discussion with Joseph Priestley, the dissenting Birmingham scientist. Milner was unhappy with this self-image, feeling perhaps that it gave too much authority to the local community, and preferring a model of Church order which was more akin to that of the Established Church. An interesting footnote to this earlier discussion is provided by a letter written at this time by Jones to Bishop Walsh, on the matter of the possibility of Catholics being appointed Churchwardens in the Anglican Church.[51] This was an issue which had been raised at the clergy meeting in Northampton. The implications of the question are rather more wide-ranging that they might at first seem. The fabric of the Anglican parish church was maintained by a local rate on the whole community and authorised by an annual meeting at which all the townsfolk were eligible to vote. In some urban areas, where Dissenting communities were strong, the blocking of this rate gave Dissenters some negotiating power against the establishment. Sometimes this led to rioting: it was such riots in Birmingham over the Church Rate in the autumn election of 1832 that prompted Thomas Arnold's alarmist declaration, 'The Church as she now stands, no human power can save'. Arnold looked to the creation of a national Church which, based on broad moral commitment rather than the ancient creeds, might embrace all Christians. This was certainly not to be, but the controversies mark a significant stage in the history of Christianity in Britain. For the first time Christians were forced to face up to the problems of religious pluralism. It was the beginning of a long and painful journey. Samuel Jones, meanwhile, made his own enquiries and wrote to the bishop that it was quite impossible for Catholics to take on the role of Churchwarden in the Established Church. It is interesting to note that Jones at least, like Milner before him, was not prepared to recognise himself as a Dissenter and speaks rather disdainfully of the fact that '*malgre nous* the *Law* considers us as Dissenters'.[52]

No doubt life within the small Catholic community in Shrewsbury was relatively untroubled by such debates. Mr Jones himself would have added nothing to the fires of controversy and his quiet manner must have won approval in the town. Pidgeon again notes in his diary:

> Mr Jones is a mild unassuming and charitable gentleman and is an ornament to the religion which he professes.[53]

On Wednesday October 24th 1827, Mr Abbott returned once more from Oscott to preach at a celebratory High Mass. This time it was to mark the installation of a small Chamber Organ in the Chapel. It had been built by G. Parsons of Bloomsbury, London. Some time after mass a short recital was given on the new instrument and a collection raised £23 towards the expense of the organ. The instrument has done worthy service for it was this, transferred eventually to the new Cathedral, that provided music for services until 1974, when it was replaced by the much larger Mander's Organ. Even now, however, the old instrument plays on, serving the small village church at Mainstone, on the edge of the Clun Forest, adjacent to the 8th century earthwork of Offa's Dyke.

Music could now enhance the regular services on Town Walls: Sunday Mass at 10.30 and Latin Vespers in the afternoon, Mr Jones preaching at both. On the first Sunday of the month, Benediction was added. During the week there was mass on Wednesdays and Fridays. At this time, also, a small school was incorporated in the buildings on Town Walls. Earlier in the century some small beginnings of a day-school were set up in a house occupied by Merryfield at the back of Wyle Cop. Some time later this was transferred to the 13th century Tower on Town Walls. Here Patrick Harding, an Irishman and ex-sergeant-of-Militia, held classes during the week and taught catechism on Sunday. The children moved to their new quarters on his death at the age of 37, in December 1827.

Poverty and Progress

Jones himself died in August 1833. The Revd Eugene Egan replaced him in Shrewsbury and remained in charge of the mission for the next twenty years, a period of dramatic change both for Shrewsbury and for the Catholic community at large. Famine in Ireland and the ever-increasing demands of Industry led to a rapid growth amongst the Catholic urban poor. This increase in numbers, together with tensions created by the Continental religious and local secular missioners, highlighted the weakness in the ecclesiastical structure and paved the way for the establishment of the Hierarchy in 1850.   At much the same time a number of important converts, including Newman in 1845 and Manning in 1851, may have helped to win some acceptance for Catholics in the nation as a whole: but the process was to be slow and often very painful.

One of an earlier group of converts was George Spencer, younger son of the second Earl Spencer.[54] An Anglican priest, he became a Catholic in 1830 and was ordained in Rome two years later.   After working in the heart of the industrial Midlands, he was appointed Spiritual Director at Oscott in 1839.   The year before this he had established his Crusade for the Conversion of England, preaching and lecturing.   The local paper records his visit to Shrewsbury in August 1839[55] when he preached at a solemn High Mass and again at Benediction.   On this occasion entry to the Chapel was by ticket rather than the usual collection, perhaps an attempt to dissuade unwelcome onlookers.   Some years after his visit to Shrewsbury, Spencer became a Passionist, attracted by the figure of Dominic Barberi, who had dedicated his life to the conversion of England.   On the latter's death in 1849, Father Ignatius (as Spencer had become on assuming the habit) became English Provincial.   One of his tasks in these years was to oversee the establishment of a new Order of religious sisters, finally approved in Rome In 1863 as the Sisters of the Cross and Passion.

The foundress of this Order, which took its inspiration from Barberi, was a Shrewsbury woman who could possibly have been present at Spencer's sermon in August 1839. Elizabeth Prout was born in Coleham on September 2nd 1820, the only child of a staunch Anglican mother and lapsed Catholic father.[56]   Edward Prout was a cooper by trade and worked at the brewery in Coleham but lost his job when it closed down in 1831.   By 1841 the family had left Shrewsbury and were living in Stone, Staffordshire, where her father had again found employment.   Apparently she had a happy childhood and received a good education at one of the many small schools which had grown up in early nineteenth century Shrewsbury. In her early twenties she had come under the influence of Dominic Barberi, who had arrived from Italy in 1841 and lived in Aston Hall, just outside Stone. Soon later she was received into the Church. Her parents could not cope with this and she was driven from home to find work teaching in the slums of Manchester. Feeling herself called to the religious life, in 1848 she joined the Sisters of the Infant Jesus in Northampton, a French community which had arrived in England in 1845 and opened a school for the poor. Soon, however, her health broke down and her doctor declared that she would remain a semi-invalid for the rest of her life. At last she was welcomed home and her mother nursed her back to health. Eventually, after turning down a proposal of marriage, she returned to Manchester to devote her life to the urban poor.

There had been a lot of changes in Shrewsbury during this period. In 1840 the chapel was again extended by turning the girls' school into a gallery overlooking the chapel below. But already in 1841, after his visit for Confirmations, Bishop Walsh was writing to Kirk:

> The chapel is lighted with gas and is become much to small. A large Church here would soon be filled, notwithstanding the bigotry of the town.[57]

A few years later Eugene Egan was writing to his bishop complaining of the poverty of the community and his problems paying for the school.[58] He was asking Bishop Wiseman for help in order to keep the school open. Many of these children must have been from the families of Irish labourers who had been brought to the town with the building of the Great Western Railway in 1845. This brought with it many problems for an already overstretched community, suddenly enlarged by possibly over 300 people. For a time Egan had some assistance from his brother, James Egan, who had been working in Lincolnshire and eventually spent some time in Congelton. In February we find Egan writing to the bishop for temporary faculties for his brother to help him in Shrewsbury. This would allow two Masses on Sunday and a regular daily Mass, as well as a period for Confessions each evening and more frequent week night instructions. In making his request, Egan notes:

> The construction of the railways here has necessarily given me more labour. In fact there is work enough for two priests in attending to the Congregation, the Gaol, the workhouse, the Infirmary and the assylum.[59]

The local paper gives a more detailed picture of at least one of these pastoral duties that Egan refers to: that of caring for prisoners.[60] On March 23rd 1836, a Mr Woodward, a malt-mill maker, was returning to Shrewsbury with his nephew after the fair in Wrexham. They were set upon by five men who had blocked the road with a thorn-bush and were waiting in ambush behind the hedge. Things might have been worse if they had not been rescued by a local man who happened to be passing but the robbers escaped with various items of booty. This proved to be but one of a series of robberies: one, a few days earlier, near Disley, and another the following day, just outside Altrincham - a testimony to the speed with which the men could travel. There had been other robberies, to, as it turned out, in Prescot and Chorley. Within a few days two of the men were arrested after a scuffle, trying to pawn some of the objects in a pawnbrokers in Deansgate, Manchester. The three others were soon picked up in a public house, The Fox, close by, in Jackson's Row. They still carried evidence of their crime about them, together with clasp-knives, tinder-boxes and clay-pipes, with tin covers, so that they could smoke in the dark without being seen.

The five men, all Irish labourers and three of whom were brothers, were brought back to Shrewsbury to await trial at the Quarter Sessions. They were met by a huge crowd of curious townsfolk. Woodward managed to identify two of them, one as a 'little man with dark coat and white buttons'[61]

Eventually they all confessed and were committed for trial. One of the youngest, John Mulholland, broke down: 'I have a wife and four children; it was a bad day when I met them and I told McDaniel when near Ellesmere not to beat them for it was pretty well to rob them'.[62] Perhaps it was for this reason that Mulholland and one of the three brothers, Owen McDaniel (alias Donnelly) were sentenced merely to transportation for life, an apparent gesture of leniency. The others, Patrick and Edward McDaniel (alias Donnelly) and Laurence Curtis, were to be hanged. Owen stayed with his brothers till the hour of their death and Egan and the Revd R Colgan, who came over from Plowden, were unceasing in their attention, spending up to eight hours a day praying or reading with the condemned men.[63]

The trail finished on 1st August but they had to wait until 13th for sentence to be carried out. A somewhat mawkish sentimentality hangs over the accounts in the paper as the weeks go by: a letter admitting their responsibility, asking forgiveness and forgiving those who had hurt them, an attempt by Edward McDaniel to write to his mother which was prevented by Egan, who promised to write later. During this time they had a visit from the father of a lad who had been sentenced in Liverpool with two others for a robbery in Rochdale. These two were now waiting in the hulks at Chatham to be transported for life. The Shrewsbury men accepted responsibility for this crime, too. On the day of execution they received Communion from Mr Egan at about 7.30. Their irons were struck and they received their own clothes for their last journey. Egan and Mr Colgan remained with them all the time. From the scaffold itself they reaffirmed their guilt for the Rochdale crime, Patrick McDaniel crying out: 'Those men in the Liverpool gaol, they are innocent of the Rochdale robbery. It was I that did it; no Englishman was at the job!'[64] Edward McDaniel kissed the priest's hand, 'May God reward you'. His brother said a final prayer: 'Good Christians, pray for us — we die in the Catholic faith. God be merciful to us sinners. Into thy hands we commend our spirits.   Lord Jesus, receive our souls'[65] After their death plaster casts were taken of the dead men's heads by a phrenololgist from Manchester. They were buried in St Mary's Churchyard.

One of the most disturbing things about the whole episode was the immense crowd that gathered for the event. It offers a telling comment on the darker side of nineteenth century England.   Indeed the *Chronicle* itself professes concern:

> We have already stated that the spectators at the awful closing scene of the malefactors was immense. Will it be believed that in a country calling itself civilized three-fourths of the spectators were young females. Several young persons were asked 'Why they attended the execution? The answers were, 'People tell us if we once see an execution we shall not be hanged ourselves'. Such is the ignorance and superstition yet prevalent in Shropshire! And a school — erected opposite our County Prison — is not deemed worthy of support![66]

It was estimated that upwards of 10,000 were present that morning. They had come from all over the county and particularly from the collieries around Wellington, Ironbridge and Shiffnal. Some had come form as far afield as Bilston. Every window and place with a view of the scaffold was crowded with spectators. Castle Walls and the bank in front of the Castle was packed, so too the terrace in front of the prison. Waggons and vehicles, 'chiefly loaded with women', had arrived in droves in the hours preceding the execution. The whole thing was a sorry and sad event.

Poverty was a crushing buden, Many in the community barely survived. Egan, as ever, did what he could. In January 1849 Egan had to apologise to the bishop for the delay in collecting money for the bishop's fund:

> The very Sunday appointed in your letter for the collection had been previously fixed for our collecting clothes for the the poor children of this Congregation. We have given clothes to about 50 of them and several others are asking for what we can't give.

The Congregation though far too numerous for our confined Chapel is very poor. Under the circumstances I have deferred the collection till next week. The last Lenten collection amounted only to £3 10s.[67]

Obviously financial worries, especially those concerning the maintenance of the school, weighed heavily. His letter concludes:

> we are very much straitened here in consequence of maintaining a school (which took about £15 of my salary last year) and keeping the Chapel as it ought to be kept. It is quite as expensive to me as a good sized Church would be. Our schoolroom in which we stow from 70 to 80 children is about 15 feet square and nine feet high, so we can't make any application for aid from London.[68]

By the time of the 1851 census, the congregation is recorded as numbering about 700, including 100 Sunday scholars. Egan appended the comment:

> The congregation some years doesn't pay the current expenses of the chapel.[69]

Restoration of the Hierarchy

Some help was at hand. Already plans for the restoration of the English hierarchy were well under way, being delayed only by revolution in Italy and Pius IX's flight to Gaeta in 1848. Shrewsbury was a suitable place for a new See, an honour also for the Earl of Shrewsbury, who had given so much to the Church in England. John Talbot, 16th Earl of Shrewsbury, was involved in a vast building project which was to make his beloved Alton Towers the largest country house in Europe. For this work he had engaged Augustus Welby Pugin and together they were responsible for the building of many Catholic churches; one of the earliest was St Alban's, Macclesfield. For much of the year Lord Shrewsbury lived in Italy in hope of saving more of his income for various ecclesiastical projects. In fact Egan must have been in touch with him. So often in his letters Egan reveals himself as somewhat querulous; pressed by financial worries, he had perhaps been rather over insistant, even suggesting that the earl had failed to come to the support of the town as he might. Pugin had little sensitivity to cost and Alton Towers devoured far more than had been planned by the earl, whose reply, written in February 1847 from St Leonard's-on-Sea, betrays an element of irritation:

> I am really as well inclined as possible to do the work at Shrewsbury and there neither is nor ever has been any one who attempted to hinder me therein, as I told you before when you made the same statement and which you need not have repeated now but I cannot do impossibilities neither am I the first person who has miscalculated his means. Judging by things present and not having the gifts to see into futurity, it is out of the question to think of building in the manner you propose with tradesmen's money. Two years are soon gone and then, please God, it will progress rapidly and securely.[70]

He added a post-script:

> Rest assured that I am not doing anything now, nor shall I engage in anything that can come in your way. Shrewsbury has no dependence on the works I am carrying on at home — those are in our regular course — Shrewsbury must be done and not with our own workmen.[71]

As things worked out Shrewsbury was to wait rather longer than two years for its new cathedral and its building was fraught with more than usual difficulties.

The Papal Brief restoring the English hierarchy was promulgated on September 29th 1850. On October 25th the *Shrewsbury Chronicle* reprinted without comment a straight summary taken from the French Catholic paper, *L'Univers*. Soon enough anti-Catholic feeling, fanned to fury by Cardinal Wiseman's provocative and flamboyant letter *From Without the Flaminian Gate*, was unleashed across the length and breadth of the nation. In the next few weeks the *Chronicle* reprinted a whole series of letters on the controversy, an open letter from the Bishop of London to his clergy, John Russell's open letter to the Bishop of Durham, endorsing the bishop's remark that this example of 'papal aggression' was both 'insolent and insidious'. Replies were also published: Bishop Ullathorne's letter to *The Times* and an article in *The Spectator*, both insisting on the spiritual nature of the issue, rather than presenting it as a threat to the constitution of the English Church and nation. These seemed to go unnoticed. An advert appeared from the clergy of Shrewsbury signed amongst others by the Archdeacon of Salop, and Kennedy (of *Shorter Latin Primer* fame), then Headmaster of the Schools. A petition was to be left for signing in Mr Lake's, in Market Square, protesting about an 'illegal usurpation of power, insulting to our most gracious sovereign . . . openly intimating a design eventually to subjugate England to papal control'. The local papers seemed happy enough to encourage the debate. Eventually, after a series of anonymous letters in the *Journal*, the incumbent of the Catholic mission, the Revd Eugene Egan, himself entered the lists, insisting that the ecclesiastical arrangements were simply a matter of internal discipline within the Roman communion:

> The bishops appointed have been all along bishops ruling us under the name of Vicars Apostolic. The difference now is, that they are not removable by the Pope, except in very extreme cases. And we priests of the second order are less liable to be moved than before. This has long been desired and petitioned for. . . . To talk of the Pope 'partitioning out' England is as absurd as it is malicious.[72]

In many places that year Guy Fawkes night took on a particular significance as effigies of Pius IX were consigned to the flames. The following week, a public meeting of protest was organised at the Town Hall. For a time at least it seemed that the chapel and priest's house in Shrewsbury were felt to require a strong guard, provided by a large body of Catholic labourers. The debate continued: Kennedy became quite heated. At the end of the month Wiseman returned to England and published his *Appeal to the English People*, which did something to undo the misunderstanding that his first letter had caused. At about the same time Kennedy was lecturing the Shrewsbury Church of England Institute on the subject of 'Jesuits', a topic always liable to incite ignorant fears. The following April, a series of anti-popish lectures took place in St Chad's, resurrecting old grievances over purgatory and indulgences.

During the winter, Parliament, under strong public pressure, found it necessary to pass anti-Catholic legislation to make it illegal for Catholic bishops to assume territorial titles. Wiseman certainly made things worse: he was no man to keep a low profile. His outspoken comments particularly threatened the delicate standing of Maynooth, the Irish College which had, since Peel's attempt to placate the Irish Catholics in 1845, been supported by an annual grant of £21,000 from the government. Shrewsbury himself was most unhappy with the situation and became quite outspoken in his comments to Bishop Brown:

> I fear the Primate is bent on a Crusade not only against the Colleges, but against the whole system of National Education. He has been the real cause of the whole row. I am more convinced of this every day. The Press, the Parliament, the ministers all say it, especially Lord John [i.e., Lord John Russell, the Whig Prime Minister]. It was very ill-advised of the Pope to send him expressly to oppose the Government — to lead the opposition against them, & give it greater force and consistency . . . You may have observed that Lord John declares that all his subsequent legislation shall be guided by the conduct of the Irish Church and the Pope in respect of the Colleges. If they go on in this present mad course, unless Providence comes to their special protection, they will infallibly loose Maynooth: and where will Catholicism be then, either in Ireland or the Colonies? Had they been quiet under this new law, the effervescence had gradually declined, & we had been precisely

where we were; for the Government had no idea of carrying it into execution. It was certainly foolish of them to say otherwise; but it was more silly of us to brave them. But the Primate is evidently a man of little judgement, of no knowledge of the world, a great anti-Englishman, and with very narrow views. He is enough to ruin any cause. But at Rome they know nothing of us or of Ireland, & therefore are entirely governed by one or two individuals to whom they give their whole confidence, and without reason.[73]

Shrewsbury was in the process of publishing a pamphlet on the question, strongly attacking the Prime Minister yet noting, rather wryly, that he 'has certainly behaved like a spoilt and angry child, though he has very much to cross him'.[74] A few months later matters seemed to be getting worse:

I am sorry to see the hue and cry against Maynooth becoming more general every day. The Candidate for Greenwich was called upon to pledge himself to withdraw the grant and he did not hesitate to do so. I fear that no Government would manfully resist it, if called for by a majority of the House. The General Elections will be the question. It would indeed be an awful vengeance on us all . . .[75]

The letter concludes with more general comments about foreign relations:

We have great pleasure of Ld Palmerston's leaving office. He did infinite mischief, more especially in Italy. His exit is hailed with great joy. The Coup d'État in France has been a most glorious thing, and will in all probability consolidate the peace of Europe more than any other circumstance could have done.[76]

The Catholic euphoria regarding the situation in France was fairly short-lived. So too was the panic in England: the legislation was never invoked and some time later quietly removed from the Statute Book.

If England was not ready to accept a newly established Catholic Hierarchy, the Catholic community was itself equally unprepared. The new posts created could not all be filled immediately. The plan had been to leave several Sees vacant for a time, until suitable men could be found. With the threat of the Ecclesiastical Titles Act, plans went ahead rather more quickly and the hierarchy was completed with the consecration of James Brown as first Bishop of Shrewsbury in St George's Cathedral, Southwark, on July 27th 1851. The Diocesan Chapter was installed temporarily in St Alban's, Macclesfield, being the only Church of any size in the diocese. Bishop Brown moved into Salter's Hall, Newport, until somewhere more suitable was ready. His first intention seems to have been to reside in Chester. It would certainly have been a more convenient centre for such a vast area.

Plans for a Cathedral

It would appear that the bishop had already secured a site in Chester for his new church. Property, standing next to the ancient parish church of St John, had been purchased. This included a large Georgian house, which he felt would make a convenient residence. Bishop Brown had invoked Pugin's help to support the cause of a church for Chester but Pugin delicately declined 'to say anything at headquarters *in Italia*',[77] and though admitting that he thinks the plan 'exceedingly good', he felt certain that the earl 'would be greatly shocked at any proposal of transferring funds from Shrewsbury to Chester and I would not venture to be the man who would make the proposition'.[78]

Pugin does, however, promise 'to get a sight of the site'[79] while journeying to inspect work in progress at another of his churches, in Pantasaph. He had scarcely recovered after a serious nervous illness and complained of lack of rest: 'I only exist by medicines and such is the pressure of work in the midst of all this that I am obliged to work about sixteen hours a day'.[80] This same letter affords some insight into the work on which he was engaged at the time:

We have many thousand feet of painted glass and the great
window of West(minster) Hall to make for the New Palace and
all this has to be drawn and coloured on paper full size before
the glass painter can begin. And now the whole of the metal
work for that building and I am obliged with my own hand to
draw all the details.[81]

Pugin had also to contend with a strike at Myers, his builders;
got up, he felt certain, to ruin his best work-force. At least he
is able to boast of the praise given to the two windows
recently put into the chapel of Jesus College, Cambridge.
One correspondent, he claimed, suggests that Pugin 'had
surpassed the glass of King's College Chapel of which they are
so proud at Cambridge'.[82]

Pugin visited the site in Chester that winter, as he
returned from Pantasaph. He was full of complaints. It
proved to have been a wretched day: ice on the rails delayed
the train for nearly two hours and Pugin could only get
within a mile of the church when he arrived at Pantasaph.
He grumbled about the house in Chester. A Georgian, rather
than Gothic house, was for Pugin, 'quite unepiscopal'.[83]

At about the same time Lord Shrewsbury wrote from
Italy, both to Pugin and to the bishop, insisting that any
thought of a church for Chester must be put to one side until
after the church in Shrewsbury was finished. Naturally Pugin
was to remain as architect:

> I desired Mr Pugin to communicate with you respecting a small
> church at Shrewsbury. I have long promised to do it; but times
> have been so adverse that I really never had it in my power: but
> now we must make every effort & I have authorised him to
> begin in the spring of '53. I promise to devote £1,500 every
> half year to it, till completed at a cost of £9,000. I wish I could
> do it quicker, but of this I see no chance. Of course, the land
> must be found *free of debt*. I can only undertake it on that
> condition.[84]

SHREWSBURY CATHEDRAL

The land was apparently obtained by a man called Perks, a hosier and carpenter, who had premises on Dogpole. He bought a garden along Town Walls, which later formed a pleasant site for a mid-summer garden party to bid farewell to Canon Egan. In 1853, after his long service in Shrewsbury, Bishop Brown decided to transfer him to Stalybridge, in the north of the diocese. Egan handed over the administration of the Mission to the Reverend John Tobin. According to tradition, Perks himself was buried in the garden and a pear tree from the site provided wood for a cross which hung in the Cathedral until the decorations undertaken in the summer of 1885.[85] The parishioners rallied round to contribute to a fund instigated by John Scott. This was to ease the financial burden on the Mission, a burden which had weighed so heavily on Egan. Even so it would have been hard to make ends meet without the aid of another benefactor, Charles Cholmondeley. The second son of the Revd Charles Cholmondeley of Hodnet in Shropshire, Cholmondeley had been educated at Rugby and Balliol and was received into the Church by Egan, eventually becoming a priest of the diocese. His three brothers were said to have cut him out of their wills on hearing of his conversion and his move to Oscott to train for the priesthood. At this time, however, he was living at Wisbech in Cambridgeshire. Cholmondeley's gift provided for the purchase of a small boys' school housed in a late eighteenth century terrace running up Belmont, adjacent to Town Walls. The two pieces of land, which even together remained rather small, made an excellent, though restricted, site for the new church.

Pugin's health was already beginning to give way: he had always been far too highly strung, as the earl comments in a letter, written in January 1852:

> I am sorry to find that poor Pugin has been so unwell: he was, however, convalescent. He would be a dreadful loss; it is a great pity he should work himself into such a state of nervous excitement. He never could take things quietly — he is too much of a genius for that. I know of no one to whom we owe

so much, or who has been so severely and unjustly treated — he has formed quite a new school, but of pupils who are supplanting the master.[86]

The two letters that Pugin himself wrote to the bishop at this time are a sad testimony to his precarious state of health. Although it is still just possible that he is discussing the Chester site, it is likely that these letters do in fact refer to the site of the future Cathedral in Shrewsbury. It seems that the bishop had sent at least a sketch of the site to Pugin, who, apologising for his almost decipherable handwriting, promised a 'useful church well protected from draughts'.[87]   In the margin of one of the letters he includes an attractive, thumb-nail sketch and a very rough plan.   Pugin's chief concern seems to have been to dissuade the bishop from insisting that the church should lie on a north-south axis:

> . . . my mind is so shaken and my nerves so sensitive that I can ill bear to find (?) such a proposition as that contained in your Lordship's letter of turning the church of God to the chilly north and disregard the traditions of so many ages. However, if this be done the church would always be damp and cold and lose the south light and heat pouring into the whole side during the day . . .[88]

It is a good example of Pugin's medieval whimsy, invariably underlined by good, practical common sense. The site was very restricted but Pugin had proved himself a genius at coping with oddly shaped parcels of land. He proposed that the tower should stand at the side of the building, on the south-west corner, and the nave was to be flanked by two separately roofed aisles. The church would be roughly square, with the sanctuary intruding inwards into the body of the building as in many French and Belgian parish churches. Although this would allow ready access to the side of the sanctuary, it would inevitably be shielded by an elaborate rood-screen, for which Pugin had battled royally for so many years. Whether the plan was acceptable, or not, this is the last we hear of a church for Shrewsbury for some months.

Work was due to begin on the Cathedral during 1852 but before the end of the year both patron and architect were dead. The work was left to their respective heirs, both still in their late teens. Bertram Talbot, the Sixteenth Earl's nearest kinsman, was as enthusiastic for the concerns of the Church as his predecessor had been. He was soon writing to Bishop Brown, expressing regret that the building programme must inevitably be delayed until he gained control of his estate on achieving his majority. It was at this time that the young earl arranged for a medieval cope to be sent as a gift to his future church. This was the magnificent Syon Cope, now to be found in the Victoria & Albert Museum, South Kensington. The diocese decided to sell it to the museum in 1864 for £100. Some of the money went towards the purchase of a set of cloth-of-gold vestments, still used for Pontifical High Mass. Edward Pugin, at nineteen, the same age as the young earl, went ahead with the plans of what was to be his first major work. There is no doubt that his father's plans had got no further than the sketch in the letter to Bishop Brown.[89] He was far too ill in the last months of his life to develop his idea. In fact, his son's design, though generally inspired by the tradition of Augustus Welby Pugin, was to break away significantly from the intentions of his father. Talbot celebrated his twenty-first birthday on December 11th 1853. The following day Bishop Brown laid the foundation stone of his new Cathedral. Tickets were on sale: 1s, or 2s, for a reserved place, a considerable price in the mid-nineteenth century. The bishop preached and the whole celebration was followed by luncheon at The Lion. The young earl had asked that the building be dedicated to Our Lady of the Immaculate Conception and to St Peter of Alcantara, the Spanish Franciscan who was, for a time, confessor to St Teresa of Avila and to whose intercession Talbot attributed many graces. St Peter remained in the dedication but Pius IX intervened to suggest that Our Lady should be invoked under her title, Help of Christians, patron of the diocese.

The event did not go unnoticed in the town and provided an excuse for another bout of anti-catholic feeling. A number of townspeople asked the magistrates to forbid any sort of open-air procession, invoking the recent Act of Parliament and pointing to the riots in Stockport that June, which were encouraged by the legislation. They were able to assure the magistrates that any Catholic procession would most probably be met with an opposing Protestant march which would inevitably lead to trouble. The mayor felt obliged to write to the bishop, forbidding the procession and declining to be present at the ceremony. When the bishop, in replying, enclosed a donation of £5 for the poor of the town, it was returned: the mayor suggested that it was inappropriate for him to act as almoner for the Catholics. A local broadsheet tried to make a mockery of the event:

> the sham-bishop, priests, boys in bed-gowns, Shrewsbury papists (all they could muster) and some rabble papists from the neighbourhood, with an audience of protestants, who delight in sight-seeing — precisely 87 persons present.[90]

This same source was went on to attack the *Chronicle* for reporting the event 'to the utter disgrace of a professing protestant press'.

The work started well in the capable hands of Augustus Welby Pugin's collaborators, Myers of London. Pugin exhibited a drawing of the projected work in the Royal Academy Exhibition of 1854. The drawing, a finely executed work, still hangs in Cathedral House. Clearly, from the beginning, the younger Pugin had abandoned his father's intention to aline the building on an east-west axis. Its Gothic facade dramatically intersects the line of Georgian houses to the rear, providing a fine contrast from across the river. *The Ecclesiologist*, in its account of the exhibition, comments somewhat condescendingly of the plans:

> generally speaking, we regret that the architect does not seem to have sufficiently considered the difference existing between the cathedral and parochial character. The cathedral before us aspires in all its features to be a handsome parish church, and nothing more.[91]

The Cathedral, intended to hold 1,000, was to be built in the Early Decorated style; its length, including the sanctuary would be 124ft. At the south-west corner a fine spire was projected, 227ft. in height. The local fine white sandstone of Grinshill was to provide the main source of stone but both Bath and Caen stone were to be used for additional interior detail. The whole work was expected to cost upwards of £10,000.[92] The young earl was full of praise for the design, thinking the spire 'truly magnificent'.[93] He had one criticism, however, breaking from the established orthodoxy of Augustus Welby Pugin's adamant insistence on rood-screens and passed on his views to the bishop in no uncertain terms:

> I have seen Pugin's design for the screen of the High Altar and I think it greatly too heavy and will very much tend to prevent persons seeing the altar, a thing I much regret. I am myself no great admirer of screens and when they are so thick they become intolerable. However the cathedral is yours and not mine so you must decide for yourself upon the dimensions of your rood-screen.[94]

Whether the letter convinced the bishop or not, no rood screen appeared in the church.

The problems that the builders had to face were rather more serious than a liturgical debate about screens. While the foundations were being dug the men discovered strata of sand a short distance from the surface. Any thought of building a tower had to be abandoned and the church itself was reduced in scale. The sanctuary was shortened from forty-one feet to twenty-four feet and the nave and aisles were shortened by six feet to seventy-five feet.[95] The building would certainly be less imposing but the seating capacity could be guaranteed. Bishop Brown obviously began to consider whether this smaller building would be suitable as a cathedral. At the same time the rapidly growing urban catholic community in Birkenhead demanded a large church. Brown decided that he could combine his need for a cathedral with their need for a church and suggested that on finishing

the inevitably small church in Shrewsbury they should build a
cathedral in Birkenhead. Obviously Rome would have to be
consulted. George Talbot, the bishops' agent in Rome, was in
correspondence with both the bishop of Shrewsbury and the
Earl of Shrewsbury (his kinsman). The Vatican seemed
unhappy with the idea and Talbot pointed to the
embarrassment caused by the tension between the respective
bishops of Southwark and Westminster. Although admitting
that the situation between Liverpool and Birkenhead was
somewhat different, he comments that 'such a neighbourhood
between two bishops has not been found to work well'.[96]
Pugin's aid was invoked and his imagination ran riot with the
thoughts of a new commission. His plans for the church in
Birkenhead ran to £20,000.   The earl seemed rather
disconcerted:

> [this] would, I am convinced really amount to £35,000 or
> perhaps £40,000. . . However this Cathedral can only be
> begun after Shrewsbury church is both completed and paid for.
> There remains enough time to consider further plans. . .
> strictly within the £15,000.[97]

Earlier he was insisting on the same point, demanding
that the bishop must stop Pugin from entering into new
financial commitments without first consulting Hope Scott,
his representative in England:

> [Pugin] has not much experience and little (?) prudence, with
> no knowledge at all of my financial condition.[98]

The new earl's priorities were rather more realistic than those
of his predecessor. John Talbot had written to Bishop Brown
in January 1852:

> I wish I could help in more ways than one, but the many calls
> and claims upon me, besides the extreme badness of the times
> for landed proprietors, render it quite impossible if I am to do
> anything on a large scale — and it seems to me far better to do
> *one* good thing which no one else will or can do, than to divide

the same means between a multitude of others to which everyone can and will subscribe.[99]

His cousin, young though he was, appears rather more down to earth in his views:

> the salvation of souls is what God is most pleased with and it is equally certain that ten simple and plain churches will save more souls and work more good than one on which immense sums have been expended to make it profusely rich.[100]

This forthright comment put paid to Pugin's design for a spire for the Birkenhead church, which would have added another £4,000 to the bill. There was no way in which Shrewsbury would agree to this. The church of Our Lady, Birkenhead, was finally opened in 1862 but it was not to be a cathedral. Propaganda finally intervened to prevent the moving of the cathedral from Shrewsbury. Monsignor Talbot wrote to Bishop Brown in January 1855 to tell him of the decision. He admitted that this new church would be a blessing for the Irish, settling in such large numbers on the banks of the Mersey, but insisted that the building of a church could only go ahead on the understanding that it could do duty as a pro-cathedral until a suitable site was found for a larger church in Shrewsbury. This is the last that we here of the suggestion.

Like the 16th earl, Bertram Talbot was thoroughly conversant with events in a wider arena and his letters are peppered with interesting comments on the relationship between the Catholic community and the nation at large at a critical moment for religious affairs. Writing from Paris at the end of October 1854, he notes the arrival of Robert Wilberforce and his meeting in secret with the Jesuit, Père de Ravignon.[101] His reception into the Church during the following month was something of a *cause célèbre*. He was the second son of William Wilberforce, the great anti-slaver, and his elder brother, Samuel, was the doughty Bishop of Oxford who was to do battle with the scientist, Thomas Huxley, over the question of evolution in 1860. Robert Wilberforce was one of the most learned of the Tractarians, connected by marriage to Henry Edward Manning.   At the time of his death in 1857, he was preparing for the priesthood.

It was an unsettling time for the Anglican communion. The Gorham case of 1850, which led directly to Manning's reception into the Catholic Church, had convinced many that the catholic aspirations of the Oxford Movement had not won acceptance within main-stream Anglicanism.   George Denison, vicar of East Brent, a staunch defender of High Church ideals, was being prosecuted in the civil courts for his teaching concerning the Real Presence of Jesus in the Eucharist.   In a letter of November 1854, Talbot adds a comment:

> I am glad that Archdeacon Denison has lost his case so far before Lord Campbell. I only hope it may prove a second Gorham and completely break up the Protestant establishment.[102]

Such hopes must be accepted as somewhat naive. After a protracted legal battle, Denison eventually won the case in 1858 and the Oxford Movement left to the Anglican Church a rich legacy of spirituality and social concern which is part of its life to this day.

These were also years marked by the campaign in the Crimea. Loss of life was a result not only of fierce fighting but also of the cholera epidemic which ravaged the encampments. Perhaps the young Bertram Talbot can be forgiven for being somewhat partisan:

> I am glad to perceive that none of our catholic officers have been hit by Russian balls or bayonets, although some have fallen victim to the prevailing epidemic.   Lord Feilding's brother, Captain Feilding, is, I am sorry to say, dangerously wounded in the thigh.[103]

This was certainly a time for ecumenical endeavour and Talbot notes with approval that the British government had sent ten priests and ten nuns to minister to the men, 'a great step in the right direction and will I hope bring a blessing to our arms'.[104]   In fact this was the result of an initiative of Bishop Grant of Southwark, who responded to an appeal published in *The Times*.   The Sisters of Mercy from their convent in Bermondsey were the first nurses to set out for the Crimea and won the esteem of Florence Nightingale.[105]

Talbot's own health was giving grounds for grave concern and revealed the reason for his long spells abroad. In March 1856 he was writing to Bishop Brown that he was just getting over a bad cold. In fact he was suffering from tuberculosis. As in many families, signs of recovery were treated with self-delusory optimism.   A little earlier, the dowager Lady Shrewsbury, was passing on good news about his health:

> he will in a year or two become as robust and vigorous as could be desired.   In the meantime the doctor strongly advises his keeping out of damp and foggy climates.[106]

It was not to be.   In the next few months Talbot's health deteriorated rapidly and on August 10th 1856 he was dead, a mere 23 years old.   A plaque to his memory remains in the Cathedral sanctuary.   With his death came the end of a line of heroic benefactors to the English Catholic community. Having no direct heir, he had intended that most of his wealth should go to the Church, but after a dramatically protracted legal battle, his fortune passed to a Protestant kinsman, living in Ireland.   Nearly 10 years later Bishop Brown received a final legacy of just over £6,000.

Shrewsbury Cathedral was opened two months later, on October 19th 1856.   Tickets were on sale for the princely sum of 5s..   The event was well reported in the *Shrewsbury Chronicle* and *The Tablet* reprinted the article some weeks later.[107] *The Builder* also contained a fairly lengthy description of the new church.[108] The presence of forty of the clergy, four bishops and Cardinal Wiseman himself added a splendour to the scene rarely experienced in such a small, rural town. Bishop Brown celebrated Mass and Wiseman preached.   It was left to the luncheon, held in the Lion Assembly Rooms, to pass adulatory comments on the new building. Wiseman took as his theme man's role in the wonder of creation:

> Has not the electric power existed and have not all the elements which the chemist has discovered for 5,000 years? The discoveries and achievements of these times are but the necessary results of the elements and faculties which have always existed, coming into contact. To God, and God alone, should be the glory. To the true Christian there could be no danger from contemplating these triumphs over nature, and these advances in science. . .[109]

The text seems rather unrelated to the event but reflects wider concern of a community coming to terms with the relationship between religion and the new scientific discoveries. This is the period nearly mid-way between Tennyson's *In Memoriam* and Darwin's *Origin of Species*. As it happens, Darwin himself was born in Shrewsbury.

The Cathedral is spoken of in some detail. Even within the limitations imposed by the site, it remains an achievement of fine proportions and Edward Pugin's first major work. The firm of Myers had given way to local contractors, Wullen of Wolverhampton. The white free-stone was local Grinshill sandstone. The apex of the nave and chancel roofs is marked by a gilt cross as is the bell-turret which surmounts the west gable.[110] It is the sense of height which so impressed the architectural historian, Nikolaus Pevsner:

> The impact is created by very tall proportions of nave and aisles and a steep gable with big bell-cote.[111]

Pevsner finds the interior disappointing but the simple dignity and uncluttered line of the building is far from unimpressive. Finer detail is provided by octagonal pillars of Painswick stone, with moulded bases. The somewhat pedestrian carving on the capitals seems to have been completed shortly after the opening of the church. The distinctly narrow chancel, not unusual in Edward Pugin's churches, is separated from the five bays of the nave by a 38ft arch, again of Painswick stone. The fine detail of the reredos, crafted in Caen stone, is the work of Lane and Lewis of Birmingham. Beneath runs a series of blue and yellow encaustic tiles, made by Minton's, for whom Pugin's father provided so many designs. The font, again the work of Lane and Lewis, was the gift of Lady Shrewsbury as a memorial to her husband, John Talbot, and the young Bertram Talbot. Cholmondeley, too, is remembered in the church: the Pulpit and Stations of the Cross, both now lost to the Cathedral, were his gift. The latter are preserved in St Peter's, Wythenshawe, whither they were transferred when the present Stations, by Philip Lindsey Clarke, were erected in 1954 as a memorial to Bishop Moriarty. The East window, with glass by Hardman, was also provided by Cholmondeley and he is depicted as a kneeling donor with blue cloak and family coat of arms.

Apart from the successful, liturgical re-ordering in 1984 and the extension of the sanctuary area in the years before the centenary of the Cathedral, the structure of the building remains largely unaltered. The original Blessed Sacrament Altar (to the left of the sanctuary) was refitted with a fine Sacred Heart Altar, by J.A. Pippet, of Hardman's in 1885 as a memorial to Bishop Brown. His work is also to be found in the Bishop's throne and sanctuary floor of 1899. A lot of the decoration in the Cathedral was also his. A cartoon for the glass of the West Window by Alphage and Pippet has been preserved in Cathedral House. This belong to another generation of the family and is possibly the work of Gabriel Pippet, who was influenced by the Arts and Crafts movement and is responsible for the mosaics in the Sacred Heart Church, Droitwich.

The main alterations were the work of the Liverpool architect, Edmund Kirby, who was responsible for several churches in the north of the diocese. Originally the south aisle ended simply with a square end and window. Kirby was responsible for extending this by the building of a new chapel in 1901. This was dedicated to St Winefride, the gift of

Florens Burke and his wife, Bridget. The chapel, with its arcading and rich stonework, is a gem. Plans were also drawn up to build a polygonal baptistry, projecting into the garden at the north west corner of the building. This was never begun but two porches were added by Kirby: first the South Porch and, a couple of years later, the West Porch. The builder was Joseph Heyes of Belle Vue. The West entrance has a flight of steps, rising from Town Walls. The heavy Porch added dignity but at the same time served as a useful buttress to the West End, standing as it does on unstable ground. The figure of Our Lady, which surmounts it, is of Mansfield stone, a somewhat yellower stone making a satisfying contrast to the whiter, Grinshill stone of the rest. The carver demanded £27 for the work. It is fine, the work of the same sculptor as the heads and figure work in St Winefride's Chapel, Under Whittingham. At this time, too, the inner porch was raised to the level of the nave and the gallery above was extended. The screen was added. The alterations were made to mark the celebration of the fiftieth anniversary of the Cathedral's opening. It was completed during the following year. These fifty years had been a period of both consolidation and growth for the Catholic community in Shrewsbury and in the country at large.

School and Parish Life

The   community which grew up around this new church reveals no dramatic increase in size. It grew steadily as did the borough. By the beginning of the last decade of the nineteenth century the population of Shrewsbury had grown from 19,681 in 1851 to 26,967. The baptismal figures for the parish were 39 in 1851. Ten years later they had risen to 83 before dropping to 45 in 1871. From that time onwards they remained fairly stable: 67 in 1881; 51 in 1891 and 54 at the turn of the century. Confirmations reflect this pattern although the number of marriages remained surprisingly low: 7 are recorded in 1861, 2 ten years later, with figures reaching a high-point of 13 in 1881 and 7 again in 1901.

Deaths in the community run from 13 in 1861, 18 in 1871, 35 in 1881 and then drop to 22 and 27 respectively in 1891 and 1901.[112]

The most significant change in the community is its gradual emergence to a full part in the life of the town. Gone were the days when Shrewsbury looked suspiciously on the comings and going of the community on Town Walls. As in earlier years the community in the town offers something of a microcosm of the larger, national Catholic community and it is perhaps not without use to reflect upon the detail of parish life at this time. Partial glimpses of the concerns and interests of the catholic community are afforded by the various brief notes and records preserved from the period. Particularly valuable are the Diaries of the Sisters of Mercy[113] and the Minute Books of the Catholic Young Mens' Society.[114] The latter run continuously from the opening meeting on December 9th 1872 until well into the present century. The community is dominated by the work of two men, uncle and nephew, first administrators of the Cathedral, then bishops of the diocese: Samuel Webster Allen and Ambrose Moriarty.

Bishop Brown had moved from Newport to the house on Belmont in September 1868, a venerable and familiar figure in the town. Here, in 1876, he celebrated his silver jubilee as bishop. That same year saw the purchase of a piece of land next to the old chapel. This was to allow for the extension of the small school. The new building was ready two years later and the Young Mens' Society offered their clock and organised a concert to raise money for the new school benches and desks. The original building was small, 40ft by 20ft, and with a class-room and gallery, 24ft in length, added later to accomodate another 60 children. Soon that too proved inadequate and in April 1891, the Duke of Norfolk came to lay the foundation stone of a new building. This was the strong stock-brick building demolished in 1987. It was designed by Edmund Kirby and built by E Wittingham of Newport. There were three class-rooms and, together with the Infant School, catered for about 400 children. The day celebrating the laying of the foundation-stone provides a good illustration of the warm relationship growing between the town and the catholic community. The Mayor's speech, for all its rhetoric, reveals a genuine enthusiasm and warmth for Canon Allen, by this time administrator. The *Wellington Journal* reported his words:

> During the short time that he has sat upon the bench as chief magistrate cases of a sad nature have come before him - cases in which Dissenters as well as members of the Church of England were concerned - and often a mysterious hand has been stretched out to them...Canon Allen has the confidence and support of many of the inhabitants of the borough who are not of the same religious belief as himself, a statement born out by the fact that he was returned at the School Board election as head of the poll.[115]

The Canon's reply reveals a warm-hearted, kindly and humorous character:

> It was our duty and privilege to take the poor in hand from the gutter and try to make him a Christian gentleman - not only with a head, but a heart.[116]

And then, referring to the old school building:

> Those who erected the first portion of the building did so with a certain amount of fear and trembling - unknown and wishing to be let alone... The school continued to grow and now it occupies the position of being a very good motherly old lady - taking care of their little children and waiting only till her more goodly, fair and buxom daughter higher up would take care of the flock . . .[117]

The school diaries reveal a vivid picture of life at the turn of the century.[118] The desks, twelve foot in length, were only a little over three inches wide, presumably mere rests for slate and chalk. Even after the revolutionary Education Act of 1870, teaching must have been pedestrian with much learning by rote. The monitorial system of pupil teachers and payment by results was still a feature of most schools. Grants were awarded to schools on the result of an annual test for the pupils. In order to move up to the second class a six year old would have to pass tests in reading, writing and elementary arithmetic. The government inspectors had the hard and thankless job of encouraging higher standards and offering what support they could to overburdened teachers. In Shrewsbury the first recorded inspection was not until 1905, when it was reported:

> This is an orderly well conducted department where the children are effectively and kindly taught.[119]

That year there were 42 boys and 33 girls in the infant department. Amongst the 3 to 5 year olds:

> three divisions were made for reading in the Babies class. All have been learning their letters during the past fortnight. There is now a spelling, a small letter and a large letter class.[120]

Poverty loomed large. In the bad weather of February 1905 breakfast was given to the children before lessons began. Dinners for the poor were given by Mrs Sanjar and the Mitchells of Kingsland gave sweets and cakes each Friday. Life was harsh. Three children left to go to an orphanage on the death of their mother; another family left to find work in South Wales; the following October five three-year-olds left school until the warm weather. The school diary notes:

> Much poverty prevails on account of the scarcity of work and the long wet season. A supply of hats, coats and other articles of clothing have been kindly given by the Convent for the very poor.[121]

The Sisters of Mercy had in fact been looking after the school and caring for the poor in Shrewsbury for many years. They arrived in July 1868, gratefully met at the station by Fr Henry Hopkins. In spite of a warm welcome from members of the congregation, life must have been bleak enough. They moved into the old mission house on Town Walls and their diary records a description of the house built for the priest at the end of the eighteenth century:

> The house consisted of six rooms, on the first floor was the refectory and small kitchen, the latter was rather dark, having a small window, it was very damp and had a bad floor. On the second floor was the parlour, on the third floor was the Revd Mother's cell, a dormitory which had four beds and a community room, and on the fourth floor was the choir, and one double-bedded cell. All the cells looked out onto the school yard, which was anything but refreshing.[122]

Nevertheless they started work immediately. The following day they had their first mass in the house and that same afternoon they started a visitation of the parish accompanied by a little girl as guide. Soon these hard-working women became a regular feature of parish life. They could be seen at the two Sunday masses in the Cathedral, celebrated at 9.00 and 11.00. Later, in the afternoon there would be Benediction, celebrated in the Convent, except on the first Sunday of the month, when they all went up to the Cathedral. With the coming of Rosary Sunday in October, one of the Sisters took over the regular task of playing the little chamber organ, which had been transported from the old Mission Chapel to the Cathedral.

The main work of the community, however, was teaching. The former headmistress of the parish school, Mrs Lyons, had retired on August 10th 1868, barely a month after the arrival of the Sisters in Shrewsbury, and they themselves opened the doors to the children for the first time.[123]

They also established a small pension (i.e., fee-paying) school in a small room near the poor school. The slight income that this offered must have eased conditions for the community. In spite of a salmon from Fr Hopkins and venison from the Smythes, gifts to mark the first anniversary of their arrival, life could not have been very easy. There was the occasional day out, including trips to Acton Burnell and once the little excitement of the return journey, during which the carriage lamp caught fire. A few years later they were able to move into better accommodation. In June 1872 the Sisters moved into property on Belmont, bought for them by the bishop. Ten years later this property was enlarged by the purchase of College House and the Sisters were able to begin another of their works and open a laundry to give some occupation to poor and orphaned girls of the area. At first one of the Sisters and two girls set to work in the coach-house, which was extensively altered in 1884. By 1912, 250 girls had passed through the Home.

The old buildings on Town Walls were finally demolished in the last decade of the nineteenth century. Until that time they remained a focus for life in the parish. Only a few months after the Sisters moved out the rooms became a regular meeting-place for the Catholic Young Men's Society. It seemed to have been a thriving organisation and shows us something of the concerns and entertainments of a community struggling against a background of poverty and hardship. It attracted a steady stream of members: in 1873 there were ninety-two and ten years later, after various fluctuations, eighty-seven.[124] Concerts were organised. The first to be held in the school-room was graced by the presence of the bishop in a crowded hall; there was a band, choir solos, comic songs and readings. A more ambitious event was held in 1876 and the Music Hall was hired for two and a half guineas. Mr Bratton's band was engaged and Signor Dobrowski conducted and played the piano. These concerts were not only fun to produce, and pleasant entertainment, but a necessary social service: regularly funds were given to the Infirmary, occasionally assistance was needed towards funeral charges. The appalling weather of February 1879 provoked a Concert for the distressed poor, the proceeds being divided between the Mayor's Fund and a Charity Organisation Society, with a further £3 towards the Soup Kitchen. In 1883 they were able to make a donation to wards the West of Ireland Distress Fund.

It was not all fund-raising.   On August 3rd 1879 twelve local members joined a national delegation of the CYMS to present a special Address to John Henry Newman in Birmingham to mark his reception of the Cardinal's Hat.   A copy of the Address was hung in the meeting-room.   In 1882 a full-size football was bought for the club.   A small reading-room was open on several nights a week and this offered a selection of papers of national and more local interest.   This also contained the parish library.   The catalogue of 1867 lists 180 books available:[125] lives of the saints jostled with more general volumes, such as *Robinson Crusoe, Shamrock Leaves, or Tales from Ireland,* and their former parish priest's *Rule of Faith,* to add weight to the collection.   As in all societies, there were problems: the decision to transfer funds to a Savings Bank led to the resignation of the treasurer in 1878 — up to this time he had the use of the funds, paying 5% interest to the Society.[126]   Picnics were organised and talks and lectures given.   On Thursday July 21st 1892, twenty-seven members set out for a trip to Grinshill:

> after games of cricket, bowls, rounders and racing had been freely indulged in, the hill was ascended...members were photographed by Brother J. Della Porta.[127]

The glass magic lantern plate has survived and presents us with a solemn, Victorian period-piece.   In fact the magic lantern shows, given by Della Porta and Canon Allen became quite a feature of meetings.   As early as October 1878 the young Fr Allen had given a talk about his visit to Lourdes. Nearly twenty years later, in March 1895, there was the excitement of a lantern lecture by Mgr Slaughter, who talked about his trip to the Alps and his ascent of Mont Blanc.   That same year Fr Moriarty was giving a series of historical and apologetic pieces, and even an astronomical lecture on 'some of the principal heavenly bodies'.   In January 1899 a Gordon Highland Bandsman, replete in full uniform, gave some descriptive verses of his own composition relating encounters on the North West Frontier under Sir William Lockhart and an account of the assault on the heights of Dargai.

But the parishioners of Shrewsbury had had other excitements of late. In May 1890 the Cathedral was finally consecrated. Seven years later, on June 17th 1897, Canon Allen received episcopal ordination as fourth bishop of Shrewsbury at the hands of Cardinal Vaughan. The new bishop's long association with the town had won the hearts of many. He was a member of the Shropshire Archaeological Society and always had a passion for Egyptology and Biblical Languages. His private library was said to be one of the best collections of Egyptology in the country. His years in Rome had coincided with the Vatican Council, which he attended as one of the official stenographers. On his return to the diocese he first became secretary to the aging Bishop Brown and then assistant priest in the Cathedral, taking over as administrator from Fr Lynch in 1874.

A New Century

The beginning of the new century saw Bishop Allen and his old parish community working closely together on an issue which was central to the interests of the catholic community at large. The year 1902 witnessed the battle over Robert Morant's Education Act, one of the most fiercely contested measures of the century. As in the past the central issue was the suggestion that Voluntary Schools should be awarded aid from the rates. It earned the bitter antagonism of the Nonconformists. Lloyd George denounced the Act as a 'fresh endowment of the Church' and advised Welsh County Councils to resist. For the Roman Catholics, on the other hand, the Act came as a Godsend, saving the community from financial ruin and protecting the huge outlay which had been committed to the education of children. The Catholic Young Men's Society in Shrewsbury wrote to their M.P., H.D. Green, expressing their confidence in him:

a friend of the education of the poor who have for 32 years successfully struggled to keep their schools from being secularised by a body whose only aim would seem to have been to harass all consciences but their own, and to add to the financial burden of the country.[128]

It is often said that the anger of the Nonconformists at the passing of the Act was the first stage of the restoration of liberal unity which bore fruit in the Liberal government of 1906.

Bishop Allen had been the victim of surprisingly bad health since assuming the responsibilities of the diocese. Already in the summer of 1903 he had to give up work for a time and take a complete rest. Perhaps the education issue and his concern for the diocese were beginning to tale their toll. He was able to preside and preach at the mass to mark the golden jubilee of the Cathedral's opening in October 1906. He was also able to witness some of the changes to the Cathedral. St Winefride's chapel had been completed in 1901 and a few years later the south-west porch. The central porch and the alterations to the gallery had just been finished before his funeral. It was said that Bishop Allen's coffin was the first to pass through it. The requiem mass was celebrated by his nephew, Ambrose Moriarty, in the presence of Archbishop Bourne and several of the other bishops.

Dr Moriarty, like his uncle, had come from Stockport. He and his mother came to live at the Cathedral at about the same time that Allen took over as administrator. It was from here that he set out to study for the priesthood and, after completing his studies in Rome, he returned in 1894 to assist his uncle in the parish He must have taken on the main weight of parish duties after his uncle had become bishop but became administrator in 1898. Moriarty followed Allen's path exactly. He became Canon in 1910, Vicar General in 1925 and finally bishop in 1932, assuming full responsibility for the diocese on the death of Bishop Singleton in December 1934.

Canon Moriarty had for a long time been on close terms with the family of one of the leading doctors of the town, Henry John Rope, FRCS. Rope had come from Suffolk, settling in Shrewsbury in 1870 and marrying Agnes Burd, a daughter of Dr Burd, of the Royal Salop Infirmary. Although Dr Rope remained a staunch Anglican, his wife became a Catholic. A quiet and saintly woman of austere habit, she is still remembered making her way to early morning mass from The Priory. Dressed in black, she carried a lantern on dark winter's mornings. Their son, Henry Edward George, read English at Oxford and taught for a time in Leipzig before coming home to be received into the Church in Shrewsbury. Soon he was studying for the priesthood in the Beda in Rome. A poet and historian, he was well known for his idiosyncratic manner, his horror of the motor car and of electricity. His happiest days as a priest were spent in the Shropshire he loved, in Plowden and Cleobury Mortimer and then amidst the Archives in the English College, Rome. His hatred of commerce led to an identification with what he saw as the spiritual vision of the Gaeltacht. He set himself to learn Irish from the washer-women in the streets which tumbled down the hill from Castle Street and Pride Hill, Shrewsbury. Writing in his Diary in Chester, the year before the Easter Rising, he comments:' one feels almost ashamed of one's nationality when one knows the history of Ireland'. [129] The following year he was visiting some of the IRA prisoners lodged in Shrewsbury Gaol. Henry's brother, Michael, was an engineer and designer. He had risen to the rank of Squadron Leader by the time that he and his brother-in-law, Irene's husband, made their fateful journey in the R101. Both were victims of that disaster of 1930.

Their sister, Margaret, entered the Carmel at Woodbridge in Suffolk in 1923, taking the name of Sister Margaret of the Mother of God. She was born in June 1882. By January 1900 Henry recorded in in his Diary that she was attending classes at the Birmingham Municipal School of Art. This was its hey-day: she was able to work under Sydney Meteyard and E.G. Treglown and study stained glass with Henry Payne. [130]

Payne studied under Christopher Whall, an undisputed leader of the Arts and Crafts Movement.[131] Margaret Rope herself was a draughtswoman of great sensitivity and a fine colourist, working equally well on a large as well as small scale. She made an important and original contribution to the movement. Having finished her studies in Birmingham by 1909, she worked first from home, The Priory, in Shrewsbury. Later she had one of the studios in The Glass House in Fulham. Whall and Payne had both had studios here for a time. The workshops were set up by Mary Lowndes and Alfred John Drury and were run according to the principles of the Arts and Crafts Movement, allowing the artist to be involved in the whole process of making a window. They had also pioneered the use of Prior's Early English, slab glass. This is opaque and of uneven and course texture yet it has a brilliance of colour which makes it a very distinctive medium. Margaret Rope made excellent use of this glass and thanks to the keen interest Canon Moriarty took in her work the Cathedral has an outstanding collection of her windows. The West window of the Cathedral was her first major commission, unveiled by the bishop in February 1910.[132] Her work often reveals glimpses of the parish and of her family: the Canon appears among the saints and bishops and her brother Michael is often the model for the younger saints. Miss Peg Poore, one time Olympic swimmer and later a hygiene teacher in the town and a great friend of the family, provided the model for many of the female figures. The whole family is to be seen together with parishioners in the Rope Memorial window in Blaxhall parish church in Suffolk. The scene is clearly the Blessed Sacrament Procession in Shrewsbury and the old processional cross depicted is still to be found in the Cathedral.

Many had been born and grown old under the kindly administration of Canon Moriarty. He had a deep love for the town and developed a rich knowledge of Shropshire and its history. His fine library of local history bears telling witness to this. With the coming of his silver jubilee in January 1919 he had become very much a public figure: vice-chairman of the borough Education Committee, member of the Free Library Committee, a member of the Atcham Board of Guardians.[133] These all point to his concern to play a part in the affairs of the town.

War had brought many changes to the parish. Fr Bleasdale, the tall and active curate who had arrived in the parish in 1912, left for the Front.[134] He was greatly missed for he had been a popular man, fond of practical jokes and music hall songs. The Convent set itself to organise sewing classes for the relief of refugees. They were but poorly attended. A new knitting machine, however, speeded up work somewhat. The Canon treated the parish to an evening talk on Nietzsche's superman doctrine. By October 1914 Belgian refugees had begun to arrive in the town and settled in The Armoury. The additional pastoral care that this involved was to some extent eased by the arrival of Fr de Ryck and two Belgian Sisters, who stayed at the Convent.

Few families in Shrewsbury must have remained untouched by bereavement and all sorts of inconveniences that tore at their lives. The winter of 1815 was exceptionally cold and coal was in short supply. It was particularly hard for the old and very young. Often the school was closed and the children sent home. In 1916 the bishop asked that all churches should be insured against Zeppelin raids: modern war and the threat of civilian casualties was closing in. In June 1918 came the news that Fr Whitefoord was dead. He had been wounded in a shell attack on the Front and taken to a Field Hospital, which had suffered a direct hit. That autumn brought peace but with it came 'the Spanish Flu'. Again the school was closed for a month. Gradually, however, things returned to something like normal. There were moments of thanksgiving and moments of mourning. The following September the Canon unveiled a memorial to the dead, fashioned by Margaret Rope. A few months earlier he was presenting a medal awarded by the King of Greece for good service in Salonika to another parishioner, Frank Beastie. July 14th was an official day of holiday for the school to celebrate the peace. There was a children's party.

A few days later they were all taken to the King's Hall for a picture show.

For many, things could never be quite the same again. The war marks a water-shed in the life of the parish and town. There was a sense of coming of age. There would be many changes. New inventions would lead the Catholic community towards other tasks and new priorities. The Sisters from the Convent would have to wait a few years yet for the excitement of the wireless installation over the road at Cathedral House:

> being a new invention the Canon has invited two Sisters in turn to go across and listen in — it is connected with Bournemouth, Birmingham, Manchester and other places. The Sisters enjoyed a splendid lecture on music as well as many musical selections from the best composers.[135]

Canon Moriarty would be delivering a series of Advent lectures in November 1924 on 'Was the Pre-Reformation Church Roman Catholic?'. They were well attended and reported at length in the local paper. Gone was the vitriol and anti-Catholic fervour of an earlier generation. Canon Moriarty would become bishop of the diocese in 1934, on the death of Bishop Singleton, and when he himself died in June 1949, at the age of 79, it was an Anglican priest, Revd Geoffrey Strange of All Saints, who wrote in *The Chronicle*:

> Being a really big man, the late Bishop was a very humble one, and blessed with a marvellous sense of humour, not being afraid to tell stories against himself. . . . To have served in the same area for over fifty years and to have passed from the diaconate to the episcopate without creating envy or jealously, and with increased affection and esteem at each stage, sets the seal to an inner life that cannot be hid. A very large number not acknowledging the absolute authority of Rome will thank God for the life of Ambrose Moriarty.[136]

It is a fitting epitaph for the man but also a statement about the community with which he identified himself. The

Catholic community in Shrewsbury had a very different relationship to the town than in the days when its first chapel was opened. It had become integral to the community at large, making its own warmly accepted and welcomed contribution to the life of the town.

NOTES

This study, now slightly revised, was originally published in two parts in *Recusant History,* October 1990, pp.239-361; May 1991, pp.380-402. The author is most grateful to the Editor of that journal for permission to reprint it here.

1.   Anon., *Catholicism in Shrewsbury*, Fides Publication, no date, Liverpool, p.7. (This pamphlet is largely taken from the manuscript history of the diocese compiled by Mgr Edward Slaughter, 1886, and now preserved in the Shrewsbury Diocesan Archives).
2.   Alec Gaydon, ed., *History of Shropshire,* Victoria County History, vol.2, Oxford, 1973, p.8.
3.   J.H. White, 'The Vicars Apostolic's Returns of 1773', *Recusant History*, vol 9, pp.213 -214.
4.   Owen & Blakeway, *History of Shrewsbury*, Shrewsbury, 1825, vol 2, p.476.
5.   Birmingham Archdiocesan Archives (BAA), A 739.
6.   *Catholicism in Shrewsbury*, p.9.
7.   Refer G. Anstruther, *The Seminary Priests,* Mayhew McCrimmon, vol 4, 1977, p.153.
8.   J. Cosin, *List of Catholics and Non-Jurers 1715,* John Russell Smith, 1862, p.110.
9.   *Catholicism in Shrewsbury*, p.8.
10.   There is a memorial tablet preserved in the sacristy of the Cathedral.
11.   John Kirk, *Biographies of the English Catholics,* ed. J. H. Pollen & E. H. Burton, Burns & Oates, 1909, p.49.
12.   Lichfield Record Office, D 56. Published by kind permission of the Bishop.of Lichfield.
13.   J.C.H. Aveling, *The Handle and the Axe,* Blond & Briggs, 1976, pp.256-257.

14. Kirk, p.86.

15. *Catholicism in Shrewsbury*, p.9.

16. Smythe Papers, 1514/1/138. Shropshire Country Record Office. The printed version of this document in *Catholicism in Shrewsbury* differs somewhat from the original.

17. *The Diary of the Blue Nuns,* ed. Joseph Gillow & Richard Trappes Lomax, Catholic Record Society, vol 8, 1910, p.342.

18. *Douai College Documents 1639-1794,* ed. P. Harris, Catholic Record Society, vol 63, 1972, passim.

19. ibid., p.353.

20. Owen & Blakeway, p.476.

21. John Bossy, *The English Catholic Community 1550-1850,* Darton, Longman & Todd, 1975, pp.334-337, 341-346.

22. Eamon Duffy, 'Ecclesiastical Democracy Detected', *Recusant History,* vol 10 pp.193-209, 309-331; vol 13, pp.123 -148.

23. J. Derek Holmes, *More Roman than Rome,* Burns & Oates, 1978, p.163.

24. See Duffy, *Recusant History,* vol 10, p.324,

25. BAA C 1520.

26. *Douai College Documents,* p.342.

27. BAA A 1487.

28. BAA A 1291.

29. BAA C 2162. Revd James Bramston writing to John Roe in 1816.

30. K.S. Latourette, *Christianity in a Revolutionary Age,* Eyre & Spottiswoode, vol 2, 1960, p.283.

31. BAA C 2185, James Corne's Will, dated February 4th 1817.

32. BAA A 32a, no date.

33. *Birmingham Archdiocesan Directory,* 1915, p.60. I am most grateful to Dom Aidan Bellenger of Downside Abbey for this and other helpful references to the French émigré priests associated with Shrewsbury. See his *The French Exiled Clergy,* Downside Abbey, Bath, 1986.

34. Aidan Bellenger, 'The French Revolution and the English Benedictines, Part 1: The French Exiles', *The Downside Review,* July, 1989, p.195.

35. Downside Abbey Archives, Burt Papers, C 364.

36. Downside Abbey Archives, Burt Papers, C 241.

37. Owen & Blakeway, p.255, note 1.

38.   Family papers in the possession of Mrs Phillipa Gray of Shrewsbury. I am grateful to her and the Misses Bourlay for access to family papers.

39.   ibid.

40.   ibid.

41.   ibid.

42.   H.N.Birt, *Obit Book of the English Benedictines 1600-1912*, privately printed, Edinburgh, 1913, p.162.

43.   *Obit Book,* p.145.

44.   *Catholicism in Shrewsbury*, p.11.

45.   Henry Pidgeon, *Salopian Annals,* unpublished manuscript, Shropshire County Record Office.

46.   Local Studies Department of the Shropshire County Library, D97/5322.

47.   *Salopian Annals*, from which much of the following is taken.

48.   ibid.

49.   ibid.

50.   ibid.

51.   BAA C 2559.

52.   ibid.

53.   *Salopian Annals.*

54.   Brenda Walsh, *Father Spencer*, Catholic Truth Society, 1981.

55.   I am indebted to Mrs Phillipa Gray for acquainting me with this fact.

56.   Anna Maria Reynolds, C.P. *Heralds of Hope: The Sisters of the Cross and Passion,* Editions du Signe, France, 1989, p.4. For a life of the foundress see Edna Hamer, *Elizabeth Prout, 1820-1864: a Religious Life for Industrial England,* Downside Abbey, Bath, 1994.

57.   BAA, B 611.

58.   BAA B 1304.

59.   BAA B 1304.

60.   *Shrewsbury Chronicle*, beginning with the edition of 25th March 1836.

61.   *Shrewsbury Chronicle*, April 1836.

62.   *Shrewsbury Chronicle*, August 1836.

63.   *Shrewsbury Chronicle* 19th August 1836.

64.   ibid.

65.   ibid.

66.   ibid.

67.   BAA B 1388.

68.   BAA B 1388.

69.   Ecclesiastical Census 1851.

70.   Shrewsbury Cathedral Archives (SCA), Letter dated 25th February 1847.

71.   ibid.

72.   *Shrewsbury Chronicle*, 8th November 1850.

73.   Shrewsbury Diocesan Archives (SDA), letter dated 25th Sept 1851.

74.   ibid.

75.   SDA, letter dated 3rd Jan 1852

76.   ibid.

77.   SDA, undated letter: 'headquarters *in Italia*' refers to Lord Shrewsbury.

78.   ibid.

79.   ibid.

80.   ibid.

81.   ibid.

82.   ibid.. See also Martin Harrison, *Victorian Stained Glass,* 1980, p.20.

83.   SDA, undated letter.

84.   SDA, letter dated 25th Sept 1851.

85.   *Catholicism in Shrewsbury*, p.15.

86.   SDA, letter dated 3rd Jan 1852.

87.   SDA, undated letter, possibly Jan 1852.

88.   ibid.

89.   Nikolaus Pevsner, following Phoebe Stanton, suggests that plans for the cathedral were discussed with A.W. Pugin (*The Buildings of England: Shropshire*, 1958, p.264). This is misleading if it is thereby thought that he had made any contribution to the design of the building as it stands.

90.   Local Studies Department, Shropshire County Library, d 97/5322.

91.   *The Ecclesiologist*, vol 15, 1854, p.166.

92.   *The Builder*, 1853, p.772.

93.   SDA, letter dated December 1853.

94.   ibid.

95.   *The Builder*, 1853, p.544. See also *The Builder*, November 8th 1853.

96.   SDA, letter dated Sept 5th 1854. The letter is from Bertram Talbot, who informs the bishop of his correspondence with Mgr. Talbot at the Vatican.

97.   SDA, letter dated Aug 25th 1855.

98. SDA, letter dated Oct 30th 1854.

99. SDA, letter dated Jan 3rd 1852.

100. SDA, letter dated Feb 22nd 1856.

101. SDA, letter dated Oct 30th 1855.

102. SDA, letter dated Nov 29th 1854.

103. ibid.

104. SDA, letter dated Oct 30th 1854.

105. See Imelda King, *Sisters of Mercy of Great Britain,* 1839-1978, 1978, p.26.

106. SDA, letter dated Jan 6th 1856.

107. *The Tablet*, Nov 8th 1856.

108. *The Builder*, Nov 8th 1856.

109. *The Tablet*, Nov 8th 1856.

110. Although the Cathedral does not have the traditional orientation to the East, throughout the description the liturgical, rather than geographical, orientation is retained.

111. Nikolaus Pevsner, *The Buildings of England, Shropshire*, 1958, p.264.

112. SCA, various registers.

113. *Convent Diary* 1849-188 1; 1814-1925; 1936-1945, Convent of the Sisters of Mercy, Shrewsbury.

114. SCA, *Minute Books of the Catholic Young Men's Society,* 1872-1922, 1936-1945.

115. *Wellington Journal,* an undated cutting, preserved in the Cathedral Archives.

116. ibid.

117. ibid.

118. Norah Jenkins, 'St Mary's Roman Catholic School 1877-1977', unpublished paper.

119. ibid.

120. ibid.

121. ibid.

122. *Convent Diary,* 1868.

123. ibid.

124. *CMYS Minute Books.*

125. SCA, Catalogue of Parish Library, 1867.

126. *CMYS Minute Books,* 1878.

127. *CMYS Minute Books,* 1892.

128. *CMYS Minute Books,* 1902.

129. Shropshire Record Office, 2031/2.

130. I am most grateful to Peter Cormack, of the William Morris Gallery, Walthamstow, for sharing with me his researches into the stained glass of the Arts & Crafts Movement.

131. Martin Harrison, *Victorian Stained Glass,* 1980, pp.64-69.

132. A leaflet was published to commemorate the event.

133. *Convent Diary,* 1919.

134. *Convent Diary,* 1916.

135. *Convent Diary,* 1924.

136. *Shropshire Chronicle,* June 1949.

PROVOST JOHN HALL

III

A CHESHIRE APOSTLE

JOHN HALL OF MACCLESFIELD

E. Maurice Abbott

John Hall was born on 10th July 1798. His mother belonged to the old Catholic family of Barrow, of Westby in the Fylde. He begam his studies for the priesthood at Crook Hall until the move took place to Ushaw, where he completed his studies on 6th April 1821, was ordained priest and, in the same year, was appointed to look after Macclesfield. Among his contemporaries were six future bishops, including Wiseman, Errington and Briggs.

John Hall arrived in Macclesfield on 17th April. There was a chapel, but nowhere to live. He found lodgings, but the landlady did not like him going on sick calls late at night and asked him to leave. He first converted part of the chapel into a dwelling, and then eventually built a house which adjoined the chapel and the school. The house still stands now, across the road from the present church.

Towards the end of 1821 Hall was asked by Catholics in Congleton to look after their needs too. In December he went the eight miles by horse to Congleton, spent the night in the home of Mr Tracy who lived in Moody Street and celebrated Mass in his kitchen the following morning. He then went regularly to Congleton to say Mass, administer the sacraments and give religious instruction.

Hall joined up with the Cheshire clergy and in 1821 they numbered five, James Blundell, John Briggs, Thomas Colling-wood, Ralph Platt and John Hall, all of old English Catholic stock. In 1825 when they held their first meeting, James Fisher was also at work in Dukinfield. They decided at their first meeting to send out an appeal in which 3,000 Cheshire Catholics were asked to subscribe a penny per week. Hall composed the letter and in it expressed the priests' concern for the poor Irish who had recently entered the country. By 1828 when a further letter was sent, the number had risen to 6,000. The aim of the fund was to help towards meeting the cost of the new chapels, schools and presbyteries. £100 was given to Hall towards the cost of the presbytery which he had built in Congleton in the hope of getting a resident priest there. In 1826 he had opened a new chapel, with a school underneath it, in imitation of the building in Macclesfield. The arrival of a resident priest at Congleton in 1830, meant that Hall could turn his attention to Bollington. By 1834 he had erected a church. This was eventually replaced in 1957 by a new church, but the one in Congleton is still in use.

By 1830 the Cheshire clergy had secured the interest of the Earl of Shrewsbury. Hall and Briggs visited him and he promised to contribute to the fund. In a letter dated 6th October 1833, the Earl wrote: 'I have long admired the zeal of the Clergy of the County of Chester', and he increased his initial contribution of £50 per annum to £200. In the years following Hall's arrival in Macclesfield, the number of Catholics increased dramatically. From 1802-1822 there were 200 baptisms. From 1822 to 1838 there were 1,427.

Even allowing for the high death rate, the Mass attendance was clearly growing rapidly and Hall was thinking of a new church in the 1830s. He was advanced £50 for the purchase of a field opposite the old chapel. In 1836 he approached a young architect from Sheffield, Matthew

Hadfield, who had submitted plans, on which Hall was initially keen. However the Earl of Shrewsbury had indicated that unless Pugin was chosen as the architect he would not give financial support for the project. Hadfield was paid £45 for his work and was, not surprisingly, somewhat put out at being replaced by Pugin. By 1850 when the hierarchy was restored there were fifteen priests in the county. *The Victoria County History of Cheshire* (Vol. III, p.93) comments 'Throughout the period of expansion, the county still depended greatly upon the efforts of individual priests. It was well served. The work of its clergy in the three decades after 1820 was outstanding'. Mention is made of John Briggs who became a bishop and others, but the writer of this section of the history said 'throughout this period John Hall was pre-eminent among the Cheshire clergy, for until his death . . . he dominated Catholic life in the county, first as a missionary priest and later as a spokesman for the Cheshire clergy. . . '.

His determination to build a new church for Macclesfield inevitably involved a massive fund-raising exercise. The field acquired in 1832 had cost £600, appeals were sent out and occasionally tea parties were organised. Subscriptions were recorded from near and far, from Knutsford and Prestbury and then Sheffield and Blackburn, Edinburgh and Dumfries. The church was opened officially on 26th May 1841. The Pontifical High Mass was celebrated by George Brown, Vicar Apostolic of the Lancashire District. He had been on the staff at Ushaw in Hall's student days. Nicholas Wiseman, the future Cardinal, who was then rector of Oscott and co-adjutor bishop of the Central District, preached the sermon, pointing out that the times were propitious for the spreading of the Faith. The service commenced at 10.30 am with tickets costing five shillings, half-a-crown, and one-shilling-and-sixpence. A luncheon was arranged at the Macclesfield Arms from 2.30 pm, with tickets costing three shillings each.

The church stands as a monument to Hall's vision and to Pugin's genius. Lack of money meant that the tower could not be completed, and the field was not large enough to give the church its usual orientation or be the length Pugin would have wished.

'St Alban's church, which was erected for the Roman Catholics in 1838 from the design of the celebrated architect Pugin, is very much admired as a specimen of good modern Gothic architecture', wrote J.P. Earwaker.

In a letter to Briggs in September 1838, Hall shows his delight that the Mayor has allowed the use of the Town Hall for a Tea Party, to raise money for the new church. Tickets cost one-shilling-and-sixpence and Hall expected that most of them would be bought by Protestants, which would not have been done ten years previously. In March 1839 he writes to Briggs to tell him that the ceremony for the laying of the foundation stone would be put into English and printed for the Protestants who would be expected to attend.

In a further letter in April 1839, Hall tells Briggs: 'We are going on very well with our building, quite astonishing the natives. They all acknowledged that there will be no building either in the town or neighbourhood to be compared with it'.

Not long after the opening of the church, we find Hall engaged in the establishment of yet another mission. While he had curates with him, he took the opportunity to go to Caldwell's Farm at Over Tabley where he was able to say Mass for several families. In his history of the Knutsford parish, Mr Harris reckoned that Hall was going to the farm from 1842-1844.

In 1846 Hall celebrated his silver jubilee and was given the sum of £82. He used this for the installation of a stained glass window in the Lady chapel and is shown in the bottom right-hand corner as the founder of the church.

In 1850 the hierarchy of England and Wales was restored, but Shrewsbury did not get its bishop till July 1851. This was James Brown, who had been educated at Oscott, and he appointed Hall as his Vicar General. When the Chapter was formed, Hall was made Provost, which shows the high esteem in which he was held. His scholarship was also recognised in 1852 when the Pope made him Doctor of Divinity (*honoris causa*) and from this time he became known as 'Doctor Hall'.

St Alban's was chosen as the pro-cathedral and here the first Diocesan Synod was held in 1852.

In 1854 Hall ceased to be Vicar General and in 1857 he resigned as parish priest. His eyesight had been causing concern and his friend John Briggs commented in a letter to Bishop Brown that he no longer wrote to him because of this. After ceasing to be Parish Priest, Hall went on an extended holiday hoping that his eyesight might improve. In the course of his travels he went to Cologne and called on the Cardinal Archbishop who instructed the priest of the church of Our Lady of Peace, where the body of St Alban was enshrined, to give Hall a rib of the proto-martyr of England. This relic is kept in the sacristy of the church of St Alban, Macclesfield, and has with it a long document testifying to its authenticity.

From the period when Hall returned, until his death in 1876, it is recorded 'in all the time of local emergencies, and they had frequently arisen, the authorities of Macclesfield looked up to Dr Hall for his opinion, his counsel and his influence'. In 1870, Hall became a member of the Macclesfield School Board and remained on it until his death.

At Hall's Golden Jubilee, Bishop Brown pointed out that the testimonial had come from members of all the denominations in the town. His remarks that Dr Hall was worthy of such a mark of respect and esteem was greeted with great applause. In 1874 a prominent Unitarian, and a very significant man in Macclesfield history, T.U. Brocklehurst, visited the Pope and enquired as to what were suitable presents for a priest. As a result he presented Hall with a missal and a set of vestments.

Hall remained in Macclesfield until his death in 1876. He had been in church on the Saturday evening preparing for Sunday Mass. He called his housekeeper at 5.30 a.m. complaining about a pain in his chest, the doctor came, but little could be done and he died at 6.00 a.m.

His funeral was remarkable. The route from the church to the cemetery was lined with five to six thousand people, according to the local newspapers of the time, and several carriages carrying distinguished people from the locality followed the hearse. His tomb was paid for from public subscription and cost £160.

There are many tributes to Hall. John Earles in his book on the streets of Macclesfield wrote: 'For over half a century this talented man and devoted priest ministered to his fold and took an active part in the affairs of the town. It is safe to say that no minister of any denomination more completely won the respect of the community, with the exception of those members who were blinded by religious bigotry'. and the local newspaper wrote 'the love and esteem entertained for him by members of his own flock, consisting at the time of his death of about three thousand, have seldom been passed in the relations between pastor and people'.

BIBLIOGRAPHY

Byrne, E. A.	*A Short History of St Alban's Debt.* Macclesfield c. 1905.
Earles, John	*Streets and Houses of Old Macclesfield,* 1915.
Earwaker, J.P.	*East Cheshire Past and Present,* Vol II p.511.
Finney, Isaac	'The Rise and Progress of Catholic Missions in Macclesfield', lecture: *Macclesfield Courier and Herald* 9, 16, 23 and 30 May 1885.
Gillow, Joseph	*Bibliographical Dictionary of the English Catholics from the Breach with Rome in 1534 to the Present Time.* 5 vols. 1881-1902. Article on John Hall, Vol. III pp. 90-92.
Harris, A.E.	*History of the Parish of St Vincent de Paul, Knutsford, Cheshire 1840-1985.*
'H.R.K' (Kelly)	'Father Hall' Article in *Shrewsbury Diocesan Year Book,* 1977.
Kelly, H.R.	'Post-Reformation Catholicism in Macclesfield' in *A History of Macclesfield,* edited by Stella Davies. Manchester University Press, 1961.
Pevsner, N. & Hubbard, E.	*Buildings of England —Cheshire,* pp.267, 268.

Slaughter, E.	*History of the Diocese of Shrewsbury.* 2 vols. mss. 1886, 1892.
Ullmann, Michael	*St Alban's, Macclesfield.* Catholic Printing Company of Farnworth, Bolton, Lancs. 1982.
Vaughan, Audrey	'The Catholic Faith in Macclesfield from the 8th Century to 1988', article in *Shrewsbury Diocesan Year Book*, 1989.
Whomsley, D.	*Churches of Macclesfield No. 1 St Alban's.*

Archives of St Alban's, Macclesfield.
Articles in the *Macclesfield Courier* and *Macclesfield Courier and Herald.*
Article in *British Architect and Northern Engineer*, 2 March 1877.

HOOTON HALL
a home of the Stanley family

IV

THE HOOTON HALL REGISTER

W.P. Jeffrey

Among the archives held in the presbytery of St. Mary of the Angels Hooton, was the register of Baptisms, Confirmations, Marriages and Burials originally kept in the chapel of Hooton Hall, for many centuries the seat of the Stanley family. This small book, kept meticulously by the last chaplain, Father Thomas Collingridge, is the only Stanley Register known to exist and it throws some light on Catholic rural life at a time when great changes, both social and religious, were starting to take place in Cheshire. Much has been written about the Stanleys of Hooton, notably a detailed description and genealogy by Ormerod[1] and it is clear that from medieval times they held great power in Wirral, building a house at Hooton in 1488 where they lived for more than three centuries. It was the Reformation that began a long and difficult period in their fortunes because, unlike most of the Cheshire gentry, they (together with the neighbouring Masseys of Puddington) would not accept the new State Religion, maintaining their allegiance to the Pope and the Catholic Faith. As a result they suffered fines and imprisonments throughout several reigns. Despite all this they prospered and continued to have great influence in the life and affairs of Wirral. There seems little doubt however that had they given up their faith, the Stanleys would most certainly have greatly increased their wealth and authority.

During the sixteenth century, while Sir Rowland Stanley was head of the family, the future of his dynasty was placed at particular risk. His eldest son, William, dedicated to a military career, had served in the Elizabethan army in Ireland for some fifteen years,[2] conducting himself with great courage and loyalty in suppressing the Irish opposition to the Queen. He was knighted for his gallantry in 1569. On leaving Ireland, he joined the campaign against Spain in the Netherlands, eventually being made Governor of the English fortress of Deventer. In 1587, he surrendered this key city, together with its garrison, to the Spanish — a drastic move which appears to have been chiefly motivated by anger at the lack of royal recognition and reward for his long service in Ireland. This act of treason meant that should he ever have succeeded to the family estates, they would at once have become forfeit to the Crown. Fortunately, Sir Rowland outlived him, surviving to the great age of 93 (reputedly the oldest knight in England) and he was able to assign the title and property to his great grandson and so ensure the family's continued tenure of the Hooton estates.

William's brothers, John and Edward, had also left for Europe, both eventually entering the Jesuit Order as priests. Possibly under their influence, William, did much to help establish a new Jesuit Novitiate at Liège in 1614, later to become the Liège Academy, which was moved to Stonyhurst in 1794.[3] The chapel in Hooton Hall was used throughout the penal times but, for obvious reasons, no records were kept and thus very little is known about it apart from a story that there was a priest's hiding place built somewhere within the house. Old Sir Rowland had a very difficult path to tread with regard to his family's known Catholic loyalties and although some authors have described him as an 'ardent' Catholic, as Sheriff of Chester in 1576 he could hardly have displayed any adherence to the Faith. Wark[4] concludes that there is no evidence at all that he shared the beliefs of his sons.

A later Sir William was reported by the Churchwardens of Eastham Parish Church that on reaching his majority (1649) he '. . . did reverentlie and devoutlie join with the congregation in Divine Prayer and Services . . .'.[5] It seems he conformed mainly out of respect for his late mother and turned to the Catholic Faith of his ancestors in later years. In 1661 he was made the first baronet.

Thomas Stanley, born in 1715, took the name Massey Stanley as a child, on succeeding to the title and estates of his godfather William Massey, who had died without a direct heir. Later he chose to give up life on a country estate to follow his vocation and was ordained a Jesuit priest in 1746. He served in many places, including Bury St Edmunds, Rookley, Stapehill, Britwell and Lulworth — where he died in 1803. His brother Henry had also joined the Order and after being ordained in 1739 he spent most of his priesthood in Lancashire at Liverpool, Leigh and Moor Hall near Ormskirk.[6] Before leaving Cheshire to study for the priesthood, Thomas had assigned all his Massey inheritance to his older brother, John, who, on succeeding to the Stanley baronetcy in 1792, therefore took the title Sir John Stanley Massey Stanley.

There is little doubt about the intensity of the faith of the Stanleys who, despite all the difficulties that beset the family, passed on their beliefs to each succeeding generation and besides providing a Mass centre for the Catholics living in and around Hooton, produced over the years four Jesuits who helped maintain the Catholic Faith in various parts of England. The family's important role in preserving Catholicism in Cheshire is emphasised by J.A. Hilton.[7]

The coming of the nineteenth century saw an easing of the restrictions on English Catholics and the beginning of an increase in their numbers. By 1800 Cheshire had five Missions with resident priests, Chester, Macclesfield, Stockport and the two older chapels at Puddington and Hooton.[8] The growth of the Catholic population at this time was almost entirely due to the increasing numbers of Irish people seeking work in the expanding industries of North

West England. This influx became much greater in the 1840s and 50s due to the Irish potato famine.

In 1805, Sir Thomas Stanley married Mary the only daughter and heiress of Sir Carnaby Haggerstone, head of one of the old Catholic families of Northumberland, which was linked through Lady Haggerstone with the Erringtons, another well known Catholic family. Thomas and Mary lived at Hooton Hall and had five children: William (b.1807), Maria (b.1808), Rowland (b.1809) John (b.1810), and Charles (b.1813). Rowland assumed the name Errington under the will of his great-great uncle, Henry Errington, who died in 1820. William succeeded to the Stanley title on his father's death in 1841 and in the following eight years lived a life of such extravagance that he accrued debts which only the sale of Hooton Hall and its estates could repay. So ended an association lasting several centuries of the Stanleys with Hooton. Sir William on leaving Wirral, lived in Paris until his death in 1863, under the patronage of Napoleon III, whom he had known while the emperor was in exile in London.

William's brother, Rowland, succeeded to the title and lived on the Errington estates at Sandhoe in Northumberland as well as on the Massey property at Puddington. Finally, in 1875, John inherited the baronetcy and also claimed the Errington estates. This claim was challenged by several other Errington descendants and after a lengthy and expensive legal dispute, the Master of the Rolls found for the plaintiffs against Sir John. However, not accepting this, John made an appeal to the House of Lords and in 1876 obtained a majority judgement from the Law Lords in his favour, with costs and so he was able to claim his Errington inheritance.[9]

Thus it was during the baronetcy of Thomas and William Stanley that the last fifty years of the Stanley occupancy of Hooton Hall took place, a period in which we can get a glimpse of the lives of Hooton Catholics through the register of Father Collingridge.

The Register, written mainly in Latin, covers the period from January 1805 until July 1849 and includes 167 baptisms, 77 Confirmations (in five ceremonies), 7 marriages and 59 burials.   The people using the chapel, apart from those actually living in the Hall or on the estate, would come almost entirely from Eastham, Hooton Green, Childer Thornton or Little Sutton, all situated about a mile from the Hall.   The obituaries include people from as far afield as Storeton and Puddington, so it seems likely that the burials would have taken place at local graveyards and Father Collingridge would have gone there to officiate.   Baptisms comprise the largest section of the book and are therefore the most informative, many entries being annotated as follows:

a) if a child died shortly after baptism.
b) if a child died whilst still young the date of death is given.
c) whether the parents had come from Ireland.
d) whether one of the parents was a non Catholic.
e) the maiden name of the mother.

In most entries, two godparents are named.

A rough estimate of the size of the Catholic population around Hooton can be deduced, using the average national birthrate for the period, of 35 births per 1 000 population.[10] In the first ten years of the register, 26 baptisms were recorded and in the last ten there were 43; which suggests that the number of Catholics in the area increased from about 75 to 120.   This is in broad agreement with a census of Papists made by the Vicar of Eastham (Rev. George Travis) in 1767,[11] who counted 50 and did not include the members of the Stanley family who were abroad at the time the count was made.   It also mirrors the increase in population in England and Wales as a whole from 9 to 16 million during the same period.   Another change which the Register reveals is that while in the early years, less than 30% of the Baptisms were performed on a Sunday, the proportion rose to 70% towards the end of the period. Whether this reflects a change in the parents' working practices or in the attitude of the clergy is hard to say.

In true Catholic tradition, 80% of the children were baptised within a week of their birth, including 13% actually on their birthday, although this latter figure does include the Stanley children. Only 7% of parents delayed baptism for more than four weeks. 46% of the boys were named Thomas, James or John, while for more than half of the girls Mary, Elizabeth or Margaret was preferred. Only four of Sir Thomas's children are in the Register, his eldest son, William — born in 1807 — was baptised elsewhere, quite possibly at his mother's former home at Sandhoe in Northumberland. 11% of the children died shortly after they were born and a further 7% died before they reached the age of 7; this is appallingly high by today's standards but lower than the child mortality rate in some large cities at the time. The frequency with which many people acted as godparents — Mary Boardman, for instance, was godmother on 14 occasions between 1812 and 1832 — suggests that the Catholics were formed into a closely knit community, although they were spread over quite a wide area. Father Collingridge himself acted as godfather to eight children between 1812 and 1830.

There were five Confirmation services:

7th June 1813: Bishop William Gibson: 17 children.

30th October 1821: Bishop Thomas Smith: 18 children.

12th July 1831: Bishop Thomas Penswick: 16 children.

20th July 1837: Bishop John Briggs: 8 children.

2nd December 1845: Bishop George Brown: 18 children.[12]

Only the candidates names, plus their chosen names, are given so not much can be gleaned from these lists. Cross checking the names, with those baptised at Hooton, suggests an age range of 9 to 17 years. The marriages also yield very little information other than that five of the seven couples remained in the area for several years. Three marriages took place on a Monday, two on a Tuesday and two on a Wednesday.

The obituaries show the deaths of five members of the Stanley family. Two of Sir Thomas's brothers died while still young, James at 17 and John at about 23. Charles his youngest son, died when he was only 21 whilst travelling abroad, he is recorded as being buried at Syra(s), presumably the island of Siros, one of the Cyclades group in the Aegean sea. Lady Frances Haggerstone, Sir Thomas's mother in law, also died at Hooton. The final death was that of Sir Thomas himself, on August 20th 1841, to be succeeded by his son William who was shortly to bring about the downfall of the Stanleys of Hooton.

The Hooton Catholics, representing only a small part of the whole population of the area, were in the main employed in the usual basic rural occupations and several are mentioned in the 1841 Census as labourer, shepherd, woodman, domestic servant etc. Only one appears as a tenant farmer in the catalogue of the Stanley estate prepared for the sale in 1849,[13] although in the estate accounts of 1806,[14] Thomas Lightbound (whose wife was a Catholic) is shown as a tenant required to perform several days 'boon work' for the estate as part of his tenancy. He appears still to have been a tenant when his wife Mary's death was recorded as occurring on the estate in 1822. A proportion of the fifty servants employed in the Hall itself were Catholics and the Register shows that Rowland Errington and Charles Stanley acted as godfathers to the three daughters of Edward Davies, one of the senior servants.

Once the Stanley chapel had been closed, the Hooton Catholics had no alternative but to walk the five miles to Puddington Hall to hear Mass.[15] It was not until 1865 under pressure from immigrant Irish Catholics working on the new Helsby railway, that Fr Baron, the chaplain at Puddington, began to say Sunday Mass for them in a shed at Childer Thornton. Shortly after this, Hooton was established as a separate mission under Canon Hilton and Mass continued to be celebrated in temporary premises until a local resident, Mr Craven, provided a plot of land so that a presbytery could be built. By 1867 this presbytery-cum-chapel was complete, financed by money collected by Fr Baron and it adequately served the needs of local parishioners.

In 1877, having finally resolved his legal difficulties, Sir John Errington offered to buy the land adjoining the presbytery on which he proposed to build a church with graveyard and four cottages, intended as a source of income for the parish. This generous offer was accepted and work on the new church commenced early in 1878. Sir John and his wife, Marie, took a personal and active part in designing and planning every aspect of the building and intended that the new church should be medieval in style and made with stone from the Stanley Quarries at Puddington, which were still in Sir John's possession. Everything was of the best material and workmanship and it was of a size to hold a congregation of over one hundred. The interior furnishings matched the quality of the building, the centrepiece being a magnificent altar, complete with six heavy silver candlesticks and supporting a most elegant French tabernacle. An imposing statue of Our Lady of Lourdes occupied a prominent place to the left of the Sanctuary. It was clearly Sir John's intention that St Mary of the Angels would provide a permanent memorial to the faith and tenacity of his forbears. A codicil to his will, added in 1893, ensured a constant income to maintain the fabric and appearance of the church.

So it was that a very English church was built to commemorate a faithful Catholic family, who throughout centuries of religious adversity had held fast to their beliefs and who were at last able to pass a small remnant of English Catholicism into the hands of a strong and rapidly growing community of Irish Catholics. Most appropriately, this was the very first church in Cheshire to be consecrated after the Reformation. Sir John must have found great comfort in the knowledge that the faith of his ancestors was at last beginning to grow unhindered in Cheshire.

Sir John Stanley died in France in 1893, aged 82 and fittingly his body was buried in the graveyard close to the church.[16] His sister, Lady Williams Bulkeley, died in 1889 and his wife in 1907, both were buried beside him. Some years later, the north side of the church was extended to accommodate this family tomb, forming what is now known as the Stanley Chapel. This is separated from the main part of the church and is lit by an imposing stained glass window, crafted by Meyer of Munich, depicting Sir John and Lady Marie.[17]

Father Collingridge's Register is now in the care of the Cheshire Record Office,[18] a photocopy and transcription is held with the parish archives in the presbytery of St. Mary's.

NOTES

For the background history of the Stanley family I have relied mainly on Ormerod and the *Dictionary of National Biography* and for the early history of Hooton Parish, upon Canon Abbott's *History of the Shrewsbury Diocese*. Specific items are listed below.

1. G.A. Ormerod, *History of the County Palatine and City of Chester*, 1882, p.410.
2. *Dictionary of National Biography*.
3. G.Holt,SJ, *The English Jesuits*, Catholic Record Society 1984, p.2.
4. K.R. Wark, Elizabethan Recusancy in Cheshire, Chetham Society, 1971, p.182.
5. *Cheshire Sheaf*, 3rd Series, Vol.2, 1899, p.37.
6. G. Holt, op. cit. p.236.
7. J.A. Hilton, *Post Reformation Catholicism in Cheshire*, North West Catholic History, Vol. 9, 1982, p.6.
8. *Victoria County History — Chester*, Vol.3, p.88.
9. *Hexham Courant*, 9th Dec. 1876.
10. C. Cook & J. Stevenson, *The Longman Handbook of Modern British History (1714-1980)*, 1983, p.98.
11. E S Warrell, *Return of Papists 1767, Diocese of Chester*, Catholic Record Society, 1980, p.179.
12. These bishops were all, at the time, Vicars Apostolic of the Northern District (or, from 1840, Lancashire District) in which Cheshire was situated. In 1850, on the re-establishment of the Hierarchy, George Brown became first Bishop of Liverpool and John Briggs first Bishop of Beverley (later divided into Leeds and Middlesborough).
13. Cheshire Record Office (CRO) D2903/5.

14. CRO DDX374/41.

15. M.A. Abbott, *History of the Diocese of Shrewsbury,* 1986, p.62.

16. *Chester Chronicle*, 25th March, 1893.

17. B.W. Kelly, *Historical Notes on English Catholic Missions,* 1907, p.217. (Reprinted, M. Gandy, 1995).

18. CRO ERC4/5071/1.

V

ACTON BURNELL

E. Maurice Abbott
and Aidan Bellenger

Acton Burnell, historically important as the meeting-place of the Parliament of 1283, lies about eight miles south of Shrewsbury, placed among many narrow roads, small villages and a network of fords. It is a wooded rural area, but close enough to the ironworks of the mid-Severn during the late seventeenth and early eighteenth century to supply charcoal for the developing Industrial Revolution.

Acton is referred to in *Domesday*, but its distinction owed much to the Burnell family, associated with the place by the late twelfth century and its most distinguished member Robert Burnell, Bishop of Bath and Wells and Chancellor of England, who died in 1294. It was Bishop Burnell, active with his mentor King Edward I in the Welsh war, who constructed the fortified manor house now known, as it has been since at least the sixteenth century, as Acton Burnell Castle. By the eighteenth century the castle had become a barn and by 1731 a small stone house had been built on the site of the present Hall. Burnell's chapel was on the first floor of the north-eastern corner tower.

The church of St Mary, described by the *Victoria County History* as 'a highly sophisticated building', owes its construction to Bishop Burnell and has some affinities with his great Gothic Cathedral at Wells in Somerset. There are numerous memorials.[1]

In the north transept there is a brass to Sir Nicholas Burnell (d. 1382) which is one of the finest in the country. Nearby is the magnificent tomb of Sir Richard Lee (d. 1591). It is worth noting that his nine daughters lined up at the back of the monument are each differently attired. In 1967 Maurice Abbott showed two descendants of Robert E Lee the recumbent figure of this representative of a collateral line of their family and they stated that they could see a family likeness. Robert E Lee, the leader of the Confederate Forces in the American Civil War was descended from a Shropshire Lee who emigrated in the early 17th century. Because of their connection, the Lees of Virginia, who form a society, made a gift in 1960 to the Church.

On the opposite side to Richard Lee's monument is that of his son Humphrey, who became the first baronet in Shropshire and a convert to Catholicism. His tomb was the work of Nicholas Stone, the master mason of Charles I. Part of the Latin inscription which commemorates him provides a challenge to those interested in this language and its translation. Here is the text and English rendering:

Hic iacet obscura clausus vir clarus in urna
Laeus et est titulus quem gerit urna brevis
Nec Mausolaeo; titulo nec dignior amplo
Ullus erat virtus si monumenta daret.

Here lies the nobleman Lee, enclosed in a modest urn. The title borne by the urn is short; neither from a tombstone nor from a more lengthy title did anyone ever acquire greater dignity, unless his own virtue bestow it on his monument.

It is possible that the reference to obscurity (*obscura*) is occasioned by the contrast provided by the tomb of his father. To the left of the Richard Lee monument there is a Smythe tablet dated 1764. It has on it a delicate cross of marble which may be unique among 18th century tablets in England.[2]

It is also possible that the lords of Acton Burnell manor have been Catholics since about 1650. In 1679 three recusants were noted in the parish, while in 1706 the number had risen to ten, all members of the Smythe household. The Smythe family, with their centre at Esh in country Durham, had married into the Lees. On the death of Richard Lee in 1660 the manor passed to his daughter Mary, wife of Edward Smythe. Their most famous family member is probably Maria Smythe who, as Mrs Fitzherbert, became wife, but not queen, to the future George IV.

It was the Smythe family's generosity which established the first and only Benedictine mission in Shropshire. There was a continuous succession of Benedictine priests from 1724 to 1923. As early as 1714. Sir Edward Smythe made a foundation for the maintenance of a student at the English monastery of Lamspring in Germany. Dom Francis Rookwood, from St Gregory's, Douai, was at Acton Burnell in 1724 and from 1748 three other monks served the mission until 1795. The last of these, Dom Thomas Ballyman, who arrived in 1774 from Lamspring, was there when Acton Burnell began its twenty years as a Benedictine priory.[3]

Edward Smythe, who had been educated at St Gregory's, Douai, came to the rescue when the English Benedictines resident in France were forcibly repatriated during the French Revolution. It was through his good offices that St Laurence's (formerly at Dieulouard, now at Ampleforth) and St Gregory's (at Douai, and later at Downside) survived as monasteries and schools. Acton Burnell Hall was offered at the favourable rent of £25 a year and the first monks, from St Laurence's, moved in by the end of 1793. The first superior was the formidable Dom Richard Marsh, Prior of St Laurence's, later Prior of Ampleforth, President General of the English Benedictines and Titular Abbot of Westminster, whose heroic escape from France was recorded in a printed memoir. The Laurentian monks moved out in 1795 when the Gregorians arrived with their seven pupils.

The early days of the small community at Acton Burnell were not easy. On 2nd March 1794, Father Marsh in a letter to Gregory Sharrock, a monk himself and co-adjutor to the Vicar Apostolic of the Western District, reflected that the neighbours were 'mighty jealous'. The house was 'almost threatened by a mob' and 'a number of the most ridiculous stories' circulated including that the newly-arrived residents of the Hall were 'French Jacobins to the number of some hundreds'. Marsh's attempts to 'contradict' them were 'quite useless'.[4] The monastery and school, which survived until its transfer in 1814 to Downside in Somerset, was on a small scale with only a few monks and never more than twenty pupils. Only seventy-six students are recorded altogether of whom twenty-four became Benedictine monks. These included Bede Polding who became the first Archbishop of Sydney in 1842 and was the founder of the Australian hierarchy, Placid Morris, Bishop of Troy and missionary Bishop in Mauritius from 1832 to 1840, and Joseph Brown, Vicar Apostolic of the Welsh District, 1840, and first Bishop of Newport and Menevia from 1850 to 1880. Bede Slater, who was Archbishop Polding's cousin, made his profession as a monk of St Laurence's at Acton Burnell in 1794. He was Vicar Apostolic of Mauritius from 1818 to 1832. A notable Catholic priest, John Kirk, had been born at Ruckley, about a mile from Acton Burnell in 1760. He was ordained from the English College, Rome, in 1784 and was to spend almost a half century as Catholic priest at Lichfield. He was a considerable scholar awarded an honorary D.D. by Pope Gregory XVI in 1841. Before his ordination he had obtained a rescript to say his office in Greek and Hebrew. His *Biographies of English Catholics* was finished by 1841 but not published until 1909. His copies of the inscriptions in the English College Chapel were used in the construction of the College Chapel at the end of the nineteenth century and provided important evidence for the beatification of the English martyrs. His sister, Mary, was the housekeeper of the Acton Burnell monks.[5]

The monks themselves in residence at Acton Burnell attempted to continue their monastic life as it had been lived at Douai in much reduced circumstances. A chapel, plainly classical with a galleried interior, completed in 1804, was constructed at the expense of Peter Holford, Sir Edward Smythe's father-in-law and later, in 1810, a new wing to the west end of the house was constructed for the use of the community. Writing on 22 August 1801 to Bishop Gregory Sharrock (whose brother Dom Jerome, formerly Prior of St Gregory's Douai, had succeeded Prior Marsh as superior at Acton Burnell), Bishop John Milner, of the Midland District, stated that nowhere did he meet 'with more kindness or more edification' than at Acton Burnell:

> it gave me infinite pleasure to find the true spirit of St Benedict mixed with that of our great apostle St Augustine in the little family under the guidance of your worthy brother the Prior, and I only regret that they are not multiplied a hundredfold.[6]

Jerome Sharrock, who had spent thirteen months in prison in France before coming to Acton Burnell, died in 1808, one of six monks who died during the period Acton Burnell was a monastic community. One of those to die was Dom Hilaire le Wengue, a monk of St Vedast at Arras, who died on 17th April 1808 and was buried in Acton Burnell churchyard. He had previously been professor of philosophy at the University of Douai. Two other Frenchmen lived with the community. Dom Martin Leveaux, a Maurist monk who came to Shropshire in 1797, entered the English Benedictine Congregation 'as far as his former vows allowed' in 1798, became Novice Master and as superior was superior when the community moved from Acton Burnell to Downside.[7] William Davies, a pupil at Acton Burnell, writing in his eighty-sixth year, remembered Leveaux: 'when at the High Mass he intoned the *Gloria* with his powerful voice, I used to think before the sound ceased that it had reached the heavens. No doubt it did'.[8] The third, the Abbé François Elloi de Malancourt, formerly of the Sorbonne, was a secular priest who found in the land of his exile a true home.

Peter Kendal, who succeeded Jerome Sharrock as Prior in 1808 had escaped from France during the Revolution and was at Acton Burnell by 1793 acting as missioner. Between 1793 and 1808 sixty seven people in the parish were received into the church. Peter Kendal, who was to acquire the Downside property before his death in 1814, established a dame school, catechised the local children and is reported to have rowed across a swollen Severn to give the Last Rites to a parishioner. Kendal is also said to have inspired Polding in his great missionary activities. When the monastery and school migrated to Downside a Benedictine priest remained. One long-term missioner was Dom Ralph Radcliffe, who as a boy had made a dashing escape from France and who had been ordained at Acton Burnell where he was to remain until his death in 1842. The chapel was Gothicised and a side-chapel added in 1846 to the designs of Charles Hansom. The chapel remained in use for worship until 1973 when the Sion Sisters who had acquired the Hall in 1948 decided to leave the district. The new owners, Concord College, adapted the main chapel for use as a dining room. The side chapel, which stands over a Smythe burial vault, was used for Sunday Mass until August 1983 when Acton Burnell ceased to be supplied with Mass.

One of those employed in the building of the chapel was a joiner, named Samuel Lee, who had left the village school of Longnor at the age of twelve. In his late teens he had determined to learn Latin because in reading books he had come across Latin quotations and failed to understand them. He naturally thought he would receive encouragement from the priests in his studies and one day he approached one of them for some information, only to receive the reply 'Charity begins at home'. In his own words 'This was very mortifying, but it only served as a stimulus to my endeavours; for from this time I resolved, if possible, to excel even him'. He continued his studies in Latin and later took up Greek and Hebrew. Archdeacon Corbett discovered this and arranged for him to go to Cambridge. He took orders and ended up as a Canon of Bristol and Regius Professor of Hebrew.[9]

After the monastic community left in 1814 the number of Cathlolic parishioners must have been quite large in proportion to the local population. In 1833 a parish school was started and this is now part of the entrance lodge to the Hall. A new school was built in 1872 but in 1923 it became a village hall. There were 250 Catholics here in 1850 and it is interesting to note that according to the 1851 census of church attendance in England, there were 150 at Mass in the Hall chapel and 100 worshippers at the morning and evening service in the Anglican parish church. From that time the numbers began to decline. The Catholic population was given as 110 in 1880 with 24 pupils in the school of whom 7 were non-Catholics. By 1898 the population was down to 72. The school closed in 1923 when the last teacher, Agnes Slater got married. Her father, when the new church was opened in 1929 at Church Stretton, asked the squire for the school bell to be given to the new building. This request was willingly granted.[10]

In 1914 a disastrous fire broke out in the Hall. It occurred as a result of constant burning of coal fires in Lady Smythe's bedroom during an illness, and also in her dressing room which was occupied by her maid. It is thought that an oak beam in the flue was ignited. This bedroom was part of an addition to the house made in 1909. The fire broke out on 14th April - Easter Tuesday - after a frosty night. Four fire brigades were engaged in fighting the flames. The squire, Sir Walter, in his 86th year, was most active in giving directions and begged that every effort be made to save the chapel. The wind changed at three o'clock and the chapel was preserved. The rest of the Hall was gutted.[11]

Sir Walter and Lady Smythe, together with their butler, Mr Slater, a footman, a lady's maid, three housemaids and three kitchen maids, went to stay at Cronkhill Hall, then at the Raven Hotel in Shrewsbury and finally rented Betton Strange Hall during the rebuilding at Acton Burnell. This was hastened on and the workmen often worked by lamp-light late into the night. The work was completed by 1915 and the rooms are still in a beautiful condition. Panelling was obtained from Frodesley Lodge, then owned by the Smythes, and is to be found in the two rooms which were used as dining rooms for the children when the Sion Sisters used the Hall as a school. Sir Walter attended Mass daily and expected the domestic staff to do so as well. He and Lady Smythe always gave a warm welcome to the old people who came to Sunday Mass from the workhouse at Cross Houses. As in those days those receiving Communion had to fast from midnight, breakfast was provided for the communicants at the Hall. There was also the custom of giving

sweets to the ladies and tobacco to the men.[12] During all Sir
Walter's time, Dom John Stutter was the chaplain. He lived in
the black and white house, now (1999) occupied by Mrs David
Bruce-Smythe, which was allocated to the chaplain from 1856
onwards. It was to this house that the Blessed Sacrament was
taken at the time of the fire. Father Stutter was much interested in astronomy and clocks. One of his duties was to play
cards on Saturday night with the squire and in doing so he
suffered from his irascibility. It is said that he used to take the
opportunity the following morning to preach on the virtue of
patience.[13]

   Sir Walter had two children. Edward was the last baronet
and died, unmarried, in 1942. His sister, the last of the
Smythes, married Archibald Bruce, nephew of the first Lord
Aberdare. In 1935 Mr & Mrs Bruce began to have plays in the
Hall. Their daughter, Mrs Dexter, an accomplished actress,
helped with their production. Mrs Bruce and a number of local
people took part in the plays. Able assistance was provided by
Kathleen Ellis, of Shrewsbury, a former member of the D'Oyly
Carte Opera Company. Father Pownall, parish priest of Church
Stretton and also responsible for Acton Burnell, helped considerably in the the first efforts. He was very skilled in stage
production, in designing and making scenery and in arranging
the lighting effects. These plays went on until 1939. They were
performed on five nights and one afternoon in the middle of
January. Much support was given by the county gentry and at
the conclusion of the last show, Mr & Mrs Bruce entertained
the whole company to supper which, with speeches, went on
until midnight.[14] The imminence of war in 1938 led the Sisters
of Sion to look for a place in the country to which their pupils
at Bayswater could be evacuated. They were recommended by
Bishop Moriarty to go to Acton Burnell. Arrangements were
made with the Bruces and the autumn of 1939 found the school
established in the Hall. Among the small boys who came there
was Norman St John-Stevas.[15] Conditions were somewhat
strange at first. Bracken was collected from the estate and used
to make mattresses. Stinging nettles were used as a vegetable

ACTON BURNELL HALL
a home of the Smythe family

and one does not need much imagination to realise how much of these would have to be gathered to feed hungry children.

The coming of the Sisters meant that once again the parish had a resident priest. In 1923 the Benedictines had stopped sending a chaplain. Franciscans supplied the place for a number of years until 1929 when the priest at Church Stretton took over. In 1939 the first school chaplain came in the person of Father Charles Hoare, N.D.S., one of the very few English-speaking Sion Fathers, who about this time wrote a book on the subject of Continuity in relation to the Reformation He was succeeded in 1940 by Dom Michael Caffrey O.S.B., who in his turn was followed by Dom Romuald Rylance, O.S.B. In 1942 a diocesan priest, Father John Gildea, was appointed. He, like his immediate predecessors, lived in the Hall until 1943 when the Sisters obtained a house in the village known as 'Number 9'. The return of the priest to Acton Burnell meant that parishioners were easier to visit. The parish, though covering a very large area, including Shipton, Sheinton, Cressage, Berrington, Longnor, Picklescott and Smethcott, had few parishioners living outside Acton Burnell. Number 9 was the residence of the priest until 1968 when accommodation was provided for him in the lodge by the front gate. It happened that about this time the priest concerned, Father Abbott, was asked by the Bishop to take over Church Stretton. For a few months, he continued to say daily Mass at the Convent, but in 1969 the Bishop appointed Father Larkin as chaplain, who was succeeded later that year by Father Handley, S.M.M., who, as a curate attached to Ludlow, looked after the area round Plowden and Craven Arms.

To continue the story of the Convent. The school remained when the war was over in 1945 and three years later the Sisters acquired the Hall and thirty-two acres of land for this work. The total number of pupils eventually reached about 100 boarders and 50 day pupils. In the March of 1970 the Sisters decided to close the school, as they were not able to find sufficient teachers from their congregation. The junior school closed at the end of the summer term and the senior school in the summer of 1971.

In 1966 a new building appeared a few hundred yards from the Hall, which was designed as a novitiate. Hitherto the novices had been housed in part of the Hall in somewhat cramped quarters and it was a great change to have a brand new building with a fine set of rooms, a pleasing dining room and a chapel which was planned in accord with recent liturgical changes. The stained glass windows behind the altar the work of Sister Marie John, display the leading themes of the Old and New Testament. This building was not destined to be a novitiate for very long. The novitiate was moved to Worthing and at the end of 1968 the house was named Sion House and became a Retreat and Conference Centre. This venture came to an end in 1973 when the Sisters left Acton Burnell.

There are two further items of interest. The first concerns the grotto which stands on the hill behind the Hall. Pevsner dates this c. 1750. It seems that we can now say that it was built a little later than 1750. Mr John Tipton, who died in 1967, informed Father Abbott that his first wife was a descendant of a Mr Bold, who was noted for his skill in building and was responsible for the walls on the estate. He built the house in the village known as 'Number 2', and the grotto which was shell- and tile-lined. He spent a year on his back fitting the shells into the ceiling and it would appear that he intended to depict the story of the wedding feast at Cana. Unhappily the building is in a poor state of repair and has been so since at least 1932. (16) Some of its tiles were removed and are now in the home of Mrs David Bruce-Smythe. This Mr Bold would appear to have been born in 1737 and baptised at the parish church. He married a Catholic and his descendants, including Mrs Tipton, were Catholics, His name was Thomas Booth or Boold.

The other item concerns the Stag's Head which was closed in 1882 as far as can be ascertained. The inn's sign still reposes at the back of the village shop and has on it the name of the licensee, Mrs Southern, who died in 1888 and was buried in the Catholic cemetery. Here one might note that this cemetery was opened in 1858 and with its fine trees and Italian cross has a pleasant appearance. The reason for the closure of the inn by

Sir Frederick Smythe, according to one tradition, was the death of a villager arising out of a brawl caused by drink.[17] A young man appears in the burial book as dying a sudden death and this seems to tie in with the story. Another tradition[18] states that the squire found men in the inn when they should have been working and so closed it. It would still be possible to take out the licence again, providing that the back payments are made. The large room upstairs continued to be used as an assembly room until a meeting of the Liberal Party took place there, with the result that the squire forbade it to be used again.

NOTES

1. A.T. Gaydon, ed., *A History of Shropshire* (VCH) Oxford, 1968, pp.3-13. The name of Dom Bernard Bradshaw, who died in 1774, is still visible on his broken tombstone on the floor of the church.
2. M. Moulder, *Shropshire Shell Guide*, London, 1973, p.47.
3. G. Dolan, 'Chapters in the History of the English Benedictine Missions 22. The Diocese of Shrewsbury', *Downside Review* 26 (1907), pp.254-263.
4. Clifton Diocesan Archives, 1794-5, Marsh to Sharrock (2 March).
5. G. Anstruther, *The Seminary Priests* 4, 1977, pp.163ff.
6. Clifton Diocesan Archives, 1801, Milner to Sharrock (22 August).
7. See D. Bellenger, 'The Benedictines at Acton Burnell': a further note, *Worcestershire Recusant* 40, (1982), pp.37-39. See ibid, 'An Anti-monastic Incident, 1794'; *Worcestershire Recusant* 39, 1982, pp.32-35.
8. Quoted by Daniel Rees in 'Reduced Circumstances', *TheRaven* (Downside School Magazine) Sept 1972-July 1973, p.30.
9. *The Gentlemen's Magazine*, January 1853.
10. Information supplied by his daughter, Mrs Rosemary Newton.
11. Some of this information came from Mrs Edwards, lady's maid to Lady Smythe and from the *History of Acton Burnell* by Sr Mary Travers.
12. Information supplied by Miss Alice Harvey, former house keeper to Father Stutter and a native of Acton Burnell.

13. Information supplied by Captain Reginald Bruce Smythe.
14. Information supplied by Mr Ernest Stockton.
15. Norman St John-Stevas (later Lord St John of Fawsley) was Leader of the House of Commons, 1979-1981.
16. Information supplied by Rev E. Sergeantson, former vicar of Leebotwood.
17. Information supplied by Mr Ernest Stockton.
18. Information supplied by Mr Ernest Higgs.

VI

POPULAR CATHOLIC LIFE

Michael Morton

Our subject is the modern devotional practices of the Catholic communion in England and Wales and their context. In particular we shall look at the time of the late Victorian era when Catholicism once again became a feature of the religious prospect of England and Wales after the restoration of the Hierarchy in 1850. From that period onwards, Catholicism expanded, thanks mainly to immigration, until eventually Catholics formed perhaps ten per cent of the whole population.

The description and study of devotional practice is a hard subject to research. The historian assembles data but is aware, more than any scientist, how inadequate the information really is. Much of the evidence on which we could base our knowledge of the past has been lost or destroyed or else was never recorded in the first place. We have to make guesses from the material available, rather like an archaeologist who tries to make up an ancient text from a few dusty fragments.

Even today, when thousands of experts and statisticians are assembling and analysing facts about the economic life of the country, government has only the vaguest idea about what has happened and very little idea what will happen. So we have little chance of reaching solid conclusions about how people saw the popular, devotional life of Christian faith in the past. Or about how their lives changed and how they reacted to that change. We cannot tell what people took for granted. Because they took it for granted, they never tell us. History becomes the great school of speculation. History is also very malleable; we often write the past to fit or make sense of the present. In that sense writers can actually create a past.

When the Catholic Church emerged from relative obscurity and casual persecution during the first half of the nineteenth century, it did so because of changes in law and demography, but it had lost its popular roots. Indigenous Catholics had become wary and retiring; Irish and other immigrants arrived in Britain just as the modern world did. They experienced an 'alienation' , which literally means to be a foreigner in your own country, and tried to create the religious world of their remembered past in their new homes. Yet during the 1700s, English Catholicism had gone underground. Mass had been said in rooming houses (even by senior churchmen like Bishop Challoner) or else in disguised churches (such as St Mary's, Madeley and Congleton) which were given the appearance of Nonconformist chapels.

By 1850, when Cardinal Nicholas Wiseman wrote his exuberant pastoral letter *Out of the Flaminian Gate*, which announced the foundation of the episcopal hierarchy based on dioceses in England and Wales, most of the secular clergy had been trained abroad. In Rome, Lisbon, Valladolid and even Douai before Ushaw was established.

Not surprisingly, then, they brought to their new missions devotional practices from the Continent. From Italy came the *Quarant' Ore* which was a devotion of prayer and exposition derived from the tradition that Christ spent forty hours in the garden tomb near Calvary. The Baroque style of Benediction also became popular, when 'Benediction' in general language meant any evening service. St Alphonsus of Ligouri, who was the founder of the Redemptorist Order (the Congregation of the Most Holy Redeemer), was influential through his priests in introducing the Stations of the Cross in a style and language that has persisted to the present day. Also from Italy, at the hill-town of Orvieto, came the practice of a Corpus Christi procession. This feast, which falls between 23 May and 26 June, was an opportunity to re-introduce open-air processions that mirrored the many such practices in late mediaeval England like well-dressing at Ascensiontide, St Anthony's Feast on 13 June and the celebrations of the midsummer solstice.

Soon after, in 1854, came the Solemn Declaration of the Immaculate Conception of Our Lady and the beginning of pilgrimages to Lourdes (in the 1860s). Both of these events gave impulse to the public recital of the Rosary, and superseded the old May-time traditions. These last had persisted from Celtic times, when the celebration of the festival of Summer's beginning or Beltane was kept with fragrant blossom or flowers and the feast of the goddess of Spring. The weather really meant something in times past, and after a dark, cold winter with vitamin-less food and the harsh fast of Lent, springtime was welcomed with great enthusiasm.

The Rosary, a name which properly applies to a rose garden, started life as a collection of devotional texts with sometimes a hint of association between the Rosary and gardens of love. The present practice (the Dominican Rosary) dates from the 1500s when the reformed or Observant Dominican Order worked to generate a revival of spirituality among the laity. However, the Rosary has roots in a more distant age. The Mediaeval fascination with the mystical nature of the rose, which became a sort of Christian *mandala*, became associated in turn with prayer-beads and a chanted repetition of prayer with which the crusaders would, no doubt, have been familiar. The Rosary also derived in part from the 'Peoples Psalter' where the 150 beads of the Rosary reflected the 150 psalms in the monastic Divine Office. Interestingly, the figure of a beadsman, who appears in John Keats's poem *The Eve of St Agnes*, as someone whom people paid to say the Rosary for them, may be more than just poetic fiction.

In 1572, the Dominican Pope, St Pius V, established a feast of the Holy Rosary on 7 October. This was the anniversary of a crucial battle in the eastern Mediterranean between a Christian and Turkish fleet. The victorious Christian forces, led by Don Juan of Austria, re-established control of the seas. The victory is celebrated by G.K. Chesterton who wrote a propagandist poem called *Lepanto*. In the East window of Shrewsbury Cathedral which is itself dedicated to Our Lady, Help of Christians, there is an illustration of the battle, with the Turkish galleys represented in disarray. All this led to making October the month of the Rosary, whilst the pilgrimages to Lourdes made even daily recitation of the Rosary a popular devotion.

This popularity was increased as a result of the foundation of a movement called The Children of Mary in 1847, by the Daughters of Charity and the Vincentian Fathers. With the approval of Pope Plus IX, the association promoted the Miraculous Medal (whose message had been reported in a vision by St Catherine Laboure in 1830 and who was herself a Daughter of Charity of St Vincent de Paul). Curiously, the apparition at Lourdes was of a lady dressed in the apparel of a Child of Mary and carrying a Rosary. This description by St Bernadette originally made some of the bourgeois women at Lourdes think that the vision of Bernadette to have been a young woman who had died the previous year and buried by her own request in her Children of Mary robes. Bernadette's recital of her Rosary at Masabielle grotto and its subsequent great popularity in Lourdes promoted the devotion immensely.

May Devotions, which derive in part from a christianising of the spring festivals of pagan Europe, also began in Italy in the 1500s with the recitation of the Rosary, the Litany of Loreto and the solemn crowning of a statue of the Virgin Mary. This last achieved wide popularity after a statue was set up near the Piazza di Spagna in Rome (with money offered by the Kingdom of Naples to pay off an historic debt). This statue was crowned by Plus IX every December 8 after 1854, but although the practice thus received new stimulation, the traditional season was retained. In parishes such as Our Lady's and St Laurence's, Birkenhead, this was a major religious event and much missed.

Also from Continental Europe, and this time from France, came the devotions to the Sacred Heart of Jesus. At the Convent of Paray-le-Monial in France during the 1670s, St Margaret Mary Alacoque (1648-90) reported a series of visions of the heart of Jesus afire with love for humanity. It was during the age of Louis XIV, when France was recovering from desperate and vicious wars of religion. At the same time, European society was on the threshold of the Enlightenment which was the philosophical reflection on the scientific revolution. The French religious, St John Eudes, began an Office and Mass of the Sacred Heart while by the 1850s a feast day had been established on the Friday after the Octave of Corpus Christi. As this day almost always occurs in June, that month was popularly devoted to the Sacred Heart. In 1950, with an encyclical entitled *Haurietis aquae* (that is "You will draw waters [from the well of salvation]") Pope Plus XII affirmed the devotion which had grown to include the dedication of homes to the Sacred Heart of Jesus.

The appearance of these post-Tridentine devotional practices in England and Wales open up the question of their introduction and the reason for their popularity. They were formally introduced neither by papal decree nor insistence of the newly-formed hierarchy. The liturgical writer, J.D. Crighton finds a psychological change implied by such new popular devotions — perhaps the high culture of the Enlightenment being un-frozen by the Romantics and an enthusiastic nostalgia for the Middle Ages. Certainly he is right to point to men like A.W. Pugin and Père Guéranger, the founder of the Abbey of Solesmes in France, who wished to bring about a religious restoration that looked to an age of faith and devotion.

There is also the matter of Catholic puritanism which had a considerable effect on the idiom of faith during the *settecento* all over Europe. Its original appearance brought out the name Jansenism which was based on the rigorous and neoplatonic moral religion of St Augustine as interpreted by Cornelius Jansen. Jansen, one-time Professor of Theology at Louvain and Bishop of Ypres, had published a book called *Augustinus* in 1640. The resulting controversy was to involve the monastery at Port-royal in Paris, and the celebrated French philosopher, Blaise Pascal, before it was officially ended in 1715. However, the famous novel by Henri Bayle (Stendhal) *Le Rouge et le Noir* ('Scarlet and Black' [1831]) has insights into the perseverance of such a puritanical outlook. The hero of the novel, young Julien Sorel, is terrified by the mien and the words of the Rector of the seminary at Besançon. The portrait of this cleric and the style of the institution contrasts sharply with the experience that Julien had had of the Church hitherto in the story. The Rector, Fr Pirard, in his speech to Julien, is suspicious even of an over-zealous study of the Scriptures since he believes it can only lead to Protestantism. He warns Julien sternly: 'Truth, sir, is austere. But is it not our task here below to be austere ourselves? You must watch to keep your conscience on guard against this weakness — *too much sensibility to vain outward graces'*.

Human character and purpose often shows itself more clearly in local activities than on a grander scale. During the whole of the nineteenth century Western Europe lived under the shadow of two radical movements — the French Revolution and the Industrial Revolution. Both were described by the same noun, but they were really two different sorts of change. The first was a variation in the way that people saw their place in society whilst the second was a change in society itself.

The Catholic Church reacted to these changes in a defensive and sometimes hostile fashion, and often not without reason. But then new ideas began to be condemned wholesale. The long pontificate of Pope Pius IX (1846-78) was an age of wariness and political bitterness between the Church and the Italian State. In fact, throughout Europe the Church of the Victorian age was not terribly successful. It was over-clerical and seen as reactionary, and lost a good deal of the influence that it had retained since Reformation times. The tendency then was to become populist and fundamentalist to compensate in an age of revolutions and anti-clericalism.

The mystery at the heart of Christian life, the Mass, was said silently and in Latin. In spite of the affection for the ritual, the working classes never got a hold on Church Latin and as Mass was celebrated early in the morning, when most working-class families were off to work or preparing for school, attendance at Mass was supplemented by other services during the week.

From the very earliest times, Christians fasted on two days a week, chosen in conscious contrast to the Jewish fast-days which were Monday and Thursday. The first century text, *The Teaching of the Twelve Apostles*, (usually known by the Greek word for teaching as *The Didache*) advises "Do not keep the same fast-days as the hypocrites. Mondays and Thursdays are their days for fasting, so yours should be Wednesdays and Fridays." The discourse goes on to recommend the Lord's Prayer, complete with its ending "for thine is the kingdom, the power and the glory", to be said three times a day.

These two days, with Friday given a special penitential nature because of the connection with Good Friday, also became the usual days for evening services in parish churches. The service of Benediction was described in Bishop Challoner's book, *The Garden of the Soul*, but was comparatively rare in the nineteenth century. Only on great feasts was Benediction given and then with slight ceremony. The priest did not wear a cope nor the server a cassock and the Latin Hymns *O Salutaris Hostia* and *Tantum Ergo* were said, not sung. Only in the later part of the century did the more familiar and solemn Benediction emerge.

Because preaching at Mass was rare, the service combining Benediction on a Sunday afternoon with the public recitation of the Rosary and a sermon began to appear. In season, too, there were May and October Devotions and the Novena of Our Lady of Perpetual Succour. This last was certainly introduced by the Redemptorists, for the painting of Our Lady that was used at these public prayers hangs in the Redemptorist Church in the via Merulana in Rome. The idea of a novena itself, however, is much older. The Greeks and Romans in Hellenic times kept the practice of nine days of mourning after a death and then held a feast. Nine-day periods of preparation, such as that in Advent from 17 to 25 December were added to by nine First Fridays, from devotions to the Sacred Heart, which was a personal devotion that was encouraged publicly.

The Church of England practice of public Matins and Evensong (Vespers) which had been carried on from mediaeval times never quite caught on in Catholic churches. The daily morning Mass replaced Matins while Vespers were tried, but never became popular. In Wallasey under Canon James McNally, there was a revival of Latin Vespers after 1945, but Vespers is a long service and the Latin psalms were difficult to sing, even though the texts were given in the old Missals and Manuals designed for private use. In fact, in the 1820s and 30s some of the clergy had turned Vespers into English and it began to be sung in churches. In 1838, the Vicars Apostolic had disapproved and ordered the practice to cease. One interesting fact is that the canticle printed in earlier Missals is the *Benedictus* rather than the *Magnificat*.

Plainsong itself had been developed for choir monks singing unaccompanied for the Mass and Office during the Middle Ages. In 1903, Pope Pius X published a *Motu Proprio* criticising the decline of church music over the previous century and calling for a return to the simplicity of the Church's earlier traditions. He condemned the theatrical style of singing that was performed in larger churches, where the music had become just a performance for the congregation, and called for the ancient Gregorian chant which had simplicity and beauty. This was welcomed down to parish level, and one reason for this was that plainsong is so unlike any secular music as to leave no doubt that what was being sung was different and sacred. It had an air of the mystical and remote beauty. However, it is also difficult to sing so that, apart from the setting that became known as *Credo III* and the common *Missa de Angelis,* it needed a trained choir to sing it well.

Hymns themselves are an interesting subject of study. Traditionally only Latin hymns from the Office, some composed in late antiquity, were used, including those for Christmas and Advent. Our modern Christmas is really a Victorian invention combining German customs (Christmas trees, Santa Claus and greeting cards) with a season of peace and goodwill where Charles Dickens' story *A Christmas Carol* was very influential. Carols (from the Middle English *caroles,* which were originally festivities) became popular during the nineteenth century. The first Carol Concert was held in King's College Chapel in Cambridge only in 1912. For Catholics, the eve of Christmas was a fast day and Advent itself very definitely a penitential season. In the *Westminster Hymnal,* which was published following the Bishops' Low Week meeting in 1936, a number of carols were included. From the Office of the Breviary came *Creator alma siderum, Hark a herald voice is calling* and a hymn for the novena period of Advent when the so-called 'O Antiphons' were recited or sung at the Office. This hymn *Veni, O Sapientia* was translated by Ronald Knox as *O come thou Wisdom whose decree* with a more accurate rendering than the modern version which is now sung during the whole of Advent. Mgr Knox contributed widely to the hymns that were sung in church, and some of his contributions had an endearing eccentricity of language. For example, a hymn to the English Martyrs which began 'O English hearts, what heart can know' has the remarkable line : 'O saints of English speech and race / caught up to heaven, of heav'nly grace / a double portion send us'.

One of the first modern English Catholic hymns was 'Hail Queen of Heaven, the Ocean Star' which was written in the 1800s by John Lingard and set to music by H.F. Hemy. Based loosely on the *Salve Regina,* it is still popular today, whereas another early hymn written this time by Cardinal Wiseman, 'Full in the panting heart of Rome' is less often used. Convert clergy, such as John Henry Newman and

Frederick William Faber, who became Rector of the London Oratory, also wrote well-known hymns. 'Praise to the Holiest' and 'Firmly I believe and truly' were taken from Newman's *Dream of Gerontius*, while Faber offered 'Faith of our fathers', 'O come and mourn with me awhile', 'Jesus my Lord, my God, my all' and 'O purest of creatures'. Coming from a strict evangelical background, Faber had a high-minded seriousness that became triumphant pastoralism, giving the ideas of the Tractarians to the growing Catholic Church. Francis Stansfield (1835-1914) wrote 'Sweet Sacrament Divine' and 'O Sacred Heart', whose words give the impression that he thought we were in the wrong world — exiles or cosmic prisoners-of-war held captive by a malignant power. The Jesuit priest and poet, Gerard Manley Hopkins, translated some Latin hymns — such as St Thomas Aquinas's *Adoro te devote* — which survived until recent times. All the same, it is interesting that poets such as he contributed so little to popular hymnology. For it was important where hymns came from. One of the earliest modern carols in original composition was 'While shepherds watched their flocks by night'; but because it had been written by the puritan Nahum Tate, it was not included in Catholic hymnals for a long time.

Another Anglican convert who was to have an important influence on the style of Catholic life in England was Henry Edward (later Cardinal) Manning (1808-92). He had been converted to Catholicism in 1851, a widower and a friend or foe in season of John Henry Newman. Manning had been a major figure at the First Vatican Council and a champion of the Papacy. He sought, it seems, to introduce changes that would make his shadow-cabinet church distinct from Anglicanism. So, for example, he began to address the secular clergy as 'Father', which was usual for the regular clergy, rather than 'Mister'. (All the same, Bishop Allen, who was Bishop of Shrewsbury at the turn of the century would still begin his *ad clerum* letter "Reverend sir"). Church Latin began to be pronounced in the 'Roman fashion' — that is to say, with the vowel and consonant sounds of modern Italian —

and Roman vestments were introduced. In such a climate it was not surprising that Manning's successor, Herbert Vaughan, strongly supported the conclusion of the Papal Commission of 1896 that anglican orders were 'absolutely null and utterly void' — a ruling which widened the popular Catholic-Protestant divide and, paradoxically, enhanced Catholic identity.

One notable feature of Catholic life from the 1920s onwards were preached Missions. These have an origin in 1807 when the Redemptorists resurrected a remarkable seventeenth century book written by one Francesco Pinamonti entitled *Hell opened to Christians*. This work, whose contents can be guessed at, was reprinted by the Redemptorists complete with graphic woodcut illustrations. One edition, published in Ireland as late as 1889 has links with the famous sermon on Hell preached in James Joyce's novel *A Portrait of the Artist as a Young Man*.

Following St Alphonsus de Liguori, their founder, the Redemptorists place Hell in middle earth — a fiery, sulphurous place which was peopled, in their account, with tormented souls and malevolent demons. One priest, Fr Joseph Furniss, published a junior version of all this in a book for children, *The Sight of Hell* — a work that would surely make a modern OFSTED inspector begin to frown.

Yet the Redemptorists were much in demand for Missions. These had originated in France during the 1830s when Jesuit priests would preach in the provinces on religious and political matters of the day. The Redemptorists took over the name, but changed the character of 'missions' to offer something similar to revivalist meetings (of Ranters in England, which had come in turn from the Quakers' and even the Methodists' meetings). They dwelt much on the fear of hell but with a purpose to encourage reconciliation. The skilful preaching, histrionics and sheer occasion made for an evening out. During the 1930s, before television, organised bingo or social clubs, the missions were even a kind of entertainment. Indeed, the style was taken up by several other groups and even independent sects, but eventually mass entertainment and other changes robbed the Redemptorists of their appeal. Jesuit priests were also in demand to conduct Missions; they were generally considered milder and more bookish and cultured.

On the matter of books used by the people, the best remembered is surely the 'Penny Catechism' . A short book which shaped attitudes of several generations, the Catechism had a last section called 'The Christian's Rule of Life'. Another popular book of devotions was Bishop Challoner's *Garden of the Soul.* Dr Richard Challoner (1691-1781) was the Vicar Apostolic for the London District during the second half of the eighteenth century, which was a difficult time for English Catholicism. He was influential not only for the introduction of the Catechism (whose real title was *The Abridgement of Christian Doctrine*), but for a modernisation of the Douay Bible which had been first published in the sixteenth century. The original, the official English translation of the scriptures, had been large, expensive and virtually unobtainable. Bishop Challoner had the Douay Version produced and made available. It was the version used by Catholics until a wave of new versions appeared in the 1960s.

The Garden of the Soul, however, became a classic. Most children received one as a First Communion present, bound in white with a picture of the Sacred heart and many place-ribbons. It was the most living and organic of books, as over the generations from when it was first published in 1740 it was added to and changed. It was a guide to the spiritual life which included pieces from the English of the Mass. There were night prayers, reflections from spiritual writers such as St Francis de Sales. Acts of Contrition and prayers for services like Benediction. When the Catholic Truth Society produced the *Simple Prayer Book* first in 1889, its format and content were, to some degree, a homage to Dr Challoner's classic.

These devotions, pious works and prayers seem nowadays to belong to another landscape. Their remembrance can be used, as we have said, to write a past. The past that is produced can be that of an 'Age of Faith'; or it can be a kind of 'Sub-culture of Catholicism', having the same relationship to the lofty scholastic theology, Latin liturgy and clerical remoteness that jazz, ragtime or the blues have to the high culture of Classical music.

Among the public in general, there is a disposition to see in the passing of the twentieth century a gradual decline of religion and a loss of faith. But there really is a misconception here — for the trouble is that people's perception of religious meaning is too rigid. The attempt to hold religious meanings as fixed must fail, because the process of historical change slowly evacuates them and turns them into historical curios. And none of what we have said can examine Christian faith in this country as a mass movement. In England, the majority of the Anglican bourgeoisie did not lose their religion until sometime between Darwin and Bloomsbury, but the working classes lost theirs much earlier. A folk church (which to some extent describes the English Catholicism both before and after the major Irish immigration) seems strong enough to survive industrialism, at least for a time. As society changes, some reject religion in favour of politics, while for others religious faith comes to be seen as concerned rather with inspiration than with explanation. It expresses itself inwardly as piety, and outwardly as ethical striving to realise its ideals. But the historic work of religion, of embodying our values, witnessing and conserving them and pointing to the transcendent mystery at the heart of things, this remains unchanged. It will find new, vibrant expressions which, in turn, may one day become the subject of another study of past and well-remembered devotions.

VII

JAMES BROWN: FIRST
BISHOP OF SHREWSBURY

Peter Phillips

Early Years

James Brown was born on 11th January 1812 in
Wolverhampton, the son of James and Winefred Brown, and
baptised, according to custom, by Walter Blount, the
missioner at St Peter and Paul's, the following day.[1] He must
have completed his initial schooling in Wolverhampton and
tradition has it that the young boy was brought to the
attention of Bishop Milner while serving Mass. In 1821,
aged nine, he was sent to Sedgley Park, following, it seems,
something of a family tradition.[2] It was a time of change at
the College.[3] Its President, Joseph Birch, died that same
autumn and Walter Blount came over from Wolverhampton
to assume the office. It was a difficult time for the school and
numbers dropped throughout the twenties. Yet there was the
odd school drama: on the day after Thomas Walsh's
consecration as Coadjutor to Milner in Wolverhampton at
the beginning of May 1825, all the English bishops dined at
College; Brown would have enjoyed fun of the claim of eight
playdays, one for each of the visiting bishops.[4] He would
have also witnessed the first of the Midland District clergy

meetings which Milner organised at the Park in 1822; these were continued each year and it was while the clergy were gathered for their meeting on 19th April 1826 that news was brought of Milner's death, a few months before Brown moved on to Oscott the following August.

Little is known of Brown's progress through the seminary, though he comes briefly into the limelight as Lady Duberly in *The Heir at Law*, a play staged for the annual Exhibition for 1828.   His reserved manner and proficiency in Classics marked him out for a career in teaching and so, after completing his studies, Brown was ordained priest by Bishop Walsh on 18th February 1837 and he joined the staff at Oscott. This was the last year of Old Oscott, and Brown had the privilege of acting as MC with Augustus Welby Pugin at the consecration of the High Altar of the new College chapel in May 1838.[5] The students moved into the new building at the beginning of August.   Brown was at Oscott when the newly consecrated Bishop Wiseman arrived to assume the Presidency in September 1840. He does not seem to have left any recollections of the event, but Acton, who spent his schooldays   at   Oscott   from   1843-1848   left   a   brief reminiscence of his impression of Wiseman's time at the College,[6] and Brown's successor as Bishop of Shrewsbury, Edmund Knight, was amongst the boys who met Wiseman at the Lodge gates to drag the carriage up the drive to the front door.[7] One might surmise that, like others at Oscott, Brown was   a   little   unsettled   at   Wiseman's   flamboyance   and somewhat bemused by the stream of visitors Wiseman's presence attracted.   Brown was by this time Prefect of Studies, a post he assumed in 1839 and which he surrendered in   1844   to   George   Errington,   Wiseman's   former   vice-president in Rome, and who, at Wiseman's request, had joined the Oscott staff the previous year. It was shortly after Brown's assumption of office that the College received the Royal Warrant admitting students to enter for external examinations in the University of London.

Brown returned from Oscott to his boyhood haunts at Sedgley Park on 14th January 1845 a few days after Henry Smith has assumed the presidency of the College.[8] Brown became both vice-president and chaplain. Three years later he himself succeeded Smith when the latter departed to follow his vocation as a Trappist in Mount St Bernard's Abbey. From the beginning, with Smith's encouragement, Brown was making changes. The summer of 1845 saw the re-introduction of the annual Exhibition, perhaps in reminiscence of Brown's own schoolboy performance. This time the boys presented Shakespeare's *Henry IV, Part I*, to which Brown contributed a topical epilogue. He did the same for a performance of *Henry IV, Part II* the following summer. On becoming President in 1848, Brown started some improvements to the building, built a new wash house, introduced iron bedsteads, and the old pewter plates seem to have been replaced by crockery. He reorganised the course of studies and, in 1848, instituted the annual school Retreat. For a short time during this period the students produced a hand-written journal, *The Parker*, one of the editors being Eugene Buquet, later a priest of the Shrewsbury diocese. Brown sought to put the school on a firmer foundation by seeking to buy the house and land. That his attempts proved to be unsuccessful must have provided grounds for his later support for Ullathorne to move the site of the College, much to Husenbeth's dismay:

> I sincerely hope that Bishop Ullathorne will not listen to the evil advice of Dr Brown about abandoning the old Park. I know that Dr Brown never had the true Parker feeling and unfortunately the Bishop of Birmingham is not a Parker. But I hope Dr Weedall will use his influence to avert what I should dread as a terrible calamity.[9]

Bishop of Shrewsbury

In 1851 Bishop Ullathorne brought Brown the news that
he had been appointed bishop of the new diocese of
Shrewsbury. Originally intending to leave some sees vacant,
Rome unexpectedly hurried him into office in the face of the
Ecclesiastical Titles Bill, an attempt to prevent the new
Roman Catholic Bishops from assuming territorial titles.
Bishop Brown was consecrated together with Thomas
Burgess, 2nd Bishop of Clifton, by Cardinal Wiseman in St
George's Cathedral, Southwark, on 27th July 1851, Bishops
Ullathorne and Wareing acting as co-consecrators. That this
event could take place a mere two days after the consecration
of Turner (for Salford) and Errington (for Plymouth) in
Salford offers an interesting commentary on the expansion of
the railways and the increasing ease and speed of travel in the
mid-nineteenth century. Bishop Brown was back at Sedgley
Park for a short break before moving onto his diocese; he was
to preside at pontifical Mass in the College on the feast of the
Assumption. The College community presented him with an
address, and a mitre and crosier designed by Edward Pugin,
the future architect of his Cathedral. Bishop Brown was able
to visit the College from time to time and was one of the
'Parker Bishops' to join in the College's centenary
celebrations. It was on one of these visits that he encouraged
thought to be given to the better preservation of the College
archives. Some of the bishop's letters remain in the archives
attesting to his continued interest in the affairs of the
College, although at least once not refusing to comment on
what he considered to be an example of sharp practice.[10]

On his arrival in his diocese, Brown assumed oversight of
about 20,000 people, with the assistance of a mere 33 priests:
'my desolate diocese', Brown calls it in a letter of reply to the
president of Ushaw's congratulations on his appointment.[11]
Brown worked hard to combine parts of three former, and
somewhat disparate, Vicariates into a new administrative
structure. The Diocesan Chapter was installed temporarily in

St Alban's, Macclesfield, the only Church of any size in the
diocese and a series of diocesan synods followed. For a time,
Bishop Brown lived at Salter's Hall, Newport, Shropshire,
although correspondence with Augustus Welby Pugin
suggests that he considered the possibility of moving to
Chester, which was far more central to the diocese. Later he
considered building his Cathedral in Birkenhead in response
to the needs of its urban population. He announced this
project in his Pastoral Letter of December 1854. The
Cathedral was to be built, together with a church in
Shrewsbury, as the gift of the Earl of Shrewsbury. The
Cathedral was eventually opened in Shrewsbury in 1856, the
first major work of Edward Welby Pugin.[12] Bishop Brown
moved from Newport to the clergy house, adjoining his
Cathedral, in September 1868. That same year the diocesan
structure has formalised into a shape such that he was able to
issue instructions regarding deanery conferences.[13] Growth
was steady but, inevitably, not always smooth: five priests, for
example, were ordained in 1880, while fourteen priests were
lost to the diocese in the eighteen months to September
1877, three dying, a number retiring, and at least three
emigrating to America. National figures compiled to mark
the 25th Anniversary of the Restoration of the Hierarchy
show a rise in the number of priests from 33 in 1851 to 98 in
1876; the 30 churches and chapels now numbered 70;
communities of religious men had risen from one to four; the
single community of religious women had become eight; and,
60 poor schools could now be listed, with 5,152 children
attending.[14]

All this was a significant achievement in twenty five years.
One of Brown's first pastoral letters draws a vivid picture of
the task which faced him: 'The Holy Sacrifice is offered in
some of our congregations in a room of a public tavern, in
one in a loft over a stable, in another over a common
blacksmith's shop... there are two counties in our Diocese in
which there is only one Chapel, and in three, in which there
is neither Station, nor Chapel, nor Priest'.[15] This letter

inaugurated an annual collection for the Diocesan Fund and his yearly appeals for the Fund chronicle the steady growth of the diocese, the opening of churches in both rural and urban areas and the opening of schools. In 1853 an August collection for the Ecclesiastical Educational Fund was initiated. The Bishop was particularly keen to encourage various communities of religious to settle in the diocese: his letter of December 8th 1855 includes a plea for religious to open schools. To this date he could point to only three diocesan schools under the care of nuns; he had welcomed the Faithful Companions of Jesus to Chester the preceding year, where they had already founded a Convent and opened a school. In June 1857 he joined the other bishops in addressing a Pastoral Letter on the issue of the Poor Schools Committee, the establishing of Ecclesiastical Inspectors and the Committee's intention of founding a Training College for Catholic Teachers at Hammersmith. In February 1857 he is appealing for funds for the Reformatory School opened by the Cistercians at Mount Saint Bernard's, a theme to which he returned at length in November 1864 when he addressed the matter of Catholic Reformatory Schools for both boys and girls.[16]

Bishop Brown had not joined the bishops in Rome for the proclamation of the dogma of the Immaculate Conception but his Lenten Indult of February 1855 is given over to this, quoting at length Pius IX's Apostolic Letter. In the January of 1858 Brown was making plans to travel to Rome with Lord and Lady Fielding and wrote to Bishop Grant about the etiquette of an *ad limina* visit: whether he needed a testimonial and asking if he take a small present to the Pope.[17] He made the journey that spring and could be well satisfied with the report he made on the state of his diocese. He was able to send news of the Pope's solicitude to his people in a Pastoral Letter from Rome, issued in April 1858, as was the custom, 'outside the Latin Gate'. a strongly worded Letter of November 1859 in defence of the Papal States deals with the increasingly precarious military and political pressure on the

Papacy and earned a warm response from Mgr Talbot in Rome;[18] in 1861 the proceeds of a collection for the Pope made in the diocese amounting to nearly £1100 was forwarded to Rome, a tidy sum when the collection for the Diocesan Fund that year amounted to a mere £387 2s.[19] Further sums were to follow, and Brown can be seen writing to Rome a few years later:

> it is difficult to form any very accurate idea of all that has passed. There is however one very remarkable fact that many of our leading papers are now turning most decidedly against Garibaldi and are speaking of him in no very measured terms of condemnation.[20]

The Bishop had raised the question of the danger of membership of secret societies and especially Freemasonry in his Letter of September 1865; in February 1868 he expostulates on the dangers of Fenianism, disassociating it in outspoken terms from Catholicism. National and international concerns are also touched on in his Pastoral Letters: Brown talks of outbreaks of cholera and cattle-plague;[21] the Crimean war provided the theme of his Pastoral Letter of April 1854; a collection was made for the poor of Syria in 1860-61; in November 1862 he turned to the plight of the cotton workers in Lancashire and Cheshire. There are occasional instructions for prayers in periods of bad weather; Bishop Brown's concern for the financial and commercial crisis which had hit the country came to the fore in 1879 yet, in spite of this, early in the following year, the Bishop was able to forward nearly £500 to Ireland for the alleviation of famine.

Such an achievement was not unaccompanied by problems. Brown seems to have been both distant and diffident and, at times, somewhat headmasterly in his dealing with his clergy. He was not an ebullient man. As most Victorian bishops, he took his responsibilities very seriously. a quip made in the course of a letter which happened to have been written on St Valentine's Day: 'Don't be alarmed; it is not a *Valentine*,' was not something he was later likely to indulge in as a bishop.[22] One of his main tasks was to ensure an adequate supply of priests for the growing number of missions in the diocese. This I have dealt with in detail elsewhere.[23] As well as the English College, Rome, Ushaw and Oscott, All Hallows, Dublin, provided a number of good men, who were to serve the diocese well. Occasionally Brown was less sure, suspecting All Hallows men of anti-English sentiments: John Brosnan, who was ordained in July 1866 by Bishop Brown in Birkenhead, seemed particularly antagonistic to his parish priest, Canon Chapman of St Werburgh's, exhibiting peculiar, even pro-Fenian, sentiments, and wanted to transfer to a religious order. Brosnan in fact soon transferred to the diocese of Albany in the United States where he was to minister to his death in 1898.[24]

A more curious and long drawn out episode was that of Robert Wright Brundrit, a Runcorn man who had studied in Cambridge and became a Catholic in 1856. He studied for the priesthood in Rome and then privately in Clifton, where he was ordained, on his own patrimony, by Bishop Clifford in 1860. After a curacy in St Werburgh's, Birkenhead, Brundrit went on to establish a new parish St Laurence's nearby; he was to spend a considerable amount of his own money on this new mission. By 1872, Bishop Brown responded to a rumour that he was appropriating parish funds for his personal use and a series of letters ensued. Brundrit cleared his name but remained unsatisfied with the bishop's acknowledgement of this and their relationship grew worse and worse. a series of altercations followed. Brundrit's health gave way. He was given as an assistant, first a Belgian priest, who, Brundrit argued, spoke neither English nor wished to be in Birkenhead, then another priest, whom Brundrit accused of drunkenness and womanising, a claim he justified by reporting that he had been 'accused in the Police Courts of murdering his paramour, and has been proved guilty of seduction, and has been sentenced to 18 months imprisonment for robbery'.[25] Increasingly overwrought and dogged by ill health as he was, it is hard to evaluate the truth of Brundrit's claims. According to Brundrit's deposition he and the bishop seemed more and more at loggerheads, the bishop becoming very cold and guarded towards him. At one stage Bishop O'Reilly of Liverpool attempted mediation. Brundrit retired to Southport but 'the air did not suit him' and he returned to Birkenhead, helping out locally and living privately, still complaining vociferously of the bishop's ill conduct towards him and whiling away his last months composing a long appeal to Rome. He died a few months after this was finished in December 1879.

Education

Apart from the general round of pastoral responsibilities in the diocese, the question of education was increasingly to the fore. I have already suggested how Brown could well have been a little uneasy at the change of tone at Oscott with the coming of Wiseman in 1840. A chance meeting on the train with Edward Bellasis reinforces the impression that Brown retained a rather old-fashioned Catholic suspicion of the Oxford Movement converts. Bellasis was on the way to visit his sons at the Oratory School and, in the words of Ambrose St John's report to Newman, the bishop:

> came out at once "I am very sorry you send your boys to that school". "They are not taught their religion". "They are not catechised, a mere half [hour] a week is nothing". "The school is not conducted in a Catholic spirit" etc. etc. etc. Bellasis got very warm, so did the Bishop. They parted at Wolverhampton, piping hot.[26]

Bellasis took up the issue again writing in support of the Oratory and the bishop retaliated, reporting that he had his information from parents who found religious education at the Oratory not 'like our other Catholic Schools'. Brown, rather ungraciously, felt this to be understandable 'since the instruction was given by converts'. Newman himself was clearly irritated by such comments, as well he might be.

A similar attitude seems to have lain behind Brown's hesitancy on the question of University Education. For some time there had been discussion within the Catholic community about the possibility of Catholic students attending Oxford and Cambridge. At a meeting in December 1864 the bishops had expressed their unease with the project and wrote a collective letter to Rome indicating their disapproval although refraining from asking for an absolute prohibition on attendance: Brown himself felt that, apart from exposing 'our youth to dangers against Faith and Morals', funds would be hard to collect.[27]   The bishops' meeting in April 1867 prompted a formal response from Propaganda forbidding attendance at the Universities and asking the bishops to make this known.[28]   This was the subject of Brown's autumn Pastoral Letter that year.[29] Interestingly, however, Brown kept an open mind on the subject and in the Low Week meeting of April 1872 was able to support Bishop Clifford's proposal to ask Rome to examine the question again following the changing circumstances resulting from the repeal of the Test Acts.[30]   Although the ensuing report to Propaganda included the fact that five bishops had thought it appropriate to reopen the question, the overall tone of the report made it clear that a negative answer was invited from Rome, a far cry from Acton's liberalism and a reflection of the direction the English Church was taking with Manning at the helm.

In 1869, in contrast to a generally negative view regarding other Christian bodies, the bishop reflected rather more positively on the question of ecumenism, pondering on the possible significance of the development of Ritualism in the Established Church.[31]   The year after the publication of Darwin's *The Descent of Man,* we find Brown taking issue with the pretensions of science: 'The discovery of a stray bone, or the finding of some strangely shaped skull, is deemed quite sufficient in these times, to overthrow the whole history of the world. . .'.[32] As an example of this attitude, the Bishop cites Döllinger, Acton's mentor in Germany, and the Old Catholics, who had recently split from Rome in the aftermath of the Vatican Council.

While the central issue for the Church universal was the Vatican Council, at home, it was the Elementary Education Act of 1870, which Bishop Brown regards as 'a crisis on which the future condition of the Catholic Church in this country, as well as the eternal interest of innumerable Souls, depend[s]'.[33] Brown devoted three Pastoral Letters to this subject at this time and more appeals for the work undertaken nationally by the Poor School Committee came later. In May 1869, Brown's appeal for the Poor School Committee betrayed something of his concern over the intended Act in so far as it would undermine religious instruction. He took up the subject more fully the following June raising not only the 'religious difficulty' but the question of the possible abuse of power by the proposed Local Boards and the power of the Education Department to compel parents to send their children to school. While admitting that the liberty of parents to send children to work is often abused, he asked for a discretionary power 'so that in cases which are not unfrequent among our poor, this obligation of sending the children to school, may not interfere with the liberty to which parents are entitled, in turning the labour of their children in all reasonable ways to profit, so as to assist in providing means for the maintenance of the family'.[34] The sentiments are disturbing but reflect a concern, evident again with the advent of the Welfare State, that the state should not interfere with the rights of the family. A Pastoral Letter of November 1870 sums up the dilemma the bishop sees as confronting the diocese: compulsory school attendance for all five- to thirteen-year-olds means effectively that these children must attend either the aided schools which allow Catholic instruction by Catholic teachers or the Board School which allow merely basic Biblical instruction and 'from which all safe religious teaching will be shut out'. In order the safeguard Catholic education in the diocese there is a need both to increase the efficiency of the schools already in existence and also to provide for an additional 4,000 school places. The exhortation to excellence which would preserve the schools from the criticism of inspectors becomes a significant theme. By September 1876 Brown is able to report that 212 candidates were undergoing training as teachers, 53 in Hammersmith, and 159 at the Colleges in Liverpool and Wandsworth. The Poor School Committee had also inaugurated a system of religious inspection. Both of these involved considerable financial demands.

Acton and 'The Rambler'

Bishop Brown dealings with Robert Wright Brundrit in Birkenhead reveal him as possessing an at times somewhat irritable and tendentious manner. If necessary, he could certainly be tough and knew his own mind. Brown's dealings with one of his more unusual subjects, the historian, Sir John Acton, however, show a different and rather more circumspect side of his character.[35] Bishop Brown, it might be remembered, was still Prefect of Studies at Oscott for a period following the arrival of the young Acton in 1843, and as his diocesan bishop had further contact with him. There was correspondence regarding a school.[36] The bishop had made the journey from Shrewsbury to Aldenham, with its vast library, on a number of occasions. Criticisms of the Catholic periodical *The Rambler*, with which Acton was closely associated, worried him, and the eventual rescript, censuring the journal, which the English bishops sent to Propaganda in 1861, he saw as 'a very solemn thing'.[37]

It was at this time that Brown appointed Thomas Green to be chaplain at Aldenham, instructing him 'to be well up in his points'.[38] Green was soon won over by Acton and Acton invariably spoke fondly of him. Acton, it seems, tried to evade his bishop at the time, commenting to Simpson: 'My bishop wants a talk with me, which I will try to avoid, and to inveigle him into correspondence';[39] Acton eventually submitted to a meeting in Shrewsbury at the beginning of September. Bishop Brown remained uneasy and again had cause to express his concerns to Acton in the hopes that he might give up the journal. Again Brown was softened up after a visit to Aldenham:

> The bishop of Shrewsbury under pretence of making his visitation has spent a week here, for the purpose of demolishing the H&F [*The Home & Foreign Review,* successor to *The Rambler*]. Wetherell, Arnold and Roger Vaughan came to meet him; and I have been too busy to do anything.
> The time was not lost however, for I converted the Bishop, who came to curse, and went away yesterday after giving his blessing to the review, and expressing himself gratified at my explanations, and satisfied with the principle *non lac sed escam.* At this moment there is a great meeting at Sedgley Park, where he announced his intention of proclaiming his altered views. He assured me that in spite of strong feelings of some bishops a reaction had been setting in among them, and that he would try to promote it.[40]

As Acton commented rather more respectfully to Newman:

> I was in communication with the Bishop of Shrewsbury respecting the whole management of the Review, and that I have hopes of preserving a good understanding with him. I am sure of it at least in the present instance.[41]

Like Green, Bishop Brown, too, seems to have been won over for when the English bishops finally came to join Wiseman in his condemnation both of *The Rambler* and of its successor, *The Home and Foreign Review,* Brown, tempered the more forthright severity of such as Bishop Cornthwaite, and censured only the defunct *Rambler,* delicately ignoring its successor.[42] The trouble smouldered on until the publication of Pius IX's Letter to the Archbishop of Munich in March 1864 convinced Acton that he could no longer continue the journal with a good conscience. This, together with the publication of the *Syllabus Errorum* of December in the same year, marked a watershed for Acton. Brown's Pastoral Letter of April 25th 1865 takes the *Syllabus* as its theme and a contains firm condemnation of liberal Catholicism.

It is David Matthew's opinion that Acton was disparaging regarding the intellectual capacity of his bishop, illustrating the point by way of a letter from Acton to Lord Emly: 'I know that Dr Grant was among those whom Newman's theory of development repelled, who thought it undermined Tradition, and was therefore rather uncomfortable with him. It was the same with my own Bishop Brown, of Shrewsbury; but he did not count'.[43] This is perhaps over harsh. Acton was rigorous to a fault in his assessment of the intellect and, from 1864, had distanced himself significantly from the ordinary affairs of the Catholic community. Bishop Brown had other priorities, other demands on him.

The Vatican Council

Most of the English bishops had set out for Rome well before the end of November in order to be there for the preliminary meetings and the formal opening of the First Vatican Council on the feast of the Immaculate Conception.[44] An oath of office administered to team of stenographers selected from the various Roman Colleges on Tuesday December 7th, a group which included Samuel Webster Allen, at the time a sub-deacon for the diocese of Shrewsbury, and James Guiron a deacon, ordained for Westminster. Most of the English bishops took up lodging at the English College, although some stayed elsewhere: Clifford and Amherst stayed in lodgings just off the Piazza di Spagna, Errington staying with the Dominicans at St Clemente, whose Prior Joseph Mullooly accompanied him to the Council as theologian. Bishop Brown came late: a serious fall during work being carried out in the Cathedral delayed the journey until February 1870.[45] Accompanied by Edward Slaughter, Brown eventually joined Ullathorne and the others at the English College, arriving in Rome only at the beginning of February 1870.

JAMES BROWN

FIRST BISHOP OF SHREWSBURY

The debate on the Constitution on the Catholic Faith was getting underway by the time Bishop Brown arrived. As Cwiekowski's study makes clear, the English bishops, Bishop Brown among them, took their responsibilities seriously:

> Their work on the schema reflected concerns that were directed more to pastoral needs than to the problems of scientific theology. It is clear, too, that the English bishops kept an eye on the ecclesiological import of the various questions that came before them.[46]

It is Cwiekowski's considered view that Brown, with several others among the English bishops, 'may be placed within the moderate-minority ambit' and he concludes:

> Generally speaking, English reserve and opposition came more from a sober Ultramontanism and an aversion to Ultramontane extravagance than from an acceptance of the tenets of Gallicanism, though the latter should not be discounted. Further, English reserve and opposition was heightened by a wounded sense of fair-play caused by some of the council's proceedings.[47]

Brown was in Rome for the interventions of March 24th on the first chapter of the decree made by Ullathorne and by Clifford.[48] Both were ill at ease at the opening words of the chapter, *Sancta Romana Catholica ecclesia*. Ullathorne, particularly mindful of the English situation, felt that such a phrase might give grounds for High Church Anglicanism to see a suggestion here of the Branch theory of Catholicism, asserting that Roman Catholics were but one branch of the Church alongside Anglo-Catholics and the Orthodox. After some deliberation and a show of hands the deputation *de fide* rejected both interventions. This prompted Clifford to organise a stiff protest in support of Ullathorne, noting irregularities in the handling of Ullathorne's emendation. Bishop Brown was one of the nine English-speaking bishops who joined him in signing the protest.[49] Brown, with five of the other English bishops, again recorded his unease regarding the phrase by registering a vote *placet juxta modum* when it came to the trial vote on the schema as a whole on April 12th.[50]   Brown, Ullathorne and Clifford were at one with some of the North American bishops, as well as the inopportunist, Ketteler of Mainz, Stroßmayer of Djakovo in Bosnia, a strong opponent of the declaration of infallibility, and others in their objections to the opening phrase of the first chapter of the document.[51]   These objections had only minor influence on the final version of text of *Dei Filius* promulgated at the public session held on April 24th at which Brown's presence was recorded.[52]

Meanwhile on January 21st the draft text of the schema on the Church had been given to the bishops for preliminary discussion outside the Council chamber. The schema itself avoided the question of Papal infallibility but this was increasingly a major topic of discussion amongst the Council Fathers and Manning, the 'chief whip' of the majority party, of course, continued indefatigably to press for the raising of the issue before the bishops. At the beginning of March the Pope conceded that the mater might be discussed and an additional chapter was to be added to the schema on the Church after the discussion of Papal primacy in chapter 11 of the schema.[53]   By 29th April the Council Fathers heard that the agenda had been altered to allow the bringing forward of the matter of Papal primacy and infallibility. The matter of the primacy and infallibility of the Pope were to form a short and independent constitution.   While this had perhaps become inevitable, many of the Fathers were ill at ease with the sense of hurry engendered by such as Manning. Brown joined Errington, Clifford and Vaughan of Plymouth, in signing a petition of seventy-one bishops presented to the Council Presidents on May 8th. This raised both theological and pastoral objections to a change which suddenly treated such sensitive issues in apparent isolation from their larger context in relation to a discussion of the Church itself.[54]

This was effectively Bishop Brown's last involvement in the Council.   He had been present at 49th general congregation a few days earlier on May 4th, voting positively on emendations for work presented by the deputation for discipline and on the schema on the catechism.[55] The heat of the Roman summer was beginning to take its toll: before the day's business was underway it was announced that Brown was among those who had petitioned to leave Rome for reasons of health and that his petition had been accepted.[56] He had left Rome by May 13th, the day the debate on infallibility opened. The heat was affecting many of the English contingent: in the next weeks Turner and Amherst were requesting permission to leave, which, with Grant's death on June 1st, left only Manning, Chadwick, Cornthwaite, Ullathorne and Vaughan present at the solemn promulgation of the constitution *Pastor Aeternus* on July 18th, amidst the thunder-storms which darkened the sky above St Peter's that day. Clifford and Errington, as members of the minority group, determined to absent themselves and slipped quietly from the Eternal City.[57] On the following day, came the outbreak of the Franco-Prussian War with the subsequent withdrawal of the French troops from Rome some weeks later. With the entry of the Italians into Rome in September, Pius was force to prorogue the council *sine die*.

Bishop Brown issued a pastoral letter the following February which emphasised the legitimacy of the Council and, at the same time, trying to calm exaggerated interpretations of the significance of the definition of infallibility, infallibility relating in no way to the Pope's temporal power but to be understood solely as a matter of 'formally and officially declar(ing) what is the doctrine of the Church'.[58] As Cwiekowski points out, one unusual feature of Brown's Pastoral is that he includes a reference to the joint pastoral of the German bishops issued at their meeting at Fulda held in September 1870.[59] We might surmise that Cwiekowski is correct in seeing here a reference added specifically with the historian, Acton, in mind. As early as December 1870, Acton was able to reported to Döllinger that Brown had written to him:

The day before yesterday my bishop wrote to me, delighted
that all were united in a submissive faith. I could not let this
comment go by acquiescing in silence, and answered: 'The
accounts I receive from Rome and from opposing bishops
represent the division in the Church as peremptory and
irreparable. I am glad that you have reason to take a more
consoling view of the future.' This is the beginning of an
offensive.[60]

Though ill at ease, Acton was to profess his acceptance of the
Council decrees.[61] The English bishops themselves delayed in
publishing a joint Pastoral on the Council until Low Week
1875 as a response to Gladstone's challenge that infallibility
raised questions regarding the civil allegiance of English
Catholics.[62] The delay most probably reflects the tensions
between differing positions evident within a hierarchy
presided over by Manning but the document is possibly more
restrained than anything that might have been published in
the immediate aftermath of the Council itself.

Final Years

With the death of Bishop Turner of Salford in 1872, Bishop
Brown, with Thomas Joseph Brown of Newport and
Ullathorne of Birmingham, had become one of the three
remaining bishops of the first generation of the restored
hierarchy. As one of the senior bishops, he was invited to
prepare a report on prayer books in use in England with a
view to deciding on a standard version: he came down firmly
in favour of the time-honoured text of *The Garden of the Soul*,
which, in spite of revisions, continued to reflect the spiritual
tradition inherited from Challoner.[63] A few years later, in
1877, he was asked to join Herbert Vaughan of Salford in
making recommendations about a revision of the catechism.
Here again, it was the traditional English catechism, which
had it roots in Challoner's *Abridgement of Christian Doctrine*
(1759), that proved to be the model, rather than the less
familiar, and considerably longer, text of Bellarmine's
catechism.[64] In the event Brown was able to do little: that

same year he fell victim to a serious attack of diphtheria. It was left to others to complete the task, yet there is little doubt that Brown's own position reflected the deep continuities of English Catholicism which had been focused and channelled in the person of the saintly eighteenth century Bishop Challoner.

Bishop Brown's health continued to deteriorate. In September 1874 he had been unable to travel to St Beuno's, the Jesuit house in North Wales, to preside at the ordinations, his namesake, Bishop Thomas Brown of Newport taking his place.[65] However he made up for the absence in September with a two week visit made with his secretary, Samuel Webster Allen, the following month: Hopkins recorded the vivid experiences of sky and scenery on the free day given to the students in honour of the visit.[66] The bishop was well enough to celebrate the silver jubilee of his episcopal ordination in the Cathedral on July 27th 1876.[67] He received a purse of over a thousand sovereigns and a gold chalice from the diocese. The Shrewsbury Young Mens' Society presented a Vellum Address. A few days later he was back at St. Beuno's for further celebrations. Gerard Manley Hopkins contributed three pieces in a volume of twenty-four occasional pieces put together by the students in a finely bound presentation album to mark the event. [68] Hopkins, still a theology student, and still hoping against hope that *The Month* might publish 'The Wreck of the Deutschland', describes the celebrations in a letter to his father:

> That event came off, I think, on my birthday but he did not visit us till the next day and on Sunday we presented him with an album containing a prose address and compositions, chiefly verse, in many languages, among which were Chinese and Manchoo, all by our people, those who had been or were to be ordained by his lordship . . . for the Welsh they had to come to me, for, sad to say, no one else in the house knows anything about it; I also wrote in Latin and English and the English was the aforesaid Silver Jubilee. Fr Morris preached first, for the presentation took place in Church, and after mass the Bishop

sat on a throne and received the address and album and a cheque for £100 with it. In the afternoon was a high dinner and music at dessert and the Silver Jubilee was set effectively by a very musical and very noisy member of the community and was sung as a glee by the choir.[69]

Bishop Brown stayed on for the feast of Ignatius Loyola, 31st July, before travelling across the hill to Pantasaph for further celebrations with the Franciscans.[70] He was back at St Beuno's the following year to ordain Hopkins and fifteen others. Following the Jesuit custom they received subdiaconate, diaconate and priesthood on consecutive days, 21st, 22nd and 23rd September, an ordeal no doubt both for the newly ordained and the ordaining bishop.[71]

Bishop Brown, increasingly frail, never fully recovered after an attack of diphtheria in 1877. Illness kept him away from the bishops' Low Week Meeting the following year. That September however he was able to make a pilgrimage to Lourdes with his secretary Samuel Webster Allen. Brown lived on quietly in Shrewsbury but felt in necessary to petition Rome to appoint an auxiliary to allow him to relinquish something of the burden of administration. He was able to announce the appointment of Edmund Knight, a Canon of the Birmingham diocese in April 1879 and Knight was consecrated in Our Lady's, Birkenhead, three months later.[72] Following his appointment Bishop Knight moved into the house in Shrewsbury and Bishop Brown moved into semi-retirement at St Mary's Grange, an estate just outside Shrewsbury, purchased in 1876 as the site for a possible future diocesan minor seminary. As he commented to Canon Escourt, retirement gave him time to look over his papers; he was increasingly conscious of encroaching age and death.[73]

The following winter Brown was complaining of the extreme weather conditions and how cold he found St Mary's Grange; he admitted that he now needed to spend part of the day in bed.[74] He attempted to keep up with his commitments in the diocese: a letter went out to clergy informing them of his intention of calling a diocesan synod at Our Lady's, Birkenhead on October 5th 1881 but within a week Bishop

Knight was sending a letter asking for masses and prayers for the Bishop's recovery after another period of serious illness. A few days later, on 14 October 1881, Bishop Brown died. His funeral, presided over by Cardinal Manning, took place in the Cathedral Brown had built in Shrewsbury; on his finger, according to the Cardinal, had been placed Bishop Milner's episcopal ring and with him also was his mother's cruxifix and rosary.[75] The bishop's body was then taken by train to be buried in the Franciscan Cemetery at Pantasaph, North Wales, accompanied in its journey by his secretatry, Samuel Webster Allen, and Hugh Singleton, both in their turn to succeed Bishop Brown as Bishops of Shrewsbury.

Bishop Brown was not yet seventy when he died, although he seemed much older; his health over the years had not been good. None the less, he had been bishop for thirty years. Manning, in his panegyric, spoke of him as 'just, merciful, firm, tender of heart, industrious, unresting, never sparing himself'. And going on to speak of their encounters at the bishops' meetings, he added:

> I rarely have seen any man who was more completely retiring and self-concealing . . . more calm, more gentle, more considerate — never breaking in on those who were giving their judgement, waiting till his time had come, and then speaking with deliberation, and with a careful selection of words corresponding to the thoughts that were carefully weighed before, and with a conclusiveness of judgement which we have all acknowledged.[76]

The words are formal but there is here a certain sense of the man. This is something picked up by Ullathorne, who like Wiseman had felt Brown's displeasure.[77] In a letter to Canon Escourt, Ullathorne wrote that Brown would be 'a real loss to our episcopal councils, for he always took the right view.[78] Certainly firm, perhaps somewhat unimaginative, even pedestrian, and not a man easy to get close to, Shrewsbury's first bishop had served his diocese well enough. There was not a need for the fiery campaigner, like the Milner of his youth, nor even someone like Wiseman, who had consecrated him as bishop. Brown's task was one of consolidation. He gave a sense of identity and cohesion to his new diocese, a hard enough task for an area drawn from three former vicariates with little to unify them. Brown had worked hard to oversee the provision of new missions and churches with priests to serve them; he had welcomed communities of religious and established schools. Here was a solid and worthy foundation for the future.

NOTES

I am most grateful to Canon John Marmion, the Archivist of Shrewsbury Diocese, who has generously shared with me his own researches on Bishop Brown and in particular an invaluable collection of copies of Brown's correspondence.

1. The baptismal register records his name as Browne, his godparents being George Dutton and Ann Onions.
2. Attending the centenary celebrations of Sedgley Park in 1863, Brown recorded that one of his great uncles had been amongst the boys in the covered cart that brought the first generation of students from Betley to settle in Sedgley Park a hundred years before. See Frank Roberts, *A History of Sedgley Park and Cotton College*, edited and completed by Neil Henshaw, [1985], p.101.
3. For the following, I am indebted to Roberts, op. cit., p.58-62.
4. Roberts, op. cit., p.62.
5. For this and other details of Oscott see *The Oscotian*, Jubilee edition, 1888, p.70ff.
6. See Wilfrid Ward, *The Life and Times of Cardinal Wiseman*, Longmans, 1897, vol 1, pp.348f
7. Wilfrid Ward, *Life and Times of Cardinal Wiseman*, vol 1, p.345.
8. See Roberts, pp.78-83. See also, W. Buscot, *The History of Cotton College* Burns Oates & Washbourne, 1940, pp.181-183.
9. Husenbeth to the President of Sedgley Park, Canon George Rolfe, 1857, cited Roberts, op. cit., p.89.
10. Roberts, op. cit., p.84.
11. Brown to Charles Newsham, 14th July 1851, Ushaw, Newsham Correspondence.

12. The building of Shrewsbury Cathedral is discussed in 'Shrewsbury: A Catholic Community 1750-1914' in this volume.

13. Pastoral Letter, 1 Dec 1868.

14. Elenchus presented in Rome, 29 Sept 1976. On Bishop Brown's death, in 1881, there were, according to *The Tablet*, 22nd Oct 1881, 88 churches or chapels in the diocese, 95 priests, 6 houses of male religious, 11 of women religious, and 63 poor schools attended by 9,273 children.

15. Pastoral Letter, 25th Nov 1851.

16. For a discussion of the Catholic Reformatory Schools which followed from the legislation of August 1854 see David Lannon, 'Bishop Turner, the Salford Diocese and the Reformatory Provision 1854-1872', *Recusant History*, vol 23, No.3 (May 1997), pp.389-407.

17. Brown to Thomas Grant, 15th January 1858, Southwark Archives.

18. See Brown to Talbot, 7th December 1859, Talbot Papers, Venerable English College, Rome.

19. Pastoral Letter, 22 April 1861. This is a theme to which Bishop Brown returns regularly. See, for example, Pastoral Letters of November 1859, December 1867 and February 1869.

20. Brown to Talbot, 17th Jan 1865, Talbot Papers, Venerable English College, Rome.

21. See, for example, Pastoral Letter, 27 Feb 1867.

22. Brown to Searle, February 14th 1850, Westminster Diocesan Archives.

23. See Peter Phillips, '"Or else we shall be bound hand and foot": Bishop Brown and the Oversight of Seminaries', *Recusant History*, October 2000.

24. Brown to Woodlock, 9th Aug 1858, 30th Aug 1860, 9th Sept 1860; Brown to Fortune 21st March 1867, 24th April 1874; (on Brosnan) Brown to Bennet, 8th Oct 1866, Brown to Fortune, 25th Dec 1866, 28th Jan 1867. See, also, Maurice Abbott, *To Preserve their Memory: Shrewsbury Diocesan Priests (Deceased) 1850-1995.*

25. The manuscript of Brundrit's long and detailed appeal against the bishop to the Office of Propaganda in Rome is in the Shrewsbury Diocesan Archives. Whether his document, dated 1879, was indeed sent to Rome is not known, but most probably it was forestalled by Brundrit's death in December 1879. See also *To Preserve their Memory*.

26. For this, and the following, see *The Letters and Diaries of John Henry Newman,* vol XX, ed. Charles Stephen Dessain, Nelson 1970, p.313, note 2. See also Ian Ker, *John Henry Newman,* Oxford, 1988, p.514.

27. See Alan McClelland, *English Roman Catholics and Higher Education,* Oxford, 1973, pp.200-215. Bishop Brown is cited on p.212. See also, Bishop Cornthwaite's account of the bishops' meeting, Dec 13th 1864, Leeds Diocesan Archives.

28. McClelland gives the context for this meeting and its aftermath, op. cit., pp.219-234.

29. Pastoral Letter, 11 Nov 1867.

30. See McClelland, op. cit., p.270-276. See, also, *Acta* of Low Week Meeting, 1872, Leeds Diocesan Archives.

31. Pastoral Letter, 2 Feb 1869. Wiseman's early, though tentative, enthusiasm for ecumenism might be remembered, though in the autumn of 1864, towards the end of his life, the Cardinal was to respond to pressure from Manning, W.G. Ward and others to condemn the Association for the Promotion of the Union of Christendom. See Wilfrid Ward, *The Life and Times of Cardinal Wiseman,* Longmans, 1897, vol II, pp.477-491.

32. Pastoral Letter, 20 Nov 1872.

33. Pastoral Letter, 15 June 1870.

34. Pastoral Letter, 15 June 1870.

35. Acton's Shropshire seat, at Aldenham, just outside Bridgenorth, lay in the diocese.

36. Acton to Bishop Brown, 22 May 1860, Shrewsbury Diocesan Archives: See David Mathew, *Lord Acton and his Circle,* Eyre & Spottiswoode, 1968, p.69.

37. Acton to Newman, 10 Nov 1861, cited in Josef Altholz, *The Liberal Catholic Movement in England,* Burns & Oates, 1962, p.172.

38. Acton to Döllinger, 27 Dec 1861, cited Altholz, op. cit., p.172. As Altholz comments, Green was soon 'won over by Acton's charm'. For Thomas Green see David Mathew, *Lord Acton and his Circle,* Eyre & Spottiswoode, 1968, pp.235-240. The two seemed to have got on well although Green must have found Acton's delight in controversy a little hard to stomach at times. The following year Acton was writing to Simpson, 'Old Green is knocked completely off his legs by the new world opening out before him when he expected that we were going to make everything comfortable', Acton to Simpson, 1 Oct 1862, *Acton Simpson Correspondence,* ed. Altholz, McElrath and Holland,

Cambridge, 1975, vol 3, p.22. Brown and Green had been on the staff at Oscott together. Neither Bishop Brown, nor Acton, it seems, were sorry to see his predecessor, John Brande Morris, moving on: John Brande Morris, 'the learned but eccentric orientalist' (*Acton Simpson Correspondence*, note 1, p.13) was a convert Oxford don and one time associate of Pusey, first becoming known to Acton, like Brown and Green, while at Oscott: as a convert he was confirmed by Wiseman at Oscott in 1846 and ordained priest in April 1848. It seems he was not an easy man. See the extended sketch of Morris in David Mathew, *Lord Acton and his Circle,* pp.65-72.

39. Acton to Simpson, 17 Aug 1862, *Acton Simpson Correspondence*, vol 3, p.6.

40. Acton to Simpson, 8 Sept 1863, *Acton Simpson Correspondence,* vol 3, p.129.

41. Acton to Newman, 31 Oct 1862, cited in *The Letters and Diaries of John Henry Newman,* op. cit., Vol XX p.333.

42. Acton to Simpson, 9 Oct 1862, cited Altholz, op. cit., p.188.

43. Acton to Emly, 10 Feb 1892, see *Lord Acton and his Circle,* p.231.

44. See Frederick J. Cwiekowski, *The English Bishops and the First Vatican Council,* Louvain, 1971, p.110ff. The following account of the events of the Council relies heavily on this useful study.

45. See Diary of the Sisters of Mercy, Shrewsbury. Brown to Escourt, 29 Nov 1869, BAA B 4782.

46. Cwiekowski, op.cit., p.212.

47. Cwiekowski, op.cit., p.322-323.

48. Cwiekowski, op.cit., p.196ff.

49. See the details in Cwiekowski, op.cit., p.202.

50. Cwiekowski, op.cit., p.209.

51. See Mansi, *Sacrorum Conciliorum Nova et Amplissima Collectio,* Vol LI, Graz, 1961, 394D-399B.

52. Mansi, LI, 443A. See also Cuthbert Butler, *Life and Times of Bishop Ullathorne,* Burns Oates, 1926, Vol 2, pp.65-67.

53. Cwiekowski, op.cit., p.222.

54. Cwiekowski, op.cit., p.234. Subsequent debate clarified this to some extent.

55. Mansi, LI, 506B.

56. Mansi, LI, 493A; Cwiekowski, op. cit., p.252.

57. Cwiekowski offers a useful discussion of the debate which led up to the promulgation on July 18th, pp.254-273. At the trial vote

of July 13th, Errington, Clifford and Vaughan had voted *non placet*, Ullathorne voting *placet juxta modum*.

58. Bishop Brown's restrained and careful language is perhaps worth quoting more fully: 'It has no reference whatever to the Pope as a private individual. It does not claim for him any more than for any one else any exemption from the ordinary weaknesses of human nature, nor does it pretend that he is not liable even to fall into sin. As far as his position as a Sovereign is concerned, it makes no difference in his relations to other sovereigns, nor in their relation to him. It has nothing to do with him as a Prince, or potentate, or as a politician. Even as a private theologian he may maintain opinions from which any one is at perfect liberty to differ, and which in themselves are not necessarily correct. It must be kept clearly in mind that this infallibility, this preservation from error, does not apply to him as a private individual, but only as the Head of the Church, and then only when he formally and officially declares what is the doctrine of the Church.' (Pastoral Latter, 18 Feb 1871).

59. Cwiekowski, op.cit., p.285f.

60. Acton to Döllinger, 23 Dec 1870, cited in Cwiekowski, op.cit., p.314, note 1. Translation from the German is mine.

61. For Acton's letters to *The Times* in reply to Gladstone and the ensuing exchange of letters with Manning and Bishop Brown see *Lord Acton and his Circle*, pp.225-233.

62. Bishop Brown's Pastoral Letter of 5 Feb 1875 raises some of the issues touched on in Gladstone's pamphlet.

63. See Mary Heimann, *Catholic Devotion in Victorian England*, Oxford, 1995, pp.73-74, 119-120.

64. See *Catholic Devotion in Victorian England*, pp.100-110, 120.

65. *The Journals and Papers of Gerard Manley Hopkins*, ed. Humphrey House and completed by Graham Storey, Oxford, 1959, p.259.

66. *Journals and Papers*, op. cit., p.261.

67. This event is described in some detail in *The Tablet*, Aug 5th 1876.

68. The volume contains a list of staff at St Beuno's and of the students both living and dead whom Brown had ordained, or was expecting to ordain; it includes an address outlining Bishop Brown's life and thanking him not only for his care of the Jesuits at St Beuno's, but mentioning his concern for the German Jesuit refugees who had taken refuge at Ditton Hall, near Widnes. The

following languages are represented in the volume: Hebrew, Sanskrit, Syriac, Arabic, Manchu, Chinese, Tamil, Greek (2 pieces), Latin (4 pieces), Italian, French (2 pieces), English (4 pieces), German (2 pieces), and Welsh. Hopkins contributed one English ('The Silver Jubilee'), the Welsh ('Cywydd') and one of the four Latin poems ('Ad Episcopum Salopiensem'). See Nos 29, 172, 173, and notes, in *The Poems of Gerard Manley Hopkins,* ed. W.H. Gardner & N.M. MacKenzie, Oxford, 1970. See, also, A. Thomas, 'G.M. Hopkins and the Silver Jubilee Album', *The Library,* Fifth Series, Vol xx, no 2 (June 1965), pp.148-152.

69. *Further Letters of Gerard Manley Hopkins, including his Correspondence with Coventry Patmore,* ed. C.C. Abbott, 2nd edn, 1956, p.140. Hopkins birthday was July 28th 1844.

70. For the celebrations at St Beuno's, see *The Tablet,* Aug 5th 1876; for those at Pantasaph, see *The Tablet,* Aug 12th 1876.

71. Alfred Thomas, *Hopkins the Jesuit,* Oxford, 1969, p.185.

72. 25 July 1879. Manning was assisted by the bishops of Salford and Nottingham. Soon after Bishop Knight had formally taken over as Bishop of Shrewsbury, following Brown's death, he moved his residence to Birkenhead, estimating that it would save him 2,500 miles of travelling each year.

73. Brown to Escourt, 20 June 1880, BAA B 7030.

74. Brown to Escourt, 26 Jan 1881, BAA B 7243.

75. *The Tablet,* 22 Oct 1881, p.675.

76. *The Tablet,* 22 Oct 1881, p.675.

77. See Peter Phillips, '"Or else we shall be bound hand and foot": Bishop Brown and the Oversight of Seminaries', *Recusant History,* October 2000.

78. Ullathome to Escourt, Oct 15th 1881, BAA B 7563.

VIII

THE CHURCH MILITANT
THE IRISH IN BIRKENHEAD IN
THE MID-NINETEENTH CENTURY

C.J. Boyle

Introduction

During the early years of the nineteenth century, the indigenous Catholic population consisted of a very small minority of unskilled town workers and a small upper-class minority. Catholics were still subject to legal restrictions such as the Test and Corporations Acts and could not sit in Parliament; Catholic chapels had to be registered with the local authorities. Dating back to the Reformation, Catholicism was seen as a threat to the liberties of free-born Englishmen and there was the ever-present difficulty of Catholics owing allegiance to two masters, Pope and Monarch. The passing of the Act of Union in 1801 brought Irish Catholics within the sphere of the Westminster Parliament and the years after 1815 saw a steady increase in the numbers of Irish Catholics arriving on the mainland. Catholic Emancipation in 1829 gave Catholics political representation and influence while, at the same time, retaining anti-Catholic legislation of the past, such as priests having to wear civilian dress and the banning of processions.

Anti-Catholic feeling was increased by events within the Established Church in the 1830s and 1840s, in particular, with the Oxford Movement and the conversion of Newman, Manning and others to Rome. Anti-Catholic feeling was to reach a peak in 1850 with the restoration of the hierarchy by Pius IX and the subsequent actions of Wiseman whose Pastoral, *Out of the Flaminian Gate,* in which every Papal claim seemed to be upheld, was published in October. It is against this background of national anti-Catholic feeling that events in Birkenhead must be placed.[1]

The Irish in Birkenhead

Birkenhead was a new town, a nineteenth-century creation. Growing around the ruins of the twelfth-century priory, the population in 1801 was 110 souls and by 1841, had grown to over eight thousand. The 1851 census recorded 24,285 persons and that of 1861, over 36,000. Initially, the township was dormitory for Liverpool merchants, who, thanks to the new steam ferries of the 1820s, could live on the Cheshire side of the Mersey and travel safely and quickly to their places of business in Liverpool. In 1823, William Laird and family crossed from Liverpool and opened the Birkenhead Ironworks at Wallasey Pool, and in 1829, built his first iron ship, so establishing the industry to which the town would ever be linked. In 1833, the infant township received its first form of government by Act of Parliament, when an Improvement Commission was empowered to watch, cleanse, light and establish a market. The growth of the township continued in the 1840s with the building of docks and of Birkenhead Park, the first such park of its kind in the country. These were labour-intensive activities and led to a large increase in the population of the township, as has been noted above.[2]

From 1846 onwards, Birkenhead was subject to an influx of Irish migrants following the Famine. The Irish-born were 12% of the town's population, while the Irish community in Birkenhead, that is the Irish-born, including British-born spouses and children, numbered some 14% of the population of the township in 1841. By 1851, the numbers of the Irish community had increased to nearly 30% of the population of the township, marginally higher than that of Liverpool, and the highest in the North West.[3] They were the largest group of migrants in the township which itself was composed of migrants from all over the United Kingdom. This is an important point, as Birkenhead lacked any traditions or customs of its own, and any dislikes or prejudices, such as anti-Catholicism, were imported.

There was a Catholic presence in the township during the 1830s and Mass was celebrated in a building next to the old Priory, the priests coming from Liverpool. Father John Pratt[4] of Copperas Hill, Liverpool founded the Mission in about 1835. On 14th September, 1835, the *Liverpool Mercury* recorded the laying of the foundation stone of St Werburgh's Catholic Chapel in Grange Lane by Dr Youens of Copperas Hill which would accommodate upwards of 400 people. The architect was a Mr Smith of Liverpool. The Chapel, 'an elegant and spacious edifice', was opened by Rt. Revd Dr John Briggs, Vicar Apostolic of the Northern District, on 15th August, 1837.[5] St Werburgh's was recorded as a Dissenters' Meeting House on 25th March, 1839, being:

> A certain Catholic Chapel in Birkenhead, of which John Pratt is officiating Priest and Minister.[6]

On 19th August, 1837, the death of an Irish child, Catherine Keogh, still-born, was recorded in the *Liber Defunctorum* of the new Chapel.[7]

Father Pratt remained at St Werburgh's until 1840, when he was succeeded by Father William Henderson who remained in charge of the Mission until 1846. When he retired through ill-health, he recorded that :

> I built two schools at a cost of £500 and during my time the Congregation increased from 700 to 7000.[8]

He was followed by Father Edward Browne who remained head of Mission until 1857. It was during the time of Father Browne that the influx of Famine Irish came to Birkenhead and numbers at St Werburgh's increased dramatically. The church was a focal point for Irish Catholics who found themselves in a strange land, many of them not speaking English, and, for those from rural Ireland, being thrust into an urban environment for the first time. Even though most of the Irish were Catholics, many of them, particularly those from the more remote areas, had little experience of formal religious worship: the 'devotional revolution' of Cardinal Cullen in Ireland was post Famine. There is also the question of how many Irish Catholics left the Church when they came to England or at least did not attend church. The traditional picture of thousands of Irish Catholics sustaining and boosting a flagging Catholicism in England is only part of a much wider picture which has yet to be fully researched.[9]

Irish Militancy in Birkenhead

In the middle years of the nineteenth century, Catholics in England were subject to much anti-Catholic feeling, which on occasions manifested itself in physical violence, such as the Stockport Riots of 1852 where anti-Catholic and anti-Irish sentiments were very much in evidence. On this occasion, two Catholic chapels were ransacked, twenty-four Irish homes wrecked and one Irishman was killed.[10] Irish Catholics in Birkenhead were to prove to be exceptional in that when anti-Catholic feeling was rampant in the township, they went onto the offensive. On three occasions between 1850 and 1862, Irish Catholics in Birkenhead took their grievances onto the streets and fought. The first of these was the 'Papal Aggression Riot' of November, 1850.

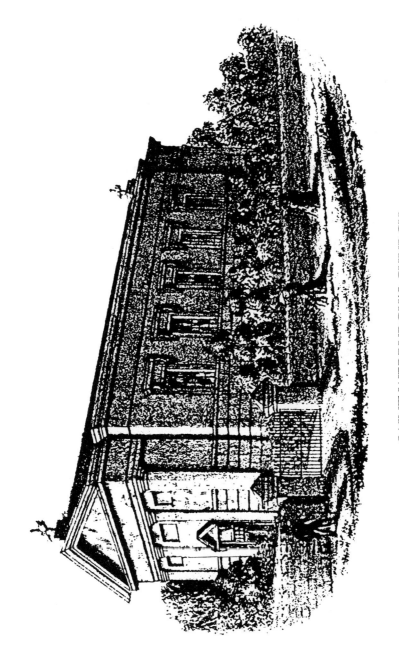

SAINT WERBURGH'S CHURCH
Birkenhead — see pages 184-5

The Papal Aggression Riot, 1850

The restoration of the Catholic Hierarchy by Pope Pius IX in September 1850 provoked a series of demonstrations and meetings throughout the country to pledge loyalty to the Queen and to protest at 'Papal aggression' and the Pope's apparent usurpation of royal prerogatives. Birkenhead was no exception and a group of rate-payers petitioned the magistrates to hold a meeting to pledge loyalty to the Crown on 27th November, 1850, at the Birkenhead town hall. However, only a select number of citizens were to attend, Catholics, and Irish Catholics in particular, were to be excluded from what was advertised as a public meeting of rate-payers.[11] Crowds had been gathering outside the Town Hall from early morning and the Birkenhead Improvement Commissioners, fearing that the small Birkenhead Police Force would be unable to deal with any disturbance, sent to Liverpool for assistance. Thirty men were despatched under the command of Superintendent Ride. The Liverpool Police were deployed both inside the Town Hall and on the road outside, opposite to where the crowd was gathering. The meeting was due to start at one o'clock, but at midday, the police moved on the crowd opposite the Town Hall to disperse them, using their batons. The people in the crowd tried to defend themselves with sticks. At this point, Father Browne of St Werburgh's and a group of leading Catholic laymen, including the solicitor Edward Bretherton, arrived. Father Browne immediately ordered the crowd to lay down their weapons and disperse to their homes. Most of them did so immediately — such was the authority of their pastor.[12]

Father Browne and his party gained entrance to the Town Hall, where Bretherton questioned the validity of the requisition for the meeting. Meanwhile outside, word of the first police attack had spread and numbers of Irish labourers had arrived from the dock area armed with sticks, clubs and pokers, accompanied by their wives, with aprons filled with stones. As yet, there was only noise and the occasional throwing of a stone. About one o'clock, the Liverpool Police emerged from the Town Hall and began to push the crowd back from the door. Those at the front could not move from the press of people behind them. The police began to use their batons and a major incident followed. A hail of stones hit the Town Hall and every window at the front was broken. The police and the crowd were engaged in hand to hand fighting.

The Birkenhead Magistrates were in a room at the front of the Town Hall when the windows were broken; they took shelter under a table. One of them, John Jackson, sent for Father Browne. The priest, stepping onto the ledge of the broken window, raised his hands and called for order. The result was immediate, the Irish labourers stopped fighting. Father Brown and Bretherton jumped through the window and the priest ordered the labourers to drop their weapons. When one refused, Bretherton tried to effect a citizen's arrest, but the labourer slipped into the crowd. Father Browne ordered the crowd to line up and he then led them in procession to St Werburgh's where they assembled in the grounds with the gates closed. The crowd remained at the church, while Bretherton returned to the Town Hall, where he found the meeting had been adjourned. Father Browne dispersed the crowd from the church, ordering them to go home and avoid trouble.[13] There were no further incidents on that day.

That was not the end of the 'Papal Aggression' riot. The adjourned meeting was held the following week, but Father Browne ensured that there would be no repeat of the disturbances. At every Mass on the Sunday he issued instructions that no Catholic should attempt to attend the meeting or go near the Town Hall. He had placards to the same effect posted in the centre of the town:

> I beg, therefore, to request of the Catholic body that they will, individually and collectively, absent themselves from attendance at such meeting, trusting, with me, that time, and more mature reflection on the part of our fellow-citizens, will, in the merciful dispensation of Divine Providence, soon tend to

assuage the spirit of irritation that has been evoked, and render more condign justice to the feelings and intentions by which we are governed.

Edward Browne.[14]

The second meeting passed peacefully and allegiance was duly pledged to the Queen. Shortly after the meeting, six Irishmen, Peter Fitzsimmons, Matthew Griffin, William Hagerty, John Feehan, Edward Smith and John Brown, were arrested in connection with the riot and tried at Chester Assizes on 7th April, 1850. John Brown was a well-known master shoemaker who had lived in Birkenhead for eighteen years. The prisoners were defended by Mr Roebuck, QC, MP, and Mr Justice Williams presided.

At the trial, Roebuck discredited the evidence of the main witnesses, members of the Liverpool Police, whom he called 'the Irish Police' (Orangemen). One defendant, Fitzsimmons, was alleged to have fought with PCs Kelly, Grimely and Cox, when, in fact, he was not in Birkenhead but at his work in Poulton. John Brown was acquitted, but the jury found the other five guilty. Mr Justice Williams stated that:

> The conduct of the police on the occasion of the first disturbance and out of which the riot took place, was not only injudicious, but illegal and unjustifiable. But the message must go out that a Court of Justice can never justify a riot of any kind.[15]

The convicted men were sentenced to twelve months without hard labour, taking into consideration the time already served. Justice Williams petitioned the Home Secretary, Sir George Grey, that Fitzsimmons had been convicted against evidence. Fitzsimmons was freed and as the *Liverpool Mercury* commented:

> In such cases the law of the land ought to afford some redress to an individual for such unmerited suffering.[16]

Perhaps the last word on the events in Birkenhead on 27th November, 1850, should be left to Mr Roebuck:

> The Magistrates, calling themselves gentlemen, get it into their heads to enjoy a little bigotry, are they to trample on their fellow subjects when they are crossed in their hobby?[17]

The Burial Board Riot, 1859

In the summer of 1859, the Birkenhead Improvement Commissioners decided to avail themselves of current legislation and provide a cemetery for the township and it was further decided that ground would not be allocated to Catholics in the cemetery, which was to be at Flaybrick Quarry, at the north end of the town.[18] An election for a Burial Board was held on Monday 30th May and Tuesday, 31st May. Voting, for the rate-payers of the town, was at the Town Hall between 8 am. and 8 pm. On the Monday, nothing of a serious nature took place, except that in the evening large numbers of people gathered near the Town Hall. There were more serious developments on Tuesday. At about 10 am., some hundreds of Irish labourers arrived at the Town Hall armed with spades, shovels, sticks and other weapons. The police on duty at the Town Hall sent for Canon Chapman of St Werburgh's, who, on arrival, defused the situation by ordering the mob to return home.

It appeared that the incident had closed at that point. The Commissioners, fearing further trouble, closed the poll at midday. They were right: between one and two o'clock a mob of thousands of Irish arrived at the Town Hall and, finding it closed, made their way to Laird's shipyard in Church Street. A number of Laird's men outside the yard were attacked, but the gatemen were able to close the gates. At this point, the police intervened and made five arrests. Had Laird's men come out, there would have been a major riot.

The police returned to the Town Hall with their prisoners, but by 3 pm, a large mob of Irish had assembled, intent on releasing them and threatening to burn down the Town Hall. The forty-one members of the Birkenhead Police Force could not have prevented an attack on the Town Hall. Canon Chapman was sent for and he bailed the prisoners, ordering the mob to disperse. On the way back to the north end, they broke the windows of the North End Bridewell. A detachment of Marines at the docks placed themselves at the disposal of the magistrates and in the evening, a company of soldiers arrived from Chester and remained in the town until Thursday. But there were no further incidents. On the Thursday, the five prisoners appeared in Court, defended by Mr Bretherton. Four of them were bound over for £20 or two months in jail. The fifth, Fallon, was sent to trial at Chester Assizes.

The Burial Board Riot illustrated a number of points. Once again the power of the priest was evident in the actions of Canon Chapman and the readiness of the police to send for him. But having stopped the mob in the morning, they returned in greater force in the afternoon and made their way to Lairds, which was not renowned for employing Catholics. There is some measure of planning evident here and credence can be given to Superintendent Birnie's fear that, if Laird's men had come out, there would have been bloodshed. Finally, the Irish were defended by Edward Bretherton in court, as they invariably were.

The Garibaldi Riots, 1862

On Wednesday, 8th October, 1862, a Debating Society at Holy Trinity, Church of England, Price Street, proposed to hold a debate on 'Italy and Garibaldi'. A few police officers were sent to the meeting, but no trouble was expected. At about seven o'clock, a large mob of Irish had collected and, when the doors were opened, they began to shout and throw stones. As the size of the mob increased, fears for the safety of the meeting grew. The incumbent of Holy Trinity, Revd J. Baylee, sent to St Werburgh's for assistance. About 8.30 pm., Fathers Brundritt and Goulding arrived.[19] The priests immediately calmed the mob and led them away from the scene in two groups. One group, passing by the side of Holy Trinity, broke the windows by throwing stones, and stones were also thrown at the Baptist Church in Price Street. The police were unable to do anything as the stone throwers were in the centre of the crowd. The meeting of the Debating Society was adjourned.[20]

The adjourned meeting was to be held on 15th October. Superintendent Bernie, acting on information received that a serious disturbance would take place, made preparations. The whole of the Birkenhead Force was placed on alert, men of the County Force, under Capt. Smith, were brought in and troops of the 49th Regiment came from Manchester. Hundreds of Special Constables were sworn in and during the day, the lathes at Laird's yard were turning out staves.

At 7 pm., Inspectors Gunning and Keenan, with sixteen men were despatched to Holy Trinity for the opening of the meeting. Large numbers of 'idle spectators' were assembling in the adjacent streets. According to Superintendent Birnie, a large body of men, armed with poles and sticks, with Father Goulding at their head, arrived at Holy Trinity. The priest called for three cheers for the Pope, the Queen and the British Dominions. That is the last that was heard of Father Goulding on the night. The Birkenhead Police were deployed and attempted to disperse the mob. There followed a series of battles between police and mob, with the police suffering severe casualties. Local premises were looted. At 11 pm., the Birkenhead and County Police entered Oak Street, the street with largest concentration of Irish in the town, and began to disperse the mob, making several arrests. The Magistrates, under Sir Edward Cust, refused to commit the military and the Specials, so the brunt of the attacks were borne by the Birkenhead and County forces. The rioters were dispersed and by 2 am. peace had been restored. The cost to the force had been heavy, with every member receiving some sort of injury.[21]

It is difficult to account for the 'Garibaldi Riots'. The occasion, a debate about the anti-clerical Italian, could be interpreted as a provocation to Catholics in the same sense as Protestants saw the restoration of the hierarchy as provocation by the Pope. The clergy, on this occasion, had little or no influence on events. No doubt, on the Sunday before the second meeting, Canon Chapman would have warned his parishioners against being present. Unfortunately, the St Werburgh's Notice Books have not survived, so there is no record in the parish archive.

There was, on the Irish side, a certain degree of planning for the riot. Irishmen came to Holy Trinity armed with sticks, pokers and spades, while their women were present with aprons full of stones. Fires in the houses in Oak Street and Eldon Place were banked up to flood the streets with smoke, making the task of the police more difficult. Perhaps the debate on Garibaldi at Holy Trinity was simply the occasion for an underclass to attack the police, something akin to the Toxteth and Bristol riots of a few years ago. The Irish were certainly easy targets for the police for offences of drunkenness, fighting and begging and, compared to other long-distance migrants in the town, were over-represented in the criminal statistics. Roger Swift found the Irish to be in a similar situation in Wolverhampton.[22]

The 'Battle of Broken Head', as *Punch* termed the Garibaldi Riot, gained a certain national notoriety and the Chairman of the Wirral Magistrates, Sir Edward Cust, was singled out for particular blame. He was accused of cowardice and received a number of white feathers for failing to use the Specials and the military against the Irish rioters. Cust maintained that, if the Specials had been used, there would have been fatalities. Given the facts that there was a strong current of anti-Catholic feeling in Birkenhead and that there were a number of Orange Lodges in the town, he was probably right. Orangemen were well represented among the Specials.

After the riot, the numbers of the police were increased and an ex-soldier was appointed as Head Constable of the force, over Superintendent Bernie's head.

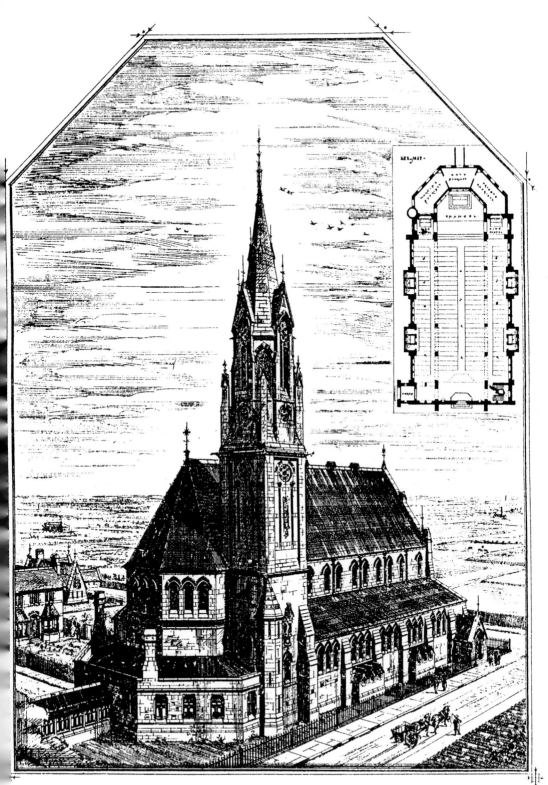

CHURCH OF OUR LADY — BIRKENHEAD
a simplified version of this design by Edward Pugin,
without tower or steeple, was eventually built

Anti-Catholic Lectures

One of the most virulent forms of anti-Catholicism in the 1850s and 1860s was that of anti-Catholic lectures. The two most militant of the lecturers were Baron de Camin (in 1859) and William Murphy (in 1867). Their attempts to deliver anti-Catholic lectures were accompanied by disturbances and rioting, as Irish Catholics protested against public attacks being made on their faith. As with the Birkenhead riots of 1850 and 1862, the issue was free speech against public order. William Murphy was an ex-Irish Catholic who devoted himself to exposing his former religion, in particular the confessional and convents. In February, 1867, his lectures in Wolverhampton were accompanied by disorder as Irishmen tried to stop them. The week before the Wolverhampton visit, there had been similar scenes of disorder at his meetings in Newcastle-under-Lyme.[23] Murphy was banned in Liverpool as a danger to public order, but in July, 1867, he began a series of lectures in Birkenhead.

Considering the number of religiously motivated disturbances Birkenhead had experienced over the years, a visit from Murphy would constitute a serious challenge to public order. An editorial in *The Birkenhead and Cheshire Advertiser* on 27th July 1867 expressed a certain trepidation:

> We know so well the inflammable character of the population, the often recurring riots of former times, the abhorrence with which Mr Murphy is regarded by a large body of our own population and by the 'Little Ireland' across the Mersey. . . With such a large and well-drilled police force as we now possess a riot ought to be simply impossible.[24]

In the event, there was no disturbance or violence during the course of Murphy's visit to Birkenhead. Canon Chapman at St Werburgh's, Father Daly at Our Lady's and Father Brundritt at the new mission of St Laurence's, had impressed upon their parishioners the need to remain calm and avoid provocation. This was commented upon in an editorial in the *Advertiser* on Wednesday, 31st July, 1867:

> We are glad that we can congratulate our townsmen upon the fact that, so far as the Murphy excitement has gone, it has not disturbed the order and quiet of the locality. With a prudence which does them credit, the Roman Catholic clergy have exerted themselves to the uttermost in seeking to restrain the more unruly of their flock from giving vent to the animosity which it is only reasonable to believe some of them do cherish against Mr Murphy and the cause he represents.[25]

In its next edition, the *Advertiser* was reporting that a novena to the Sacred Heart had taken place as an act of reparation for Murphy.[26]

Although no violence had taken place in Birkenhead on the occasion of Murphy's visit, anti-Catholic feeling ran high in its aftermath. *The Advertiser*, which was not known for its pro-Catholic views, had decided to print all the Murphy lectures for the benefit of people who had been unable to attend. Canon Chapman took exception to this and denounced the paper from the pulpit of St Werburgh's. No record of the Canon's address survives and it is only from the *Advertiser* itself that information may be obtained. According to the paper, 'the bile of the worthy Canon, who wields the power and thunders from the Grange Lane Vatican, was stirred by the fair and impartial reporting of Mr Murphy's lectures'. He warned his following against 'investing a penny in the purchase of this journal or of reading so dangerous a print'. The whole tone of the editorial was summarised in the lines:

> The Roman Catholic clergy fear Mr Murphy, they hate to hear the truth about themselves, or let others hear it . . . Romish priestcraft hates a free press and free expression of opinion. Where the Papal keys rattle there are chains and slavery for free minds.[27]

The Advertiser was voicing the anti-Catholic feeling which had been ever-present in Birkenhead since the opening of St Werburgh's mission in 1837.

Summary

There had been an undercurrent of anti-Catholic feeling in Birkenhead since the township began to grow in the 1830s, particularly among people with Orange connections from Liverpool who settled in the new town, bringing their prejudices with them. The influx of Famine Irish Catholics during 1847 brought a new dimension to the Church in Birkenhead in so much as the congregation of St Werburgh's increased. Most of the Famine refugees were poor and lived in over-crowded conditions in the poorest parts of the town, took the lowest paid employment, when it was available, and in many cases, so the English perception was, brought sickness into the town. Furthermore, they were seen as a drain on the local Poor Law finances. The majority of them were Catholic and their presence in the township served to increase anti-Catholic feeling. It is in this context that the Irish Catholic disturbances in Birkenhead in the middle of the nineteenth century can be placed.

Apart from the Garibaldi Riots, Irish Catholics were willing to heed their pastors, Father Browne and Canon Chapman, who did exercise some degree of control. At the Chester trial, Roebuck summed up the position of Irish Catholics in Birkenhead:

> The poor man in the eyes of a policeman is like a beggar in the eyes of a dog. . . he always snaps at him. The poor were to be excluded from the meeting. A large portion of the inhabitants of that town are poor . . . and they are Catholics.[28]

NOTES

1. E.R. Norman, *Anti-Catholicism in Victorian England,* London, 1968, pp.52-65.
2. P. Sully, *History of Birkenhead,* Liverpool, 1907, pp.96, 144, 179.
3. 1851 Census, Enumerators' Sheets.
4. The title 'Father' is used for secular priests throught this article although its use did not become widespread until the second half of the nineteenth century.
5. M.S. Slaughter, *History of the Diocese of Shrewsbury,* pp.7-8.
6. Register of Dissenters Meeting Houses, Cheshire Record Office, Chester.
7. St Werburgh's *Liber Defunctorum,* 19 August 1837.
8. Slaughter, op. cit., p.8
9. For a full discussion, see G. Connolly, 'Irish and Catholic: Myth or Reality? — Another Sort of Irish and the Renewal of the Clerical Profession among Catholics in England, 1791-1918', in Swift and Gilley, eds, *The Irish in the Victorian City,* London, 1985, pp.225-55.
10. Swift and Gilley, op. cit., pp.207-24.
11. The narrative is based on 1. the reports of the *Liverpool Mercury,* 2. *Liverpool Pamphlets,* 'The Trial of Catholics at Chester', Sydney Jones Library, University of Liverpool, Special Collection.
12. *Liverpool Mercury,* 29 November 1850
13. ibid.
14. ibid. Letter of Father Browne, .
15. ibid. 16 May 1851
16. *Liverpool Pamphlets,* op. cit., p.16
17. ibid.
18. The narrative is based on the Superintendent's Report to the Watch Committee, 6 June 1859: Superintendent's Notebook, Merseyside Police Headquarters, Canning Place, Liverpool.
19. Father Brundritt was soon to be the first Head of Mission at St Laurence's, a few hundred yards from Holy Trinity.
20. The narrative is based on the Minutes of the Birkenhead Watch Committee, 29 October 1862, pp.134-36. Commissioners' Minutes, 1859-1870, B/001/3, Birkenhead Reference Library. For a full discussion of the riots see F Neal, 'The Birkenhead Garibaldi

Riots, 1862', *Transactions of the Lancashire and Cheshire Historical Society,* Vol 131, (1982) pp. 87-111.

21. Among the more seriously injured was P.C.42 Patrick Kearney. He was the father of the late Canon Kearney, of Shrewsbury Diocese, who died in 1946.

22. Swift and Gilley, op. cit., pp.179-207.

23. ibid. pp.188-195.

24. *Birkenhead and Cheshire Advertiser,* 27 July 1867.

25. ibid. 31 July 1867.

26. ibid. 3. August 1867.

27. ibid. 6. August 1867.

28. Liverpool Pamphlets, op. cit., p.6.

IX

THE CHRISTIAN BROTHERS

N.D. O'Halloran

The first foundation of the Christian Brothers in the diocese of Shrewsbury was at Carlett Park, Eastham, Wirral, which was opened and blessed by Bishop Singleton on 26th May 1924. It was to act as a novitiate for the Brothers who would teach eventually in Britain itself, in India, Australia and South Africa. It was not their first novitiate in England: the 19th century had seen a novitiate in Preston which had lasted from the time of the founder, Blessed Edmund Ignatius Rice, until the Brothers withdrew from Britain in the 1870s. Previously their schools had been 'all age', in effect, primary schools. The Brothers were supported by the parishes which provided them with lodgings and 'coals', and £40 a year per man. Their training as teachers had been undertaken in Ireland for the most part and in this respect they had not been a financial burden on diocese or parish. Nevertheless, there is no doubt that the support which they needed and were given made substantial demands on the resources available to parish priests in the poorer areas of towns and cities where the vast majority of their people lived, and it must have been an enormous relief to hard-pressed clergy when after the 1870 Education Act, a Catholic Training

College was established in Hammersmith and priests were able to send prospective teachers there to be trained at public expense. Not only that, but when they came back to their parishes and worked in the schools their salaries would be paid by the Local Authority. Needless to say, the Brothers were no longer needed, and as one parish after another came to have teachers who had been trained in London the Brothers became superfluous to needs and were withdrawn.

However, the twentieth century saw a remarkable growth in secondary education and religious orders were once again asked to provide teachers and schools to meet the growing demand. While the 'all-age' school was still in existence, it was for the most part a school which would offer a more academic type of education that the bishops were now asking for. Where the Local Authority had its own grammar schools, bishops were concerned that Catholics should have available a comparable type of curriculum in a Catholic ambience and with Catholic religious instruction available for their flocks. Vocations were numerous not only from Ireland but from England, and the schools in Liverpool and Crosby as well as those in the south-west, Bristol and Plymouth, were sending many young people to Carlett Park willing to try their calling as Christian Brothers. Carlett Park soon became too small for the numbers and a decision was taken to open another house within a short distance which would accommodate younger candidates for the Congregation, where they could be prepared for matriculation before undertaking the intensive spiritual training of the novitiate. The Brothers were no different from other religious orders at the time who tended to take recruits at an early age. It should be remembered that diocesan seminaries took aspirants to the priesthood at the age of 10 and 11 before they went to secondary schools. In general, boys who applied to the Brothers were aged between 14 and 16 and had already done several years of secondary schooling. The practice of taking young people at such an early age has now been abandoned by the Congregation, though there is still considerable debate as to its efficacy in fostering a sense of self-discipline which would later help to overcome the many temptations to return to 'the world' which are inevitable in any vocation to the religious life. In 1933 a property, 'Brooklea', a fine nineteenth-century red brick building, together with about twenty acres of land, became available in Ledsham, about three miles from Eastham. It was thought that this would be suitable as a 'juniorate' for younger candidates to the Congregation. Its proximity to the novitiate was obviously an advantage and the re-location of juniors elsewhere would ensure that the more tranquil atmosphere, then considered essential to the single-mindedness of the novitiate, would be created in the elevated and tree-enclosed surroundings of Carlett Park. 'Brooklea' (to be known thereafter as St Joseph's) was officially opened and blessed by Bishop Moriarty, the Coadjustor Bishop of Shrewsbury, on 18th December 1933. Owing to the increase in the number of applicants to Carlett Park it was clear that 'Brooklea' would be inadequate and immediately on its purchase the building of extensions was begun. These were completed early in 1934 with a three-storey building on the west side, with Chapel and sacristy on the ground floor and dormitories overhead. To relieve the pressure on Carlett Park a group of novices, about 25, were temporarily transferred to Ledsham. But on the completion of their novitiate, it was intended that they should undertake further studies elsewhere, either at training college or university. When they left Ledsham in August, the building would revert to what it was intended to be — a college for junior aspirants to the Congregation. This is precisely what happened and for the next forty years it functioned as a secondary school, preparing young people for matriculation GCSEs and the novitiate. In the meantime, not far away in Birkenhead, the Brothers were establishing another foundation in the diocese. The lack of a Catholic Secondary School in Wirral had been felt for years. In fact there was not a single school of this type for boys in the whole Shrewsbury diocese. The main reason was lack of money. Neither the Government nor the local authorities were permitted, as the law then stood, to give any financial help towards the construction and equipment of such schools, even after recognition. Unless a diocese was in a position to give substantial help, the opening of a new school could not be undertaken.

It was on June 30th 1931 that the Very Rev. H.E. Provost Hazlehurst, the Parish Priest of St Joseph's, Birkenhead, wrote to Brother Stanislaus Roche, the Superior of St Edward's College, Liverpool, recommending the application of a boy seeking admission to St Edward's. In the course of his letter, he said

> Also on the larger question (speaking as one without authority) is there any chance of your Brothers opening a Secondary School in this town? I should be grateful for your opinion. What are the terms on which you usually undertake to start a school? The question is an acute one in Birkenhead and particularly in this parish. I am continually approached and reproached.

It is important, in view of later developments in the structuring of education and the categorising of schools, to understand that the expression 'Secondary School' at that time meant what is now called a grammar school. There were several such schools for boys in Birkenhead and district: Birkenhead Institute, Park High School, Rock Ferry High School, all within the town, Calday Grange Grammar School and Wirral Grammar in the neighbouring areas of Wirral, and Wallasey Grammar and Oldershaw Grammar in the adjoining borough of Wallasey. All these schools were under the Local Education Authorities for the areas concerned. Apart from these there was an independent grammar school, Birkenhead School. So Provost Hazlehurst's request was for the Brothers to provide a Catholic counterpart to these, all of which provided courses leading to School Certificate and Higher School Certificate examinations.

On November 4th, 'Outwood', a mansion standing at the junction of Egerton Road and Manor Hill, was purchased by the Brothers and the chronicler of the time describes the house and its situation in fulsome terms:

> Though the house is seventy years old, it is in excellent condition. It is substantially constructed, comfortable and commodious, but in some respects almost too ornamental for a religious house. . . .

On January 4th 1932 the balance of £3600 (the total cost was £4000) was handed over and the deeds were signed. 'Outwood' had become the property of the Congregation.

> The district round about is very beautiful. It is the best part of Birkenhead. Here dwell the Merchant Princes of Merseyside. The beauty spot, Bidston Hill, is within fifteen minutes walk. There are some fine secondary schools in the neighbourhood.

The Superior General had undertaken to open the school not later than September 1934. In the summer of 1932, William Ellis, FMSA, of St Helens, was engaged as architect. He was a brother of Br Patrick Ellis, a member of the congregation, who was later to act as Headmaster of Redcourt, the preparatory school for St Anselm's. The building was planned to accommodate 420 pupils and was to be built round a central quadrangle. Two sides of the quadrangle were considered adequate for the numbers originally expected and these were completed by 12th September 1933. Br Boniface McDonald was appointed Headmaster in August; his community arrived in early September and the school was opened on 18th September with 63 pupils, quietly, without any ceremony whatever. By the following September the number had risen to 116.

The Diocese, under the terms of agreement with the Brothers, undertook to contribute £10,000 towards the initial cost of the school. This sum would be levied from the parishes who hoped to benefit or who were thought able to afford a contribution. As some parishes were considered more affluent than others, this arrangement was not universally popular and was to lead to some argument later. The first phase of new buildings for the school would cost £16,445, and the complete building would cost £25,300. This meant that the house, grounds and school would cost altogether about £30,000 of which the diocese would contribute £10,000 and the Congregation £20,000. Once the diocese had fulfilled its obligations under the original agreement it would be for the Brothers to pay for any future expansion of the school. On 19th October 1933, Br Boniface McDonald, the Headmaster and Superior, received a letter from the Superior-General, Br Pius Noonan, and with it some letters which had passed between the latter and Provost Hazlehurst concerning the contributions from the various parishes to St Anselm's. The payments made by the Congregation to this date were as follows:

Purchase of the House	£ 4,000 0s 0d
Mr Hoskinson, Solicitor	£ 106 17s 5d
Fleming & Co, builders	£10,950 5s 0d
Bennet Furnishing Co	£ 173 3s 2d
Mr Ellis, architect	£ 9,959 1s 0d
	£16,189 6s 7d

It had been suggested that scholarships be given to boys from the parishes contributing to the school — one Parish Priest suggested an enormous number — whereas the superior proposed five in all.

The following is the text of a letter from the Superior-General to Provost Hazlehurst on 19th November 1933:

Long periods of absence from Dublin and pressure of other business since I returned have prevented me from replying to your letter of September 25th, which Br Butler (the Vicar Superior-General) acknowledged on September 27th.

It would be better for us as well as for you to have the dates fixed for the parish contributions. I accept your proposal to send £2,000 at the end of this year. This will make the total received from you £6,000. I suggest that the remaining £4,000 be paid in four equal annual instalments commencing in

December 1934. I think it will be easier for the parishes to continue the contributions in this way than to revive them after a few years. Moreover, the school will require the financial help during the difficult early years of its life. As an incentive to the raising of the contributions, I propose to give five free places annually in St Anselm's. The total will be 20 in four years - the normal period of pupils in secondary schools. I fix this number of free places from returns I have got from St Edward's College, Everton, giving the relation between the number of the roll of the school and the number of free places. The method of admission to these places will be as nearly as possible the same as obtains in schools under the Board of Education. Details of the method will be sent to you later by the Principal of St Anselm's.

I should like those people who think they have been too generous towards St Anselm's to remember what the Brothers have done in cash and in undertaking all the risks of an uncertain future. To date a sum of £18,850 has been expended. Of this the parishes have contributed £4,000. To pay the remaining £14,850 I have raised a loan in a Dublin bank. A sum of about £6,000 is still required and must be paid in the next month or so before the first part of the building is completed. The running expenses will be very great even when the building has been paid for. The only income the Brothers will have for years is the fees of the pupils To judge by the returns of the first term these will not be enough to meet the moderate living expenses of the five brothers now on the staff.

It is not easy, even if it were desirable, to make comparisons between the help given to make other foundations and that arranged for St Anselm's. In others we received grants, loans without interest for long periods, we were beneficiaries from bazaars and fetes and the like. St Anselm's differs from all the others we have opened in the north. In these we began in a small way; classes were conducted in the residences for several years until the school had grown. And, most important of all, the Board of Education paid grants even before any extensions were made, provided the school satisfied the requirements of Inspectors. Now the Board refuses to pay grants to new schools even when recognised as 'efficient'.

I appreciate all the parishes have done and are prepared to do for the school. It will need their support and their sympathy at all times especially in the early years and in the difficult times in which we live. With their active cooperation I have no fears for its success. It had to be built to receive pupils; the Mansion would not have housed them for even one year - as the roll shows.

I hope to be in Liverpool during the week and to avail myself of the opportunity of calling on you lest there might be any outstanding points requiring discussion.

With respectful kind wishes,

Yours sincerely in JC,

J.P.Noonan,   Superior-General.

PS   I should like to point out what St Edward's College (Liverpool) is doing for boys of the Wirral. It gave free places to six from that area this year bringing the total of free places in the College to boys from the Wirral to 27. The College has 43 scholarship holders from it and only 22 fee-paying pupils. St Edward's undertakes to give six free places to boys from the Wirral annually until St Anselm's is recognised by the Board of Education.

J.P.N.

St Anselm's was fully recognised by the Board of Education in the summer of 1938. This recognition was to have the effect of local authorities being able to take up places at the school should they so wish. Needless to say this is exactly what the diocese and the parishes had been hoping for, as they would then be relieved of having to make additional contributions should the school expand. Nevertheless the school was placed in the earning category of secondary schools, 'non-provided'. This category would ultimately after the 1944 Education Act become what was called 'Direct Grant', ie, a school whose pupils would all attract a grant directly from the Department of Education, while the Local Authority would be entitled to take up, if it wished, a certain percentage of the annual admissions. The Local Authority would pay the fees of the boys whom they sponsored at the school, while others would pay fees according to their means. In practice therefore, the school remained an independent school at which local authorities could take up places. The persuasive powers of the clergy were soon brought to bear on the local authorities of Birkenhead, Wallasey and Cheshire, and before long all three areas had representatives at the school and in fact took up a majority of the places. It was an admirable arrangement which gave the school a considerable degree of independence and provided Catholic boys from Wirral with the opportunity of an academic education which hitherto had been denied them unless they went to the Local Authority grammar schools. The school could dispose of its income for whatever aspect of its educational activities it saw there was a need, without the leaden hand of a Local Authority dictating in what precise areas, eg sports, library, text books, scientific equipment, furniture, particular sums were to be allocated annually. In fact, it anticipated by about thirty years the freedom that was eventually given to most schools to assign their monies to those areas where there was need.

Br Boniface McDonald, the first Headmaster, was succeeded in 1936 by Br J Bertrand Thompson, an interesting and somewhat eccentric character, very much ahead of his time, who believed passionately in the educational merits of drama and music. He was a prolific composer of pageants which involved every boy in the school. These had a twofold advantage: boys were given the opportunity to develop any histrionic abilities they had and build up their self-confidence, and as well, since every boy took part, every parent had a personal interest in the presentations, and therefore attended, contributing in no small measure to the school finances. As in drama, so in music: Fred Boraston, singing master at St Edward's, Liverpool and St Mary's, Crosby came to Birkenhead twice a week, and Eugene Genin, a former leading player with the Liverpool Philharmonic Orchestra taught orchestral music. Fred, who had an acerbic wit, had a love-hate relationship with Br Thompson, which nevertheless never got in the way of what they both regarded as advancing the image of the school. They collaborated in the composition of school anthems, Thompson composing the words and Boraston the music, but when Fred heard many years later that Bertrand had died he could not resist a pseudo epitaph which read: 'Here lies J B Thompson, as he always did'.

In the meantime, at the eastern end of the diocese there had been further developments. Among the evacuees from Guernsey in 1941 was a party of schoolboys and de la Salle Brothers from their school, 'Les Vauxbelets'. Under the care of the Ministry of Health, they arrived in Altrincham, Cheshire, and were put up for a short while in a large house in Hale. Canon Donnelly, parish priest of St Vincent's, Altrincham, purchased a detached house, 'Oakleigh', about a mile outside the town and to this the Brothers and boys were transferred. The local people supplied them generously with bedding, furniture and books. In the course of time local Catholic boys were permitted to join the school and the number on the roll at one time was 170. The house, needless to say, was entirely inadequate for such numbers and the lack of grounds must have proved a serious handicap. At the end of hostilities in Europe, the Superior of the College was directed by the Bishop of Shrewsbury to close the school in the summer of 1945. This came as a great shock, as the de la Salle Brothers were contemplating the purchase of a large property with the intention of building a permanent school. The parents of the local boys, obviously very much upset by the contemplated closure, organised protest meetings which the Brothers attended. Nevertheless, the school was closed in July 1945 and the boys, on leaving, were expressly told to secure admission to other schools in the area as the school would definitely not be reopening.

The Bishop invited the Christian Brothers to reopen the school in September 1945. This was an interesting development, which clearly must have created some resentment in the minds of the de la Salle Brothers who had been running the school, and certainly contributed to a coolness in relations between the two congregations which lasted for many years. After all, there was hardly a decent interval between their being told to leave and the Christian Brothers' acceptance of the bishop's invitation to reopen the school. Anyway, there would appear to have been some insensitivity on all sides in the hurried re-provision of secondary grammar education in the Altrincham area — or at least, so it seemed on the surface. Later it emerged that discipline in the school had deteriorated rapidly with the result that the Bishop and clergy were receiving frequent complaints. After a Mr Gooch, HMI, had inspected the school he made a very damaging report, a copy of which reached the Bishop who decided that a change of adminitration was necessary.

Possession was taken of the former premises of the school early in September 1945 and on the 14th of that month 81 boys, all former pupils of the school, presented themselves. The implications of the following sentence in the House Annals can be left to the imagination: 'The boys were very undisciplined but quickly responded to the requirements of the new staff'. These premises were to serve as a temporary school pending the purchase of an excellent property in what was then a rural area named Hale Barns, about two miles outside Altrincham.

On Christmas Eve 1945, when the purchase was completed of this property of 22½ acres, named 'Woodeaves', the Brothers took possession of the house. Two of the large rooms were converted into double classrooms while the outbuildings were converted into dining-room, cloakroom and toilet facilities for the boys. One of the rooms became the community chapel and from the outset about 50 people from the neighbourhood attended Sunday Mass here. Canon Donnelly who, from the beginning, had been so helpful in furthering the project, celebrated a *Missa Cantata* sung by the pupils on the Feast of the Annunciation. The Brothers' communities in the north all contributed to the beautifying of the chapel, the Superior of Blackpool with a lovely oak altar, the superior of St Anselm's a set of five vestments, a cope and humeral veil, the superior of Stoke-on-Trent the many requisites for the altar and the superior of Crosby the prie-dieux.

The school was intended to serve the three large parishes of Altrincham, Sale and Timperley, as well as the neighbouring towns of Northwich, Knutsford, Warrington and Stockport, in none of which was there a Catholic grammar school. The location of the school was excellent and the fine property was large enough to afford all the amenities of a first-rate secondary school. As Br J.Justin Dowling, the first Headmaster, wrote: 'The plans are being prepared, but the erection of the building must be deferred till the ill-effects of the war begin to ease off'.

There was a further interesting development at this time in Canon Donnelly's request to the Brothers to take on the management of a Secondary Modern School in the district. Br Dowling passed on the request to the Superior-General. According to the terms of the Agreement between the Bishop and the Superior-General, the Christian Brothers undertook to build and staff a Secondary Grammar School on the property at Hale Barns. Br Dowling received a letter dated 29th January 1946 from the General:

My very dear Br Justin,
Yours of the 19th inst. was received on the 23rd, but as I was a few days absent from here, the reply has been delayed until now.

We have no record of any arrangement with the Bishop of Shrewsbury about our taking charge of a Modern School. The Secondary Grammar School on the 'Woodeaves' property was the only school agreed on. The Brothers make themselves responsible for the erection of this school and since it will be a Brothers' property they will appoint two-thirds of the Governors who will control it.

Along with the Woodeaves property which is being handed over to us, an additional area of 7½ acres (beyond the path over which there is a right of way) has, I understand, been purchased by the Diocesan authorities. If they erect on this area a Modern School and hand over its management to us it would be as well to accept it so as to have in our hands the whole Catholic Secondary Education for boys in that part of Cheshire. . . .

Your affect. Br.
J P Noonan, Superior-General

It is clear from this letter that while Br Noonan was prepared
to have the Brothers responsible for the building of a
grammar school, he was not prepared to pay for the erection
of a secondary modern school. Likewise Canon Donnelly was
not prepared at this stage to commit the Diocese to the
building of the school and handing it over to the Christian
Brothers to administer. Subsequent meetings between the
various parties centred for the most part on the boundaries of
the site which would be used for the Grammar School and
those parts set aside for the erection of a new parish church,
but eventually in September 1949 it was decided that the
Brothers would take on the management of the Secondary
Modern School. At this meeting a decision was also taken
that the status of the Grammar School should be
independent. There the matter rested for the time being: no
modern school was built on the site and priority was given to
the development of the Grammar School. This became a
matter of some urgency as the number of Catholic boys
qualifying for Grammar School places was beginning to
stretch the resources of the existing Catholic Grammar
Schools in Manchester. It came to a head in July 1952 when
ten boys from Sale and Altrincham who gained the Cheshire
Common Entrance examination could not secure places in St
Bede's, Manchester or the Xaverian College. The parents of
these boys sent a joint letter to the Minister of Education
asking that the Cheshire County Authority transfer the boys'
scholarships to St Ambrose. The Minister wrote to Mr Erroll,
the local MP, referring to the application for a licence to erect
science rooms, but pointed out that the granting of a licence
would not necessarily mean that she would be able to
recognise the school as 'efficient', still less, that recognition as
'efficient' would necessarily be followed by a change in the
Cheshire Authority's attitude towards taking up places at St
Ambrose. It became clear that the problem would not be
solved until there were permanent school buildings providing

adequate facilities for science as well as the traditional arts subjects. Some attempt was made by September 1953 to meet these requirements with the building of two prefabricated teaching blocks which would cater specifically for the sciences. It would, however, be another ten years before full recognition as 'efficient' was granted, as the Ministry, through its inspectorate, was as yet not satisfied that the existing premises were adequate. In 1958, following an inspection requested by the then Headmaster, Br D. Phelan, the school was placed on the Register of Independent Schools. When Br Phelan finished his period of office as Superior and Headmaster in 1958 there were 326 on roll. It was during the Headmastership of his successor, Br C Carey, that the Provincial, Br P C Curran, agreed that permanent buildings be erected with a view to recognition as 'efficient'. On October 20th he and the local Superior visited Canon Donnelly to outline to him the proposed development and recognition of the school. The Canon was happy at the suggestions and said the Brothers were welcome to launch appeals within the parish for the raising of funds. During the year following, Br Curran spent a considerable amount of time on the project, discussing plans with the architect and suggesting various modifications. His enthusiasm as well as his practical knowledge of school building was a decisive factor in seeing the project get off the ground and in its realisation as a fine building in a fine setting. The lowest tender submitted was that of Messrs Wm Thorpe of Manchester —- £159,844. Some minor changes were effected which would reduce the figure by about £14,000. In March 1968 building work started.

From 5th to 7th December 1962 there was a full inspection of the school for the purpose of recognition and word came on February 5th 1963 from the Ministry of Education that the College was now placed on the register of independent schools recognised as 'efficient'. In the following month the Headmaster wrote to various local education authorities offering places for Catholic boys who had passed the 11+ tests. The response was varied, but generally promising: Cheshire County would send not more than ten boys a year as it was committed to sending forty-five boys annually to a Grammar School to be built in Wythenshawe; Stockport LEA would take up places; Warrington LEA would pay for every boy admitted from their list of successful candidates; Manchester LEA and Lancashire LEA were not interested.

With the backing of the Bishop, the Headmaster, Br W. de Sales Foley, OBE, wrote to all Parish Priests and Heads of Catholic Primary Schools in the catchment area of St Ambrose suggesting that parents write to the Local Education Authority asking for a place for their son at the College. He also suggested that parents ask for a transfer of their sons from County Grammars to the College on grounds of religious belief. The effect was amazing: from April onwards there came a ceaseless flow of letters from the Education Authorities asking for places. Cheshire County (after promising ten boys) asked for 68 places! They took over responsibility for the fees of 45 boys who had passed the 11+ in the previous year but who had stayed on in the college. Stockport took 13 places and Warrington 11. Even Manchester and Lancashire (though the latter, very reluctantly) agreed to help with the fees of boys from their areas. Altogether 128 boys were admitted to the first year and four classes had to be formed. This immediately put a strain on the new accommodation, and Music, Science and Art Rooms had to double-up as classroom bases. In September 1963 the College opened with 435 boys on the roll. Among the new teachers brought onto the staff to cope with the increased numbers was Father F McGuinness, MA, at the request of the Bishop who wished him to take over the Headship of St Augustine's School in Wythenshawe when it would open in 1966. As it became clear that there was a likelihood of a big annual intake, the Christian Brothers had once again to consider the need to enlarge the College further. They accepted that the extended school should provide for a three-stream entry with a large Sixth-form. The National Bank agreed to an additional overdraft of £90,000.

So, even twenty years after the 1944 Education Act, the Catholic Church was continually engaged in trying to cater for its consequences both in buildings and money. The increase in the number of Catholic children qualifying for Grammar School education was forcing the clergy and the hierarchy to provide more schools and persuade the Government to increase grants for their provision. In the Shrewsbury diocese, the satellite town of Wythenshawe and the increase in population of Ellesmere Port meant that despite the expansion of St Anselm's, Birkenhead, and of St Ambrose, Altrincham, these schools could no longer offer the places necessary. In the case of Ellesmere Port and district, the diocese proposed that the Christian Brothers open a school at Hooton to deal with the problem. In the first instance this would be a preparatory school which would prepare boys to enter St Anselm's at 11+, and to this end the diocese bought a property at Hooton which the Brothers took over and staffed. This was in 1955 when it was quite clear that St Anselm's would no longer have the capacity to take the extra Catholic boys qualifying for Grammar School places. The Bishop thought that an ideal location for another such school would be somewhere near Hooton Cross; hence the purchase of the property there and the invitation to the Brothers to staff it. It was hoped that its catchment area would include New Ferry, Ellesmere Port, Chester, neighbouring parts of Cheshire and even across the Dee into Flint. The latter area was considered tappable as several boys were already attending St Anselm's from the southern side of the Dee, though later, when the proposal was put to the Bishop of Menevia, it became clear that he did not take kindly to the idea that numbers of his diocesans should be used to justify the case for a new Grammar School at Hooton. Some other territorial problems in relation to the catchment area were to arise later on when plans for the school were more precisely outlined. In any case it would seem that the purchase of Hooton Chase itself may have been undertaken rather prematurely as there would appear to have been little consultation with the Cheshire Local Authority about the site. When the matter was put before the Authority, they had two serious objections to the suggestion that a school could be built there: (i) the fact that the site was part of the 'green belt' and (ii) the danger to children of having to cross the main road to Chester at a particularly busy junction. They would not, however, object to a small private school being conducted there. Mr Velarde, the architect commissioned by the Bishop to draw up plans for the school, had these objections emphasised to him at a meeting he had with the Planning Authority on July 5th. Three days later he reported to the Bishop, the Right Reverend John Murphy, whose reaction was to tell him to get on with the necessary alterations: 'We will open in September. . . . We will fight the case of the Grammar School'.

The beginnings were not auspicious. Apart from the small number of applications for admission to what would be called Plessington School, surveyors found evidence of dry rot throughout the building. Consequently, plans for classrooms and dining room had to be modified considerably while repairs were carried out. The opening was delayed until 19th September. When told of the small number of applicants for admission, the Rt Rev Mgr Curran VG expressed regret that the school was not in Wallasey. It is not clear whether his views or those of the clergy in the rest of Wirral had been canvassed as to where a second grammar school should be sited. In view of the fact that the original intake included boys from New Brighton and Wallasey, as well as from Birkenhead, New Ferry, Rock Ferry, Bromborough, Hooton, Little Sutton, Great Sutton, Ellesmere Port, Connah's Quay, Chester, Upton and Mollington, perhaps he had a point. The tuition fees were a modest £12 a term. The roll was 35 boys between the ages of 7 and 9 in June 1956. As the Brothers became more familiar with the building, the sorry conditions in which they had to live and work became more apparent. Br Moss, the first Headmaster, was ordered by the Provincial to advise the architect, Mr Velarde, of the situation. His enumeration of the things requiring attention were listed graphically in the house annals:

the patchwork and creaky floors, the unpainted scullery and vegetable room, unfinished boys' cloakroom, the garage and stable from which the ceiling had been removed, unfinished boys' lavatory, dilapidated greenhouses, unfinished central heating chamber, the ruinous condition of the outhouse and other less important items.

This pitiful catalogue, which should have moved the most hard-hearted to action, had little effect. On the advice of Mr Hoskinson, the Diocesan Solicitor, all expenditure on extensions and improvement was to be put on hold while negotiations were going on behind the scenes between the Diocesan Commission and the Ministry of Education about the need for a Catholic Grammar School at Hooton. The building belonged to the Diocese, not to the Christian Brothers, and it was the responsibility of the Diocese to keep it in reasonable repair and to provide adequate facilities. It never became a profitable venture, even though the numbers increased to about 100 by the time the school was closed. Whatever improvements were made were achieved through scrimping on the part of the Brothers and the generosity of neighbouring communities. Uncertainty about the future coloured the attitude of the Provincial authorities, who would not authorise any major expenditure on a property which did not belong to them. Despite these shortcomings, the dedication and determination of the Brothers to make the place succeed resulted in the school, after a general inspection by HMIs, being placed by the Ministry of Education on the Register of Independent Schools. This was only two years after opening.

It was in the February of 1963 that the Hooton project began to impact on St Anselm's, Birkenhead. A letter from the Director of Education set out the conditions that Cheshire laid down before they would include the school on their building programme. It was quite clear that these conditions had been negotiated with, and agreed to by the Diocesan Education Commission, which in effect was composed of two people, Mgr P Rees and Canon A Rigby. In reply a letter was sent by the Provincial and his Council, the Central Governing Body, asking for further information about some of the issues raised by the proposals. Copies of these letters were sent to all members of the Local Governing Body. Canon Rigby, who was a local Governor, immediately wrote asking for a meeting at which he and Mgr. Rees, the Chairman of the Diocesan Education Committee, and Canon Quinn, the Chairman of St Anselm's Governors, would be present. On the Brothers' side it was arranged that a member of the Central Governing Body, Br J V Crease, would be present, though Canon Rigby had not mentioned any other brother apart from the Headmaster when he fixed the meeting. From the outset the atmosphere was tense and the two Commissioners were quite taken aback when Canon Quinn asked them whether, in view of the proposed developments in Runcorn and Widnes, the Hooton project should not be scrapped altogether and a school erected nearer the new centre of population. When they hedged on this he asked them how far they were committed to the Hooton site, so unsuitable from a safety angle. There was no satisfactory answer. One of the more bizarre proposals was that Rock Ferry was to be excluded from the St Anselm's catchment area, an arrangement which apparently had been agreed between the Commissioners and the Cheshire Director of Education without any reference to the Birkenhead Education Authority which was responsible for Rock Ferry, a part of the Borough of Birkenhead. If the Birkenhead Authority was to be ignored then, *a fortiori*, so were the Christian Brothers who had poured the equivalent of hundreds of thousands of pounds into St Anselm's. In any case it was made clear to the Commissioners that St Anselm's would under no circumstances surrender its right to take fee-paying pupils, 11+ scholarship holders or not, from the areas excluded from its catchment area. The assumption that they would get agreement on the proposals either from the Christian Brothers or the Local Authority, neither of whom had been consulted at any stage, was mind-boggling. Re-organisation had raised its ugly head and was being complicated, on the one hand, by the Labour Government's plans for comprehensive education in the pursuit of egalitarianism, and, on the other, by the desire of the Brothers to continue with the provision of competent grammar schools to meet the aims of the 1944 Act. The Diocese was to some extent caught between the two, having to try to meet the pastoral needs of areas unprovided for in Catholic Secondary education and the ongoing demands of the Religious Orders to fulfil the role they had been invited by the Diocese to undertake. Furthermore there was no general agreement on the part of educationalists, religious teaching orders and politicians about the merits of comprehensive schools. The Shrewsbury Diocese, like most of the other Catholic dioceses in England and Wales, was still having to find millions of pounds to pay for the Secondary Modern Schools that were being built or that had been built to cater for pupils who had failed to pass the 11+. That financial considerations were ultimately to determine the Church's attitude became clear before long, especially when the Labour Government agreed to increase the governmental contribution towards the building of new comprehensives. Whatever the Catholic authorities' reservations may have been on the ideology of comprehensive schools, their objections faded in the face of the promise of more money.

Despite the tensions that arose as a result of the Hooton project, fences were mended and a new Birkenhead working party to consider reorganisation was set up with the Headmaster of St Anselm's, Brother Joseph Cowley, as its Chairman. Gradually a plan was being agreed, but it became clear early in 1969 that the Birkenhead Education Authority, while perfectly happy to see a wholesale comprehensivisation of Catholic schools, was nevertheless going to continue to take up places at Birkenhead School for Boys and Birkenhead High School for Girls. So, comprehensive education was all right for Catholics, but was not for non-Catholics. This would mean that any Catholic child could at the age of 11+ sit the entrance examinations for Birkenhead School or Birkenhead High School and, if successful, could receive a grammar school education at one or the other of these fine schools. With the vigorous support of Canon Rigby, Father Burgon and Mr Livesey, the working party put in a clause or condition stipulating that no Catholic reorganisation plan should be implemented while any form of selection was retained in any other sector. The strength of support for this clause was so overwhelming that the Education Committee was forced to accept it. As Br Cowley expressed it in his contribution to the community annals of St Anselm's: 'the adroit politicians were foiled'.

On March 7th 1970 a meeting was held between representatives of St Anselm's Parents and Staff and Fr Burgon of the Diocesan Commission to discuss the implications of the schools reorganisation programme. It was not a very comfortable meeting for Fr Burgon who found himself in the unenviable position of having to try to defend actions taken by the Commission before he became a member. Assurances that Direct Grant and other non-LEA teachers would get representation on the Commission were given and that the intention in enlarging it was to ensure that 'past mistakes would not be repeated'.

During the late 1960s it was becoming apparent that the Brothers would have difficulty in maintaining a presence in all their English schools. The Congregation was going through a phase being experienced by religious orders throughout the first world: many abandoning their vocations and very few recruits presenting themselves. The defections were mostly in the 25 to 35 age group, the group that would in the ordinary course of events take over the administration of the province and the schools It was calculated that within ten or fifteen years most of the remaining brothers would be of retiring age, and death and old age would reduce the number of active brothers so drastically that closure of some communities would be inevitable. The uncertainty regarding the future and siting of the school at Hooton (it was eventually sited in Ellesmere Port) triggered the first closure. In February 1971 the following joint communication was issued by the Brothers and the Diocesan Education authorities to all parents of children currently at the school:

St John Plessington School

Owing to the shortage of Brothers and their commitments elsewhere, the Provincial has, with reluctance, found it necessary to inform His Lordship the Bishop that the Christian Brothers will be unable to continue staffing the St John Plessington School beyond July 1973. Enquiries are being made as to whether any other Religious Congregation would be able and willing to staff the school. Pupils on roll will be able to continue at the school. New pupils can be enrolled only with a view to acceptance should it be possible to continue the school.

During the late 1960s and the early 1970s innumerable meetings of 'working parties' were held to discuss various schemes of reorganisation which would incorporate existing Catholic Grammar and Secondary Modern Schools. There is little doubt that the many schemes put forward both in the Altrincham and Wirral areas were considered in great detail by the various bodies which had been set up to consider the possibilities. After the defeat of the Labour Government in 1979 plans were put on hold. The introduction of the Assisted Places Scheme by the Conservative Government seemed to presage a period of helpful financial support for parents wishing an academic grammar school education for their children, but who could not afford to pay the ever-increasing fees. Moreover, it is fair to say that the Brothers, who had striven for years to bring their schools to a high standard of academic achievement, and were still in the 70s continuing to provide extra facilities at considerable expense, were very reluctant to accept that their efforts should be dissipated in an amorphous expansion of a comprehensive system, the value of which was beginning to be increasingly questioned. At a Working Party meeting held at St Ambrose College, Altrincham, in September 1975 of the 160 parents present, 135 favoured the retention of independent status and by implication the continuation of the school as a Grammar School. And yet despite the undoubted support of the parents and the dedication of the Brothers to the principle of an academic school, the circumstances affecting the community of St Ambrose were of no small significance in the process of disengagement which the Provincial authorities had perforce to pursue after the Hooton closure. In the ten years between 1975 and 1985 at least three members of the Community died, one in very tragic circumstances when a fire broke out in the Brothers' house 'Woodeaves', in which a highly regarded member of the Community, Br Baptist Doyle, lost his life. There were no young men to take their places and it was rapidly becoming clear that the number of brothers able to take over headships was in very short supply indeed. Nevertheless, Br Thomas Coleman, who had given sterling service in Crosby and in Plymouth, was appointed Head in September 1984 and threw himself wholeheartedly into the further develoment of the school academically and materially. It was under his leadership that St Ambrose College was admitted to the Head Masters Conference. He was the last Christian Brother to hold the post and in September 1991 he was succeeded by Mr Eric Hester. The Community house 'Woodeaves' became the Provincial Headquarters in October 1992 and the province has been administered from there since that date.

The closure of Carlett Park in 1949 as a novitiate was not due to a lack of vocations. Rather it was the fact that the Manchester Ship Canal and its importance as a commercial artery had necessitated the presence nearby of detachments of troops during the war years. The military had requisitioned parts of the grounds and the house itself. The novices were transferred to Ledsham during the war, and in 1948 to Toddington, Gloucestershire. Soon after, the property was bought by the Local Education Authority as a Further Education College. In the meantime the number of 'postulants' at the juniorate in Ledsham, 3 miles away, remained steady and even continued to grow through the 1950s and early 1960s. In 1964 there were 65 aspirants in residence, but numbers began to slump after that: there were only 47 the following year, and from then onwards the numbers declined rapidly. The 60s were undoubtedly having their effect. The supply of applicants dried up during the 70s and the effective end of Ledsham as a juniorate came in the summer of 1972. The novices would take over the building for the rest of its existence as a Christian Brothers foundation. Some juniors continued to live in the house but went daily for classes to St Anselm's, Birkenhead. The property was put on the market in the summer of 1980 and was bought by the Sacred Heart Fathers from Malpas who wished to have a retreat and conference centre nearer to the centres of population in Liverpool and Wirral. On 29th July 1980 the transfer of the property took place and the Brothers left Ledsham.

From 1979, when the Labour Government was replaced by the Conservatives, the fortunes of St Anselm's, Birkenhead and St Ambrose, Altrincham, ran more or less in parallel. New Government policies enabled both schools, which were now independent, to become part of the Assisted Places Scheme which enabled children of less well-off parents to take advantage of the grammar school education offered by the two schools. Despite this, however, it became increasingly clear that both schools would need frequent and substantial injections of money if they were to continue to develop. The inexorable onset of old age and death meant that by this time very few brothers were teaching and thus earning salaries whereby the provincial coffers could be replenished. Consequently, it was decided that the two schools should apply for 'Grant Maintained' status which the Conservative Government introduced after the election in 1979. The schools would lose their independent status, but all fees would be paid by the Department of Education and Science. The admission of independent schools to this category was due in some measure to the efforts of Br John Sreenan, OBE, the Headmaster of St Anselm's. It was a tremendous boon to the school, enabling it to open its doors to a more academic pupil and ensuring for it considerable financial help for the provision of new facilities. The Brothers would still help while they had funds though they had to inform the schools that this could not be available indefinitely. Br Sreenan retired in 1993, having steered St Anselm's through some troubled waters. The future promised to be a relatively calm, for he could not have known that Grant Maintained status would soon be abolished. There was no brother to replace him as Head.

SOURCES

House Annals of the following communities:

St Joseph's, Ledsham
St Anselm's, Birkenhead
St Ambrose, Altrincham
St John Plessington, Hooton

The annals of the Novitiate of Carlett Park, Eastham have not been traced at the time of writing and it has been necessary to rely on reference to Carlett Park in the annals of other houses, especially those of St Joseph's, Ledsham, for the little information that there is.

The sentiments expressed in the foregoing article are the author's, and not necessarily those of the present provincial leadership of the Christian Brothers.

X

THE STRUGGLE FOR
THE SCHOOLS

EDUCATION IN THE DIOCESE

J.P. Marmion

PART 1

The restoration of the English Hierarchy in 1850 caused an outbreak of prejudice. The arrival of normal Catholic diocesan bishops on the scene was heralded in *The Times* as an act of Papal aggression, to which the Prime Minister, Lord John Russell added that it was 'insolent and insidious'. The uproar went as far as the production of a Bill against anyone assuming titles to pretended sees in the United Kingdom.[1] But there was no bishop as yet for Shrewsbury to face the opposition in Cheshire, Shropshire and North Wales. Bishop Brown did not arrive until July 1851. Schools however were already in the picture, and some of them did experience the rioting in the country.

The Catholic community early in the nineteenth century was the poorest section of society. For three centuries the recusant tradition of education had been one of schools abroad for the children of the richer Catholics and, by the eighteenth century, an efficient system of catechising in the English missions.[2] Various charities tried to assist orphans and the poor and by the middle of the century the St Vincent de Paul Society was beginning to spread in the country. In 1811 a number of charities had been brought together to form the Association of Catholic Charities with a total income of about £2,000, and a commitment to education, orphans and apprentices.[3] But if this were to represent the total finance available for the education of poor children, then the situation was well nigh hopeless. Far more than a merger of existing charities was needed. Vision, policy and initiative alone could begin to grapple with a problem of such magnitude.

For some the action of Daniel O'Connell in Ireland must have suggested other approaches. In July 1839 in the Freemasons' Hall, Great Queen Street, London, there was a public meeting of Catholics; perhaps the first such meeting for three hundred years. O'Connell was the driving force, which to some of the traditional Catholic squirearchy, Tories to a man, was a scandal. The resolutions at the meeting concerned: 1) appropriation of public money to education; 2) rights of all to share in such funds; 3) that moral and religious education must be combined with literary and scientific instruction; and 4) that it would be iniquitous to grant money to particular denominations and exclude others.[4] A policy and a programme were beginning to emerge. In August 1839 a petition was presented to the House of Commons. If this had no effect on the Commons, it certainly helped to form opinion among Catholics.

In 1843 the Catholic Institute, the last of a line of transitory bodies with an interest in Catholic education, made a survey of all the Catholic poor schools in England and Wales, and concluded that of 63,307 children in need of schooling only 30,207 were actually receiving it. The most significant moment came in 1847 when the Vicars Apostolic established the CPSC, the *Catholic Poor Schools Committee*, to replace the Catholic Institute.[5] The CPSC was to negotiate with the Committee of Council on Education. Since 1904 the CPSC has been known as the *Catholic Education Council*, while the Committee of Council on Education in 1856 became the *Department of Education (and Science)*. Both have more recently changed their titles (and roles) to the *Committee for Schools* (in the Department for Catholic Education & Formation of the Bishops Conference) and the *Department for Education* (DfE) in the State.

A number of features distinguished the CPSC from any previous Catholic charity or association with an interest in education. 1) It was established by the bishops; 2) It was directly under their authority and it was mandated to negotiate with the Government for a share in the education grants; and 3) significantly, it was staffed almost exclusively by converts. As David Matthews wrote, 'converts began to penetrate the new bureaucracy a full generation before the hereditary Catholics of any grouping had found their way there'. It is quite clear that the success of the CPSC owed a great deal to the confidence and ability of these men. Of the key figures associated with the CPSC, Stokes, Allies, Langdale and Marshall, only Charles Langdale (1787-1868) was from a recusant family, and as President his role was more that of a chairman than executive.

Scott Nasmyth Stokes (1821-1891) was the first secretary from 1847-53, and then for the next thirty-eight years an H.M.I. for Catholic schools. He was educated at St Paul's and Trinity College, Cambridge, and became a Catholic, probably in 1847. Father Faber was instrumental in getting him appointed to the CPSC.[6] Thomas William Allies (1813-1903) followed Stokes as secretary and served in this office for thirty-seven years. He was a son of the vicarage, went to Bristol Grammar School, Eton and then Wadham College, Oxford. From 1833-1841 he was a Fellow of Wadham, travelled abroad and learned Italian. He took orders in 1838, and four years later became Rector of Launton in Oxford. But in 1850 both he and his wife became Catholics, moved to live in Golden Square in London, and took in private pupils. In 1853 he was appointed first Professor of Modern History at the Catholic University in Dublin. But in the August of the same year he was called to follow Stokes at the CPSC. It was a fine appointment, and Allies made it his life's work.[7]

The last of the triumvirate was Thomas William Marshall (1818-1877), who was the son of the Governor of New South Wales, educated at Archdeacon Burney's school and Trinity College, Cambridge. From 1841-45 he was an Anglican curate in Wiltshire. After being received into the Church in December 1848 he was appointed Her Majesty's Inspector for R.C. Schools in England, Scotland and Wales. This post he held until 1860. In common with Allies he was a writer on religious matters. The appointment as inspector was made by the Committee of Council but on the recommendation of the CPSC. Marshall worked with both committees, and his lengthy and important reports were published also by the CPSC. They reveal a man who had a deep concern for poor children. On one occasion, examining a school in Wade's Place in Poplar, he found the children so starved that he first sent out for food and encouraged them to eat before he continued to examine them.[8]

In contrast to Stokes, Allies and Marshall, the Hon. Charles Langdale (1787-1868) was from recusant stock, educated at Oscott and Stonyhurst, and after the Emancipation Act he was one of the first Catholics to sit in Parliament. In 1838 he had presided over the first meeting of the Catholic Institute, and for many years he was chairman of the CPSC. At his funeral Cardinal Manning praised him as 'the far sighted and inflexible defender of the religious character of education, and of the strict denominational system'. It was a well deserved tribute. In the August of 1850 the tumult raised by Lord John Russell in an open letter to the Bishop of Durham met a defender of the Faith in Langdale. Later in that year in a meeting at York, he won the cheers of the crowd by his calm and resolute defence of his faith. Although he is given a notice in Gillow's *Biographical Dictionary* he deserves a fuller study as one of the founders of modern Catholicism in England.[9]

A first monument to the work of all four men is a publication, *The Catholic School*, which was clearly intended to form Catholic opinion, and to educate the clergy on the principles and practice of the Committee of Council on Education, and the necessary Catholic response:[10] and from 1848 the *Catholic Poor Schools Committee Annual Reports*.[11] These are invaluable, since nearly all the records of the CPSC were lost during the last war, when the London offices of a solicitor were destroyed by bombing.

The Schools at the Foundation of the Diocese

In 1850 the new diocese of Shrewsbury comprised the counties of Cheshire and Shropshire (in the old boundaries) together with the six northern counties of Wales. In Cheshire and Shropshire public Mass was only available in thirty one centres, eleven in Shropshire, and twenty in Cheshire.[12] This was just as well as there were only twenty six diocesan priests, with the Benedictines looking after Acton Burnell. This Benedictine Community which was to find its home at Downside, had sheltered with the Smythe family at Acton Burnell after the French Revolution. There was thought to be about twenty thousand Catholics, and the Annual Report of the CPSC for 1848 gives some first indication of the general school situation. Some of the parishes had poor schools, dependant on charity for their very existence. To help them the CPSC collected money and gave grants. The beneficiaries that year were Edgeley, Stockport £20 which was noted as having 70 children; Macclesfield likewise with 102 weekday pupils and 240 on Sundays; and Congleton £15 with 40 to 50 pupils. Also interesting is the collection list (which helped to provide the income for the grants) Bollington £1; Macclesfield £2.2.0; Nantwich nil (thus listed) Neston and Park Gate (*sic*) £1.12.0; Shrewsbury nil; Staly-bridge (*sic*) nil; Upton House (Birkenhead) £2.3.6. The CPSC Reports all contain long lists of individuals who support the financing of schools, some of them very generously. Later among these is to be found a collection of £2.2.10 from Congleton and a further £1.0.0 from the Rev. J.Hall of Macclesfield.[13]

Looking at these statistics two items are clear; Dr Hall's influence in Macclesfield and Congleton is outstanding. And in Birkenhead the Faithful Companions of Jesus (Upton House in the list) represent the arrival of the first of the Teaching Orders. Sadly there were no grants to school building in the Diocese that year, and, compared with other areas, a small number of three grants to maintenance. While the Committee of the CPSC did include the Earl of Shrewsbury, there were no clergy from the area which was to become the new diocese.

The report for the following year (1849) gives some details previously collected about Birkenhead (then in the Lancashire District):

Collections and subscriptions on half of gross amount from Lord Shrewsbury; school not fully adapted, there being only one for girls and another for boys, and no gallery in either, and no room for a gallery. Number of children increasing weekly. Number of children requiring gratuitous education, 306; number of boys attending school, 120; number of girls attending school 73. Are Boys and Girls in Separate Rooms? Yes.

The Report covers Chester, said to support the school with a charity sermon; and adds that statistics are needed. Total 125; boys 58?; girls 45, with separate accommodation. Congleton has 100 with a question mark. Edgeley asks for 'a charity of 2d a week for scholars'. This year support grants are given to Neston, £12; Macclesfield £20; Edgeley £40. And the collections coming in from the area now include (for the first time) Crewe and Chester. As the statistics are not the same for all the parishes, I think this indicates that not all returns were complete.[14]

A new development in the 1850 report is a list of Catholic masters and mistresses. A Miss C. Duggan from Stockport gained a 3rd class in the 1st Division and an augmentation of

£12.0.0.   She was the only teacher identifiable from the Diocese.   A building grant of £70.0.0 went to Chester to increase the accommodation in the school there   by 200. Support grants went to Northwich £20, Stockport £15 and Bridgenorth (?) £15.   The acknowledgements of money received by the CPSC showed increased support from parishes and among individuals named in Birkenhead are W.Hilton £1; W.Cafferata £1; W.Austin £0.10.0 and Rev. E. Browne £1.   While there were grants towards school books this year, none went to the Diocese.[15]

There was a change in 1851 of the representation to the committee with the departure of the Earl of Shrewsbury, and the Diocese was represented by Viscount Feilding, Sir Pyers Mostyn and the Rev. John Hall of Macclesfield.   Among Catholic masters Mr T.Crotty of Macclesfield and Mr W.McCurry of Middleton, Shropshire are listed; but no mistresses.

It is perhaps worth looking just once at the returns from the areas of the Diocese:

Shrewsbury	£2. 5.0	Knutsford	
Acton Burnell	£2.10.0	Lindale House	
Aldenham	£0. 7.0	Macclesfield	£3. 0.0
Bridgewater	£0.15.0	Nantwich	
Madeley	£0. 5.0	Neston	£6.14.0
Middleton		Puddington	£2. 3.6
Newport	£3. 2.6	Runcorn	£0.14.9
Plowden		Liscard	£4.10.0
Wellington		Edgeley	£3.17.6
Wenlock		Stockport St M	£0. 9.6
Chester	£5. 0.0	Bangor	£2. 2.3
Altrincham		Wrexham	£7. 0.0
Birkenhead		Holywell	£2.18.0
Bollington	£1. 8.0	Benarth	£2.10.0
Congleton	£1.10.0	Mold	
Crewe		Talacre	£6.14.6
Hyde	£2.13.11 [16]		

I suspect that the blank after Lindale House merely means that the FCJ Sisters had sent support in under another's name in the individual subscriptions. Grants were paid out to Wellington £15; Ness £5; Bridgenorth £15; Wrexham £15, Bangor £15 and Oswestry £10. Both St Alban's Wallasey and Edgeley got grants towards the purchase of school books. And to pupil teachers J.Kearney and W.McCormack, and Miss M.Barton at Macclesfield, £36.10 in all; and at Stockport J.Staffard and A.J.Marsden. The calendar of certificated teachers included Miss C.Duggan in Edgeley.[17]

Bishop Brown and Education

Bishop Brown was to be the last survivor of the Hierarchy of the restoration of 1850. By 1864 he was reporting with satisfaction in his February pastoral letter that 'now [there is] scarcely a Mission or even a Station . . . in which there is not a Catholic school'.[18] He rejoiced that teaching nuns now numbered not just the FCJ at Upton, but also the Sisters of Charity at Liscard, and an order of men, the Oblates of Mary Immaculate, were looking after Rock Ferry. Additional accommodation had been made in schools in Shrewsbury and Stalybridge. But he had comments about the 'school penny' and the reluctance of some to find it.[19] He had instituted a policy of giving an annual report on the buildings in his diocese and so it is possible to watch the gradual spread of schools and often see a parish begin with a school chapel, with the accent on education during the week and liturgy on Sundays. In this he was following something of a national policy among the bishops. The Provincial Synod of Westminster in 1852 had not only indicated that every mission should have a school, but extended this principle by preferring the establishment of a school before that of a church. 'It is the good school that secures the virtuous and edifying congregation'.[20]

What sort of schools did the Diocese have? They were mostly poor schools, often built without any state aid and surviving on charity. There was a struggle both to find and to salary suitable teachers. In one early moment the Hierarchy dreamed of church schools staffed by nuns, brothers and priests, and even thought that the great task of teacher training might be left within the Religious Orders. A knowledge of what was happening in some Catholic countries in Europe fuelled the dream, but English reality soon forced the bishops to fight not just for schools, but also for training colleges. Shrewsbury was fortunate to have the great college at Mount Pleasant, Liverpool on hand.[21] But the training of male teachers was to prove far more difficult, and St Mary's College, Hammersmith struggled for a long time to survive before becoming a well established influence in the Catholic schools.[22] The poor schools tried to get pupil teachers sufficiently trained to go on to college, gain a certificate and even get an extra grant for good qualifications. The girls were far more successful at this than the boys, and Marshall, an inspector, was to note:

> Our female schools are taught by a class so immeasurably superior to those who teach the males, that the final result is that they are a totally distinct class of persons altogether.[23]

And the other inspector, Stokes, was reporting in 1865 that Hammersmith was in danger of collapse:

> If intelligent well-conducted boys will either not become pupil teachers, or not complete their apprenticeship, the ruin of the training school [St Mary's] is but a question of longer or shorter time. . . .[24]

Much later in 1902 the diocesan report on Religious Education lists the results of pupil teachers and out of 66 names only four are male.[25] Like the new bishops throughout the country, Brown was in effect involved in creating a whole group of professional Catholic teachers, without which there would be no real Catholic schools.

The age of the pupils would probably be between five and eleven and the attendance irregular. Compulsory education was not even fully law in 1870, but when some grants became available to Catholic schools the question of attendance became a significant issue and a teacher's income could be affected. The picture is one of poverty and struggle. The first school in the Diocese was in Stockport in 1803, in what was then the parish of St Philip and James. Macclesfield followed seven years later, and a third school in Congleton began in 1826 in a cellar. There followed schools in Stalybridge, 1839, Neston 1840 and two years later in Liscard, Wallasey. There was a second school in Stockport in St Joseph's,1845. Then in a significant moment for the Diocese the FCJ nuns opened in Birkenhead in 1845, to move to Upton convent school in 1863.[26]

The CPSC, especially in the person of T.W.Allies, had negotiated with the Committee of Council for Education an agreement that inspectors must be Catholic, and that laymen must not be involved in religious inspection.[27] But it was as late as 1856 before any dioceses appointed such inspectors. And Westminster, Southwark, Liverpool and Salford were the first four. It is not clear from the directories, or remaining papers, when the first Shrewsbury priest became a religious inspector. We have a full printed report in 1874/5 from Canon Hilton (then at Hooton), which is to be found in an appendix.[28] He was followed in 1883 by Canon Clegg, who handed over to Canon Singleton in 1887. Later schedules of inspection are numbered, and would suggest the first was in 1864 or 1865, and gives a probable date for the beginning of the diocesan schools inspectorate.[29]

There was an annual collection for the CPSC which was sent to Allies until 1892, when Hunnybun took over the post. There were a few meetings each year to support the work of the Committee. From the reports it is possible to trace first the Earl of Shrewsbury helping to support the national policy and voice Catholic needs; then in 1851 Viscount Feilding, Sir Pyers Morris and Canon John Hall (of Macclesfield).[30] In 1857 Canon Chapman replaced Canon Hall, and he was to serve for many years as one of the Shrewsbury representatives.[31] Soon in addition to this CPSC collection there was one called Peter's Pence in Advent, and, as the bishop began to be concerned about educating the future clergy for the Diocese, another called the Ecclesiastical Education Fund. But most interesting of all is the annual Diocesan Missions Fund collection, as the yearly letters gave accounts of the new buildings, and usually there was an appendix of between seven to eleven pages giving details of the collections, parish by parish, and naming individual donors.[32]

By 1869 the Catholic Hierarchy of England and Wales was looking towards Rome with invitations all round to the First Vatican Council.[33] Bishop Brown could be pleased that nearly every mission had a school, even if it was a ,major struggle to maintain them, and to find suitable teachers. Perhaps as he packed for Rome he was not aware that the great struggle for the schools was only just about to begin. 1870 was the year of the Council; it was also the year of major legislation about education. Battle was about to commence.

PART 2

School survival after the 1870 Education Act

The English Bishops in Rome were engaged in the affairs of the First Vatican Council, but met in February 1870 to discuss the Education Bill, and Cardinal Manning confessed he knew nothing about it. He wrote to Gladstone for details, and received a copy of the Bill in reply. Gladstone also told him, while the Council was in progress, that the impression of what was going on in Rome was creating an atmosphere in which it was becoming harder to do justice to Catholics, whether as regards the Irish Land Bill or the Education Bill.[34] There was not a lot the bishops could do while in Rome, and it was left to T W Allies and the Catholic Education Council to meet the challenge at home.

The hope in England on the part of William Edward Foster, Vice-Pesident of the Committee of Council on Education, was to bring some order into a very mixed scene. The British & Foreign Schools Society, founded in 1808 was inspired especially by Joseph Lancaster, and most often supported by Nonconformists; the National Society of 1811 was the main work of the Anglican church and owed its inspiration to the monitorial system of the Rev. Andrew Bell. Both these societies had been in receipt of grants from the Council for the building of schools since 1838, and though Catholics became eligible the following year, they often lacked the basic requirements to be able to claim grants. In addition there were in the country a very considerable number of private schools. The Radicals of Birmingham in 1869 provided a powerful organ for national agitation, and launched the National Education League seeking a universal system, free, compulsory, and unsectarian, supported by rate aid and subject to public management. There was a major debate about religious teaching free from any doctrinal formularies. The Nonconformist were particularly aware that the village schools were almost exclusively Anglican in ownership and teaching, and resented this.[35]

Foster made a number of suggestions for rationalising the education scene, which were somewhat modified in Parliamentary debate. He considered that the time was not ripe for one overall system. A year was to be given for the voluntary bodies to fill the gaps in the educational provision of the country; thereafter Local School Boards would be able to raise rates and build whatever was needed to complete provision for all. Foster was strongly criticised by the radicals for failure to deal completely with the situation. The voluntary societies quickly realised that School Boards could prove to be an expensive challenge. There were about 6,000 National schools, 1,500 British and Wesleyan, and 350 Catholic. The Catholic community was the poorest, and catering for the lower strata of society, and with the least resources, it was facing the greatest challenge. Could it survive the threat of rich School Boards?

Bishop Brown returned from the Council in Rome in the summer of 1870 to write about the Education Bill, and join in the national attempt to consolidate Catholic schools to a sufficient standard to be able to survive, and also to try and cater for the children not yet provided for in the Catholic sector.[36] Time was short as now only six months was left for the voluntary schools to provide education where none existed; thereafter the situation would be assessed by local school boards, who would build their own schools where necessary. Manning was able to tell Gladstone in March 1870 that

> in the past three years we have opened in London 30 new schools, and have gathered out of the streets 3,000 children. Give me time and just proportionate help, and there will not be one of our children without a school.[37]

Denominational schools could still get grants from the Privy Council, and although these were increased, they were meagre compared to those which school boards could bestow on their schools from the local rates. On the 6th February 1877 Bishop Brown sent out his customary letter on the Diocesan Mission Fund.

> The great work of this year has been the erection and enlargement of schools, and in this we have derived most valuable assistance from the Central Crisis Committee, as well as from our own Diocesan Collections. Commodious and excellent schools have been built at Chester, Rock Ferry, Northwich, Mold and Altrincham. Additions have been made to schools at Flint, Crewe, Hyde and Runcorn. A building has been purchased for a school at Over, and the foundations of a school have been laid at Dukinfield.[38]

Year by year Brown continued to appeal for funds and to record the building and extensions to schools. On the 24th Feb.1876 he adds:

this year we have had to introduce a new system of expenditure, in consequence of the system of Religious Inspection of Schools which has been established, and which as the results most clearly show, is attended with the great advantage.[39]

He then enclosed with the letter the official reports of the visits and inspections of the schools by Canon Hilton. The annual collection was now no longer just one Sunday's collection in church at the beginning of Lent, but since February 1875 had to include the results of four door to door collections in the parish, known as 'out-door collections'. Some of these survived until well into the 1950s.[40]

Clearly the Bishop was deeply concerned about the debts on the Diocese, with the difficulties of supporting both church and school expenses. But since 1869 he had been dreaming of a seminary, with Newport as the first possibility, and in 1876 he purchased a farm near Shrewsbury which he titled St Mary's Grange, as both a residence and a site for the seminary. A reformatory had been envisaged since 1864, and an orphanage was seen as a necessity. The CPSC collection needed to be increased to cover the expenses of training colleges. And by 1876 Bishop Brown was complaining in his pastoral that collections were declining.[41] Seven priests had died, but he had 27 seminarians to support. The following year he noted that he had lost 14 priests in just eighteen months. The next year recorded the opening of a school chapel at Whitchurch, in contrast to the church of Our Lady's, Birkenhead now finished, and one at Rock Ferry opened 'after the design of the late Mr Pugin'. And an intriguing note added that the mission at Oswestry will reopen. Also in this year the Bishop was noting with pleasure that the Sisters of the Immaculate Conception had taken care of the Infants and the Girls in St Joseph's, Stockport, St Alban's, Macclesfield and St Alban's Liscard. Another note that year states that a pupil need not attend school once he or she has reached the 5th standard according to the Code of 1876 and is so certificated.[42]

National Catholic leadership; diocesan reflection

Cardinal Manning gave continuous leadership in the fight to keep the schools, and it was under his inspiration that the Crisis Fund was set up and very quickly raised £28,000 (and ultimately £390,000), creating 71,518 school places.[43] The philosophy on which the Hierarchy agreed was perhaps first expressed by T W Allies at the CPSC; he used three maxims; 'There can be no sound education without religion; As the teacher is so is the child; As the trainer is so is the teacher'.[44] And when the Education Bill was introduced in 1870 Allies agreed that compulsory education was necessary, and that this made denominational education a right, as any other compulsory system would be a violation of freedom of conscience.

> The moment this truth is made clear, the question of primary education   is settled for Catholics.   "Catholic schools for Catholic children" must be their motto.

It became a famous formula, and the bedrock of the Catholic response to the Education Act. Manning saw eye to eye with this, and it was a blessing to the Catholic community that two of the principal defenders in the metropolis were in such agreement. On the first anniversary of his consecration, as the second archbishop of Westminster, Manning issued a pastoral on Catholic and national education, commended by *The Times* as free from exaggeration, and he began his education fund to build the necessary schools.[45] In response to the 1870 Education Act this became the Crisis Fund for all the dioceses.

With his background and university connections, Manning was uniquely placed to argue the Catholic case with the government and especially with Gladstone. He was sufficiently practical to judge that some voluntary schools might fail as inefficient, and he restricted the crisis grants to those schools which were prepared to accept the government's terms. He was very publicly in dispute with the workhouse guardians who blocked access to Catholic children, and to orphanages who were proselytizing the Catholic poor. Eventually the justice of his argument was accepted and *The Times* agreed that the situation here needed attention. He argued against the local rates being used for non-denominational instruction according to the Cowper-Temple clause; 'An educational rate raised from the whole people ought to be returned to the whole people in a form of education of which all may partake'. So he saw the Board School system as essentially sectarian.[46]

In 1886 both Allies and Manning were giving evidence and working with the Cross Commission. They were arguing in favour of all voluntary schools. Manning had led a movement to make the schools an issue in Chamberlain's election campaign of 1885. This was followed in the dioceses, and the Home Secretary, Sir Richard Cross, had announced that his party, if elected, would appoint a Royal Commission to study the working of the Act and the voluntary schools. So it was very much due to Manning that the Cross Commission came into being, and was strongly denominational in character. As a member, Manning was able to explain the Catholic philosophy and argue the case for the diocesan schools. Between 1870 and 1880 Catholic schools had increased from 350 to 758, and most of this development had been carried out without Parliamentary grant because of the condition that grant was only to be paid if no debt would remain on the fabric thereafter. And as many schools were badly in debt, further extensions to meet public need would not clear all debts. Nationally the Catholic schools charged the lowest fees, and had the largest number of free admissions. The balance had to be made up from voluntary contributions from the poorest section of society. The reports of the Cross Commission provide both an appraisal of the country at 1880, and also a clear expression of the Catholic position and its philosophy.

In addition to his repeated appeals for finance for the schools through the annual letter on The Shrewsbury Diocesan Mission Fund, Bishop Brown was also asking his clergy to be involved in local elections to school boards, and in any election to raise the schools issue.[47] He also made it a policy in his visitations of the missions (parishes in modern terminology) to look at the school, and he asked twelve questions about the existence of a school, its size; are the boys and girls separated in the playground? evening or Sunday schools? When he reached the subject of school income and expenditure he wanted all details; income from endowment,   subscriptions,   donations,   school-pence, Government grant, charity sermons and other sources. Equally expenditure was to show interest on debt, salary of teachers, books and apparatus, repairs, fire and light, insurance, rent, rates and taxes, cleaning, and finally rewards and treats.   He wants to know if the school is under inspection, the number of pupils and their daily attendance, how often the priest visits the school, are registers carefully kept, the   date of the last religious examination; are there other schools besides the poor school, and is there a lending library connected with the mission?[48]

The clergy were expected to know what bye-laws were made locally in connection with education, hence the Shrewsbury Cathedral collection of Bishops' Pastoral letters includes a copy of the Borough of Shrewsbury Bye-law of January 1878 relevant to the Elementary Education Act of 1870.   In 1881 the Rev. Samuel Webster Allen offered himself as a candidate for a seat on the local school board.[49] In the same active tradition, the clergy in Shropshire met in 1906 and wrote to all candidates for the election:

Dear Sir, At a Meeting of the Rectors of the Catholic Churches of the County of Shropshire, held in Shrewsbury on the 2nd January, 1906, it was resolved that the following question be put to each of the Parliamentary Candidates, viz :- Will you, if returned to Parliament resist any interference with the right of Catholic parents, AS AT PRESENT SECURED BY LAW, to have their children educated in the Elementary Schools of the country in conformity with their religious convictions? The favour of an answer at your earliest convenience is requested by them, as it is deemed useful for their own guidance and that of others. Signed.   Edward John Stutter, Acton Burnell.   Austin Tremmery, Bridgnorth.   John Thompson, Plowden and Lydbury North.   Chichele Giles, Newport.   Firmin de Vos, Whitchurch.   Thomas Mullins, Oswestry.   Thomas O'Connor, Shifnal and Madeley.   William Ellis Jones, Wellington. Ambrose Moriarty, Shrewsbury.   Charles Canon Langdon (Dean)   S.S.Thomas and Stephen, Market Drayton;   To the last of whom it is requested the answer should be sent.[50]

Sir Clement Hill answered 'yes', which was deemed satisfactory.   Mr E.G. Hermerde answered at some length. And his letter indicates Catholic pressure:

> In answer to your question I beg to state that while I do not think that it is possible or even honest for me, on the eve of what I hope will be a final settlement of our educational difficulties, to give any pledge which would cover details touching finance and public control of secular education, yet, if I may direct my answer to the broad principle, I shall certainly resist any interference with the rights of Catholic parents to have their children educated in the elementary schools of the country in conformity with their conscientious religious convictions.   I shall be obliged if you will let me know whether the above answer satisfies your requirements, as I am receiving letters constantly upon the subject from Catholics.

Canon Langdon wrote that the answer was not satisfactory, as what was at issue was the parents' rights as at present secured by law.[51]

It was not surprising that the word was being taken up by the Catholic parishioners, as at least once each year they were getting a report in a pastoral letter. Each new bishop, as his predecessor retired or died, chose to write first about the education of the future clergy and the support for the elementary schools. In addition to all this in May 1882 they were told about a petition to the House of Lords, and after Bishop Knight had introduced himself in November 1885 on the education question, there was in December a letter from Pope Leo on the same subject addressed just to England.[52]

And the Shrewsbury Diocesan Schools Association published their statement of grievances against the School Board System.[53] This was clearly echoing the document from the Hierarchy. The parishioners were kept informed about Cardinal Manning and his advice to the Cross Commission, and in February 1893 there was an interesting document on defence against HM Inspectors of schools.[54] And in June the clergy were to consider a teachers' superannuation fund. In April 1894 there was a Hierarchy resolution on public education, to be followed the next year with two documents from the bishops on the same subject. November 1896 produced three memorials on education with Cardinal Vaughan spelling out yet again the rights of parents. There were three national letters in favour of the Catholic Education Council (no longer the CPSC) in 1898, 1904 and 1906. Meanwhile there had been a major encyclical from Pope Pius X on Teaching Christian Doctrine. There had been much lobbying in 1902 about the new Education Bill, and comments the following year on the Act itself. For well over thirty years Catholic schools had clearly been a major issue in the Diocese of Shrewsbury.[55]

At a national level the number of voluntary schools had changed. The Church of England schools, from 6,382 in 1870 had risen in 1903 to 11,687; the Methodist schools however from 1,549 at the start had declined to 452, while the Catholic schools had risen from 350 to 1,058.[56] This growth had been achieved by the most disadvantaged section of the English and Welsh society of the day, and in the face of the severe competition from the Board Schools which were so well financed. It was an achievement which owed a great deal to the leadership of Cardinal Manning, and the solidarity of the English Hierarchy, and not a little to the 'school-penny' which helped to fight off bankrupcy.

Specifically within the Diocese, during this thirty year period new schools had been built at Seacombe, Latchford, Upton, Chester, Rock Ferry, Northwich, Altrincham, Dukinfield, Whitchurch, Wellington, New Brighton and Middlewich, with an Industrial School at Stockport; there had also been extensions and additions of varying sizes at Crewe, Hyde, Runcorn, St Joseph's Stockport, Our Lady's Edgeley, Northwich, Liscard, Errwood, Seacombe, St Werburgh's Birkenhead, St Francis Chester, Edgeley again, and Altrincham, and through some alterations to the Church of St Laurence Birkenhead, a further room was made available to the school.[57]

It is difficult to cost this building programme at the moment. Some of it was done in an economical way so that in Sale, Latchford, Upton, Whitchurch and Crewe school-chapels were built which could be used on week days for school and at the weekend for liturgy.[58] It was also done against a background of appeals for relief for those out of work during the cotton famine, further famine in Ireland in 1879, famine in India and an appeal from the Pope for support for seminaries in the East Indies. The Bishop Brown Memorial school was opened in 1896 for the orphans, and a further orphanage fund developed over a number of years to found the St Edmund's orphanage in the Wirral.[59]

The 1902 Act did finally establish the dual system in law, and is judged by the historian of the roles of Church and State in English education, Marjorie Cruickshank, as 'thoroughly sound and constructive'.[60] The voluntary schools were now full members of the national system. But the accession of the Liberals to power in 1906 under Lloyd George immediately suggested a threat to this hard won position and the Catholic community viewed with some alarm the Education Bills of 1906, 1907 and two in 1908.[61] But the dual system survived and the Great War caused these threats to recede in the face of the conflict for national survival.

While the Diocese had developed a system of schools, it was left to the religious orders to found grammar schools. The work of the Faithful Companions of Jesus had been followed by other religious, Sisters of Charity, Sisters of the Immaculate Conception, the Institute of the Blessed Virgin Mary (also called the Loreto nuns), the Ursulines, the Sisters of Mercy, and eventually the De La Salle Brothers assumed

charge of a Catholic approved school in Nantwich.[62]   The
notable omission was any grammar school provision for boys.
This imbalance between provision of a secondary nature for
academic boys was true nationally, but in few dioceses was it
as absolute as in Shrewsbury. A move towards improving the
situation was the foundation by the Irish Christian Brothers
of St Anselm's College in Birkenhead in 1933, to complement
the Diocesan central school for boys, St Hugh's.[63] Formerly
the more academic pupils usually tried to win a place in St
Francis Xavier's School in Liverpool, and at the other end of
the Diocese in St Bede's, Manchester.

The Haddow Report in 1936, *The Education of the
Adolescent,* raised the whole question of appropriate secondary
education (as against all-age schools), and an Act in 1936
empowered Local Authorities to make grants of up to three-
quarters of the cost of reorganising voluntary schools. The
Act was permissive, not mandatory, and its implementation
was to vary considerably. So Bishop Moriarty wrote in 1936
that 'the ever increasing burden of the schools is still with
us'.[64] In 1938 he was finding in the work of the New
Education Act 'a friendly response on the part of most Local
Education Authorities, but a deplorable exception is to be
found in Dukinfield, Hyde and Stalybridge areas'.[65] And in
his preface to the *Diocesan Year Book* in 1939 he is concerned
that Cheshire Education Committee will not cooperate
'unless we concede 25% of the class teachers in the Senior
Schools'.[66] A further deep concern which he did not mention
at this time was that many of the schools were growing old,
and the Government was looking critically at the provision
and had a 'black list'. The raising of the school-leaving age,
and the provision of secondary modern schools (as distinct
from the grammar schools), combined with restrictions placed
by Local Authorities, left Bishop Moriarty gravely concerned
about the future of secondary education in the Diocese at the
outbreak of the Second World War.

At this time Monsignor Kelly of Liscard was representing
the Diocese on the Catholic Education Council together with
the Hon. Mr Clifford of Market Drayton, and a young Father

P.Rees was diocesan inspector of schools. There were eighty two parishes in the Diocese with six all-age schools in Shropshire and thirty in Cheshire, and twelve secondary or high schools. As the Second World War broke out, education building was suspended, but even during the conflict planning began for what was to become the 1944 Education Act of R.A. Butler. Once again the Catholic community in the Diocese would be called upon to face the rising cost of education and to fight for its schools.

PART 3

The 1944 Education Act

R.A.Butler became   President of the Board of Education in July 1941, and his negotiations with representatives of the Anglicans, Free Churches and Catholics are well documented. During this period Archbishop Lang was replaced by Archbishop Temple on the Anglican side, and Cardinal Hinsley and Archbishop Amigo by the young Archbishop Griffin at Westminster. There were about 9,000 non-provided Anglican schools in the country, and 1,200 Catholic, educating 22% and 8% of the population respectively. Any settlement had to take these schools into consideration.[67] The outcome, in religious terms, was that the Anglicans mostly opted for 'controlled' schools with a minority on the governing body, and Catholics for 'voluntary aided' status with a majority to defend the religious nature of the school.   Once this basic agreement was negotiated, together with the possibility of long term loans to face new building costs, the stage was set to look again at the necessary provision. All building had been suspended during the war, and in the early days afterwards there was a grave shortage of building materials. The first problem was to gain a place in a building programme, against much public need and occasionally against local prejudice.

The great negotiator for Catholic schools was an Assumption priest, George Andrew Beck (1904-1978), who had qualified in history at London University, and taught at St Michael's College, Hitchin, for fourteen years before going as headmaster to the Becket College, West Bridgeford, Nottingham.   He was consecrated coadjutor bishop of Brentwood in 1951 and was later bishop of Salford,(1955-64) and then Archbishop of Liverpool. From 1949 he had been chairman of the Catholic Education Council, a post which he held until 1970. His contribution was of major significance to the Catholic community, and the post war reconstruction and expansion of the Catholic schools in the country greatly benefited from his leadership and the good working relations he established with the Ministry and officers of the Department of Education and Science.[68]

At a diocesan level the schools commission was headed by Monsignor Curran with Canons Byrne, Ryan, Bell, Donnelly, Welch and Hazelhurst (secretary), assisted by Mr T Quirk, and Canon H R Kelly as the diocesan treasurer.[69] And by 1947 there were regular meetings considering the development plans, all the normal questions of school management and especially the provision of sites for voluntary schools. The schools commission looked like a part of the diocesan Chapter with a few assistants. Its character was to change considerably.   Within a few years the Commission was in the hands of Father P. Rees, who with his experience as a religious inspector since 1937, had a working knowledge of the schools of the Diocese. He was fortunate in being able to call upon the assistance of Terence Quirk, a Liverpool teacher who had virtually been the founder of the Catholic Teachers Federation and had become a recognised authority on education law and proceedings.[70] Father Rees was made a Canon in 1953 and a Monsignor (domestic prelate) in 1960. The schools commission became his life's work.

Having seven Local Authorities (Wallasey, Birkenhead, Chester city, Cheshire, Shropshire, Stockport, and Manchester for Wythenshawe) made negotiating difficult, but much of the work was with Cheshire, and Mgr Rees became a well known figure in County Hall on the Education

Committee. By 1952 Bishop John Murphy, was advising in his preface to the *Year Book* that

> the birth of a school these days is a most complicated affair. It first attains a flimsy far away look in a development plan. It is no mean feat to attain this chrysalis stage. From that date its growth remains completely arrested until it appears, still only in print, in a building programme, of a particular year. When that particular year arrives, the proposed new school queues up behind all the unborn schools of the previous year. And when the first stone is laid, it struggles for existence with the usual shortage of materials.[71]

The Bishop had very much in mind the Education Minister's circular 245 of 1952 which cited 'the need for financial economy, the shortage of steel and the temporary overloading of the building industry' as the reason for a drastic revision of the school building programme which effected both 1951 and 1952 building in the Diocese. Florence Horsburgh, the Minister, placed all these on hold until the previous backlog of school building was complete.[72] So while Bishop Murphy could welcome some new schools, only four were in effect to be built in the next few years. Coming to light in the midst of these difficulties were St Peter's, Baguley and Holy Cross and St Werburgh's, Birkenhead. To follow were St Werburgh's, Chester, St Columba's Secondary school, Wythenshawe, Our Lady's at Latchford (special agreement), St Alban's, Liscard, SS Peter and Paul, New Brighton, Sacred Heart, Moreton, St Hilda's Secondary school, Wallasey and a further school, now called Sacred Heart primary, in Wythenshawe.[73]

Circular 245 had specifically looked at the status of voluntary schools, and refused to include in a building programme schools

> to meet the wishes of parents for denominational instruction, unless the building of a voluntary school can be justified as meeting the needs of new housing development or the increasing school population.

There was a lengthy correspondence between the Minister and Bishop Beck who pointed out that local Authorities would oppose the building of Catholic schools in certain areas on the grounds that the children were already catered for in existing state schools. And, under pressure, the Minister promised that

> where it can be seen with reasonable certainty that the number of Roman Catholic families moving to a new housing estate will justify additional Roman Catholic school accommodation, the Local Authority will be justified in submitting such a proposal for inclusion in a building programme at an early stage; and I am quite sure you will find that this is what in fact is happening in areas, for instance in the North West, where the proportion of Roman Catholics is high.[74]

The result was that between 1953 and 1959 the building programme in the Diocese was greatly restricted, but there was future promise.

For more than a century the cost of school building had been a burden. The 1944 Education Act had made provision for long term loans (30-40 years) and a low rate of interest, and there was to be a grant for displaced pupils. In some cases it was suggested that in a new housing estate like Wythenshawe the pupils in question would have had to come from one specific area to qualify for the school's grant. The Catholic Education Council had to work for clarification in this definition to win a possible financial future for our school building programme. The problem was not immediately solved, and the Catholic Education Council was still dealing with matters arising from this issue at the end of 1976.[75] But even with this help debt was mounting fast, and the realistic question was whether the Diocese could afford to build the schools it needed. By 1956 it is thought that at least £860,000 of schools' debt had accumulated around the Diocese, some of it weighing very heavily on individual parishes.[76] The figure for Shrewsbury in the Catholic Education Council memorandum to the end of 1957 was

£986,000, with an estimated cost of future projects of
£3,735,550.[77] A primary school would normally be the debt
on one parish, while the secondary schools were at that time
debts shared among a group of parishes.

There was a national memorandum on the whole question
of finance in January 1959. At the Diocesan level Canon
Rees was assisted by Canons Nixon, Rigby and Mr W.
Livesey, (and eventually Mr J. Callendar as well) while Canon
Kelly, quite separately, was in charge of matters financial. In
the late sixties when Canon Nixon resigned from the
Commission a new recruit asked for a briefing and some idea
of the future plans.[78] Monsignor Rees had been looking at
the needs of three possible New Towns, Runcorn, Winsford
and Telford, together with the existing needs of the Diocese.
In terms of further provision of primary streams of education
this was estimated as a possible twenty-three forms of
primary, and forty of secondary. The question was asked as
to how much the Diocese already owed for the schools and
how much of this programme could be afforded? There was
no precise information as debts were known at a parish and
not at a diocesan level! However, it was eventually resolved
to re-assess the picture and gain a broader vision of the
situation. A number of commission meetings were spent
gathering information and trying to estimate how much more
the Diocese could afford to build. At this time, the
Department of Education and Science was promoting Middle
Schools and the idea of a three tier system of primary, middle
and top-tier schools looked promising for the Catholic pupils
who normally had further to travel for their secondary
education. However a switch to this three tier system would
inevitably involve further cost.[79]

The School Religious Inspectors

Father Rees had been our religious inspector from 1939 to
1945 and he was followed by Fr Murphy, the future
archbishop. From 1949 Canon C.Hickey, with a support
team, was the inspector until 1962, and was followed by

Canon Mooney. Father Tom Hartley came to the work after a course at Corpus Christi, London, in 1968, to be followed in 1973 by Canon J.H.Stratton. Under Fathers Hartley and Stratton the inspectorate changed its role, and became a support agency to the schools, the Diocesan Religious Education Team, with various centres opening around the Diocese.[80] All the schools were visited and courses were run especially for the staff directly concerned with religious teaching. In addition a number of books were produced for use in school, which were in circulation for the next twenty years. By 1985 the late Father Paul Glendinning was head of the team, assisted by Sister Marcelle. And a year or two later Canon Peter Morgan began his work in this field. The role of the inspectorate had changed completely, and there seems to be very little archival material on the school inspectors after the series of published reports at the end of the nineteenth century.

Towards a solution of the Financial Question

Bishop Beck, with the information collated by the Catholic Education Council, was aware of the problems of financing schools in all the dioceses of England and Wales. In 1959 he was able to report to a meeting of the Council that:

> A deputation saw the Minister again on 9th March when he said he had obtained the approval of the Cabinet to the following statement of intention, which, however, was still confidential :- "The Minister has been authorised — (1) to raise the rate of grant on voluntary school building work eligible as the law now stands from 50 per cent. to 75 per cent: and (2) to offer 75 per cent grant to new aided secondary schools needed wholly or mainly to match voluntary aided primary schools of the same denomination that exist now or schools built to replace the latter schools.[81]

A calculation suggested that the effect of the Minister's proposals would be a saving of some £22m to £25m. Instead of having to find £52m, the Catholic body would be responsible for about £30m. The 1967 Education Act brought much of this to a reasonable conclusion and at the Council meeting that year 'on the motion of Canon Emery the Council placed on record its deep appreciation of the work done by Archbishop Beck which had resulted in the 1967 Education Act, and its hope that he would for many years be able to continue it'.[82]

The increase in grant aid probably made the difference between continuing with the school building or beginning to opt out of voluntary aided status. After the Act of 1944 it had been the Catholic body, especially, which had sought voluntary aided status in order to preserve the religious nature of education in a Christian context.

Secondary School Developments in the Diocese

The legacy of the 19th and early 20th century had been secondary schools (mostly for girls) built by various religious orders.[83] There were only two for boys, both in Birkenhead, St Hugh's, which was a diocesan provision; and St Anselm's College, founded by the Christian Brothers in 1933.[84] By the 1970s all these schools had their traditions, and grateful ranks of past pupils. The first diocesan developments, mainly of Middle Schools did not present a major challenge. The main difficulty with these Middle Schools was that the existing primary schools, and the accommodation available, suggested different ages of transfer in various regions.[85] But real problems arose when the Diocese sought to implement the policy of the Ministry circular 13/68. This was a call for full comprehensive secondary education. What would the future be in such a scenario for grammar schools like Upton Convent, Holt Hill, Maris Stella and St Anselm's in the Wirral? These schools did not belong to the Diocese, but to the Orders, and many parents dreamed of their children going to their old school. There was a major conflict of interests between Government policy, Diocesan needs and local groups.

Regional Groups and Consultation

The nineteen-seventies were a time both of development and considerable local concern. It was in no way restricted to the Diocese and the Catholic Education Council produced a number of studies on patterns in secondary education. At a Diocesan level to meet these needs, there were eventually five regional groupings with the Wirral and Chester City the concern of Fr Burgon, Shropshire of Fr Bowskill and later Fr Roper; Cheshire Fr Marmion; the North East of the Diocese was looked after by Fr Prendeville, and Fr Russell was involved in Stockport.[86]   Secondary developments in Wythenshawe and Stockport involved the Diocese with Manchester and the Salford Diocese; and Latchford Warrington with the Liverpool Archdiocese. But in addition to the work of programming schools, the Commission was also mounting training days for managers, governors and head teachers. The finances of the Diocese were in a developing state with first Leonard Ross and then others looking after covenants, and Cathos promoting 'planned giving' in the parishes. Repairs became an increasing concern in 1974 with high alumina cement and concrete (known as HAC) causing some beams to collapse, (though not in the Diocese), eventually necessitating the underpinning of some schools, such as Blessed Thomas Holford School in Altrincham.[87] As Cheshire comprehensive schools began to grow, two, St Nicholas, Hartford with M.D. O'Connor as head, and All Hallows, Macclesfield, under W. Blackledge, became the flagships in the Diocese in opening up the way for their pupils into the world of Oxbridge. They had the advantage of a well supported and fully comprehensive system.[88]

There was much support for the Grammar schools of the Diocese and the situation reached boiling point in Birkenhead with a group, the Birkenhead Eduction Rights Committee, calling into question the authority of the Bishop of the Diocese to make provision for Catholic education. The extent of this protest and the manner in which it was made was a matter of interest far beyond the Diocese. In Birkenhead, the Director of Education, Reg Price, had only two selective streams for the whole of Birkenhead and on the normal parity system that would have indicated only eight places for the Catholic sector. However, as a result of all this agitation the Group negotiated with the Education Committee a full stream for both Upton Convent and St Anselm's College.[89] This has left the three Catholic comprehensive schools now in this part of the Wirral, St Mary's College, St Benedict's and Plessington, without some of the top academic pupils. A final failure in this area was the inability to found a Catholic comprehensive school on Deeside, which proved impossible with the two religious grammar schools in existence.

Organisation and Reorganisation

There was considerable parental support for single-sex secondary provision in the Diocese and this affected the first moves from secondary modern schools towards comprehensive schools in areas like Wythenshawe, Wallasey and Birkenhead. Eventually the numbers needed to make a really viable comprehensive school mitigated against this, and various schools had to be replaced by a single bigger unity. In the Manchester area both Wythenshawe, Trafford and Tameside had to take into account the schools in the neighbouring diocese of Salford, and the work towards a plan here involved some forty-six primary schools and twenty-nine secondary in an area of forty-five square miles.[90] A multitude of meetings produced no easy solution or single plan.

One sixth-form college, Aquinas in Stockport, was in sight of opening when the newly appointed head decided that the job was not really for him, and resigned. It was already too late for a new and well considered appointment and the head of St Nicholas's High School, M.D. O'Connor, stepped into the breach to win time for the governors and effectively launch the new college.[91]

Local and regional schools councils around the Diocese worked well while these issues were causing concern, and provided useful training all round in cooperation and shared responsibility. A great deal of dedicated service was given in the work of building up the secondary schools of the future. Sadly some schools had to fade away, such as Maris Stella, St Hilda's and St Bede's in Wallasey: Holt Hill convent school, St Hugh's, Campion and Ladycross in Birkenhead.[92] Perhaps none so spectacularly as the primary school at Errwood Hall, which years ago gave way to a reservoir.[93] Some schools achieved a new lease of life in catering for a different age group, so that St Winefride's Girls Secondary school now provides splendid accommodation for the pupils of St Joseph's, Birkenhead. St Thomas Becket in Moreton became a school for the handicaped under the LEA. In Wythenshawe St Columba's, All Hallows and St Augustine's grammar school served their time, and ceased in favour of St Paul's which became the sole Catholic comprehensive school there under the new name of Newman, and then finally changed to St Paul.[94]

Administrative Reorganisation

The Diocesan Schools Commission eventually appointed a full time lay director in the person of Tom Helvin who had worked as an officer for Trafford LEA, and had wide experience. Various priests worked after Mgr Rees, Fathers Marmion, Walton and O'Neill to carry the work towards the twenty first century. Meanwhile, in 1988 the Diocesan Religious Education & Schools' Religious Inspectorate had changed its name to the Diocesan Religious Team, with Fr Peter Morgan and then Fr R. Strange as directors and with some full time assistants.[95] Almost a decade later the two services were combined by Bishop Noble into the Diocesan Education Service with Michael Clarke succeeding Tom Helvin, and with a group of supporters taking education beyond the schools and into the service of the adult population too. By the end of the twentieth century the

Diocese was being served by a wide range of schools, almost one hundred and twenty, and was ready to move into the new Millennium.[96]

Retrospect and Prospect

For almost two centuries the Catholics in the area of the Diocese of Shrewsbury (roughly Cheshire and Shropshire) have struggled against the odds to create a Christian system of education. On many occasions the financial pressures seemed impossible, and the reader who considers the difficulties is left with admiration for the faith and commitment of those who fought for the schools. Many of the greatest of the philosophers of education from Plato to Newman and beyond have considered that education is basically moral in what it must first achieve, prizing a saint beyond an Einstein. It was reported in *The Tablet* (27 Feb. 1999) that

> of the top 20 state-aided primary schools in London, rated in a league table this week, all but two are religious schools. The tables compare the results of 11-year olds who took National Curriculum tests in English, maths and science. Of the top 20 primary schools, 11 were Catholic, four were Jewish and three were Anglican.

There is a lot of information now available on the academic success of church schools. But this also serves to raise the question of their religious success, which is not so easily quantified.

The strength of the Catholic struggle for the schools has lain in its constant philosophy that education is a right of parents long before it is in any way a right of the state; that education is a religious matter as it is concerned with the whole person, and not just with intellectual formation.[97] St Bonaventure said; 'he is a true educator who can kindle in the hearts of his pupils the vision of beauty, illumine it with the light of truth and form it to virtue'. Perhaps the only real

Christian educator is a saint, but teachers will take heart contemplating the Gospel and the problems Christ himself had in training his apostles. Over at least one hundred and fifty years there has been considerable unity of purpose with regard to a schools' policy among the bishops of England and Wales.   In a series of joint pastoral letters they have reiterated their philosophy regarding the nature of education, and continued to press for reasonable financial support.[98] The final achievement of an 85% grant for schools represents a reasonable settlement of 'the schools question' and the accent now is on the maintenance of Christian life in school communities.[99]

The answer to rising secularism had already been given in the Commons over a century ago when, in 1846, Mr Borthwick was advising that 'education wrongly imparted only has the tendency of making a criminal a more clever criminal', and by Mr Henley, in 1858, with a more biblical approach, saying that 'God has pointed out to us in the clearest manner, from Genesis to Revelation, that life is not to be gained [just] through the tree of knowledge'.[100] The ideal is finely expressed by St Thomas More who, in his scale of values, preferred 'learning joined with virtue to all the treasures of kings', and instructed the tutors of his children 'to teach virtue rather than to reprove vice'. He defined the end of education as 'piety towards God, charity to all, and Christian humility'. And his own education and virtue stood him well in the rising tide of Tudor despotism.

SOURCES AND BASIC BIBLIOGRAPHY

There is no history of education in the Diocese of Shrewsbury. We are fortunate in having in the Archives a copy of the thesis of Colin Anthony Humphries, *The Development of Catholic Education in Wallasey during the Nineteenth and Twentieth Centuries.* Med. Liverpool 1972. There are a few pages in *Education in Cheshire 1870 to 1970*, with a good photograph of St Mary's early school in Congleton.

For the Diocese we have the reliable study of Canon Abbott, *History of the Diocese of Shrewsbury 1850 - 1986* (1986), and the *Victoria County History: Cheshire III* (1980) edited by C.R. Elrington and B E Harris has the Diocese well covered by S J Lauder pp. 88-100.

For the general English scene I have used especially H.C. Barnard, *A Short History of English Education 1760 - 1944* (1947), and for the question of the dual system I am much indebted to Marjorie Cruickshank, *Church and State in English Education, 1870 to the Present Day* (1964). A.C.F. Beales article in *The English Catholics 1850 - 1950* (edited George Andrew Beck, 1950) is important.   For Cardinal Manning I have used Robert Gray's *Cardinal Manning. A Biograhy* (1985) and V. Alan McClelland, *Cardinal Manning, His Public Life and Influence 1865 - 1892* (1962), and also E. St John, *Manning's Work for Children* (1929).

The Archives has almost a complete set of *The Laity Directory* which very soon became *The Catholic Directory*, and with these many of the reports of the Catholic Education Council.   These complement the Diocesan year books, and they all provide a background for the many bound volumes of pastoral letters of the Bishops of Shrewsbury. The set in the Archives is complete, but I am grateful to Canon Pullen for the loan of the three volumes from the Cathedral which cover the period 1865 to 1908. They are especially interesting for the additional material included. The pagination is not always sequential.

Finally as an indication of what might be achieved, the thesis by David Lannon is recommended, *Bishop Turner and Catholic Education*, MPh. Hull 1994.

NOTES

1.   For the restoration of the Hierarchy, and the reaction in England see Gordon Albion, "The Restoration of the Hierarchy 1850" in *The English Catholics 1850-1950*, (1950) edited George Andrew Beck, pp.86-115.

2.   A.C.F. Beales *Education Under Penalty. English Catholic Education from the Reformation to the Fall of James II*, (1963) ; J.C.H. Aveling, *The Handle and the Axe. The Catholic recusants in England from Reformation to Emancipation.* (1976). John Bossy, *The English Catholic Community 1570-1850* (1976).

3.   J. Kitching, "The Catholic Poor Schools, 1800-1845" in *Journal of Educational Administration and History*, 1/2 and 2/1 June and December, 1969; this reference is from 1/2 p.5.

4.   John P. Marmion, "The Beginnings of the Catholic Poor Schools in England" in *Recusant History* 17.1, May 1984 p.69, with a reference to *Catholic Institute Tracts*, vol.1 (1843-41), pp.1-3.

5. c.f Beck, *The English Catholics 1850-1950*, p.366 in an article by
A.C.F. Beales.
6. Re Stokes see *The Tablet*, August 1891, p.228 for his obituary.
7. For Allies, see V.Alan McClelland, *By Whose Authority?*, Section
XIV, 1996; also Mary H. Allies, *Thomas William Allies (1813-1903)*
(1907). The former is mainly concerned with the process of his
conversion, the latter is a tribute by his daughter which reveals the man
but hardly touches on his great work in education, though there is a
chapter on the Poor School Committee.
8. Marshall has been studied by M.J. Illing, "An Early H.M.I.,
Thomas William Marshall, in the Light of New Evidence" in *British
Journal of Educational Studies*, 20 (1972), pp.58-69.
9. Langdale is in Gillow's *Bibliographical Dictionary of the English
Catholics* (1885), IV pp.118-123.
10. For some indication of what is to be found in *The Catholic School* see
Recusant History, 17.1. May 1984, pp.71-74.
11. The *Catholic Poor School Committee Annual Reports*, from 1848 are
available on microfiche.
12. For a history see E. Maurice Abbott, *Diocese of Shrewsbury, 1850-
1986* (1986), and also *Victoria History of the Counties of England:
Cheshire*, edited C.R. Elrington and B.E. Harris, the article by
S.J.Lauder, pp.88-100. There is a two volume manuscript in the
Archives, the work of Canon Slaughter in the nineteenth century.
13. These details are from the microfiche, 695 of the *Catholic Poor
School Committee*, using the first annual report of 1848.
14. ibid. for 1850, p.514 & 25.
15. ibid. for 1850, p.514 & 25.
16. ibid. for 1851, p.35.
17. ibid. for 1851 pp.88,89 & 93.
18. Brown's pastoral letters are in a bound volume in the Diocesan
Archives. The letter of February 1864 gives a useful survey of the
developments in the diocesan schools.
19. The 'school penny' was a much used but fluctuating part of the
income for the schools, and Brown regularly gave a general financial
survey in his pastoral letter before Lent. Those in January 1865 and
February 1866 are good examples.
20.Westminster Diocesan Archives, Res. of the V.A. 1846 *Decreta
Quatuor Conciliorum Provincialium Westmonasteriensium, 1852-1873*
(Salford, John Roberts, n.d.), pp.4-6.
21. See Denis Grady, *Notre Dame College, Liverpool: the Origin and
Subsequent Development of a Teacher Training College, 1851-1904*. Med
University of Manchester, 1980.

22. The report of Stokes for 1865; in 1857 more than half the candidates for St Mary's College, Hammersmith had failed the vital Queen's Scholarship examination. Stokes reported to Archbishop Manning in 1866 on the same subject that 'we cannot after thirteen years of increasing effort fill so much as a fourth of its rooms with candidates for the office of schoolmasters'. Reports of the Committee of Council 1866, pp.506-07. And the next year that only 15 students were in residence. For much detail see John A. Britton, *The Origin and Subsequent Development of St Mary's College,(Hammersmith), 1847-1899*, M.A.(Educ.) London, 1964.

23. Marshall to the Newcastle Commission; 4, p.177. Initially this was in his report for 1852, printed in *The Catholic School, III.1. Oct 1853* pp.9ff.

24. Stokes's reports for about ten years are a lament for St Mary's College and expand the information given in reference 22 above.

25. The results of the pupil teachers' examinations for 1901 and 1902 are given in the printed *Twentieth-Eight Annual Report . . . of the Examinations in Religious Knowledge* for the Diocese. There is a copy in a bound volume of reports in the Archives.

26. The subject of the article in this volume by Sister Mary Campion McCarren f.c.J.

27. Some of the details are in early issues of *The Catholic School*. And see Marjorie Cruickshank, *Church and State in English Education. 1870 to the Present Day* (1964) on the negotiations between Kay-Shuttleworth and the Archbishops of Canterbury and York, p.3ff.

28. Canon Hilton's report in the appendix is offered as an indication as to what may be found in these interesting reports in the Diocesan Archives.

29. It is only later copies of the Diocesan Inspectors' reports which are numbered. The Archives do not appear to contain information relevant to the inspection of schools other than these printed reports.

30. The large collection of *Laity's Directories* (which was soon tp become *The Catholic Directory*) enable identification of those from the Diocese working with the Catholic Poor School Committee

31. *The Catholic Directory*, 1857

32. Bishop Brown's Pastoral Letter, 22 April 1861, is a good example. In June 1857 he was writing about religious inspectors and the training college (St Mary's) at Hammersmith. Both January 1865 and Feburary 1866 are full of financial details. In May 1869 he addresses the role of the Government Inspectors.

33. Cuthbert Butler, *The Vatican Council 1869-1870* (1930) does not cover the bishops concern with the school question in England. For this see Robert Gray, *Cardinal Manning. A Biography* (1985) pp.237ff.

34. Gray op cit p.237

35. Marjorie Cruickshank, *Church and State in English Education* (1963) p.14.

36. A Pastoral of June 1870; copy in the Diocesan Archives.

37. Gray op cit p.239.

38. Pastoral 6 Feb.1872 in Archives.

39. The Pastoral of the 24th Feb. 1876 in the Archives.

40. From 1952 onwards in Wythenshawe there was the outdoor collection in St Anthony's to try to meet the debts on the schools, long before the church was built.

41. And in a note to the clergy, (of Nov.20,1876)

> the sums sent in from several of the largest congregations in the Diocese, where two, or perhaps even three Priests are stationed, are so small that they ought to be felt as a reproach to those places, when they see the amount published, and when at the same time they compare what they have given with the contributions of other far smaller congregations.

Also in a letter to the clergy, 27 March,1877, on the Association for the Propagation of the Faith, the Bishop notes that

> there is scarcely a Mission in the Diocese which has not, in one way or another, received assistance from this source, and it is most painful to see that, in some cases, those Missions which have received even large sums to assist them in their necessities do not contribute one shilling towards the support of the Association.

42. Pastoral of 9 Feb. 1877.

43. A.C.F.Beales, 'The Struggle for the Schools' in Beck (ed.) *The English Catholics 1850-1950* (1950) pp.372, 374.

44. Beales, op.cit. p.372.

45. Beales, op.cit. p.372.

46. Beales, op.cit. p.379.

47. Knight, Brown's successor as bishop, on the 11th Sept, 1885 wrote to all his clergy

> You will receive with this a packet of Statements printed by our Diocesan School Association relative to the grievances of which we claim redress. I have to request that you will do your best to distribute them, so that each of the men of your congregation may receive a copy. This may be effected by your out-door collectors, where there are such, or by giving them to the elder children in your schools to take to their parents, or in such other way as you consider most likely to secure their reaching the hands of all. I shall be obliged by your taking all fitting opportunities of explaining more fully the nature of these grievances, and the grave dangers with which our Catholic Schools are threatened by the action of the Secularist party.

And additional copies were available from the Secretary, J.H.Treston, Esq., 15 Lowwood Road, The Woodlands, Birkenhead.

48. The document on *Visitation Questions* is dated 1879 and printed in Shrewsbury. Section eleven is on the school. A copy is bound in-with

the Cathedral collections of pastorals before a letter to the clergy of 18th Feb.1879

49. Allen's handbill is to be found in the same collection, and is dated 1st Dec.1881.

50. This is in the Cathedral volumes of Bishops' Pastorals, December 1905.

51. The note about Sir Clement Hill and the reply to E.G. Hermerde are on what appears to be part of a carbon copy of a reply, with some further red underlining. Dec.1905.

52. Knight's pastoral of 19 Nov.1885. 'the question of our Schools on the eve of a Parliamentary election, which in its result may change for good, or for greater evil, the entire working of the present system'. This is a letter to the clergy instructing that the Resolutions of the Bishops on Catholic Education is to be read to parishioners at Mass, together with special prayers to be said.

53. The undated document of the Shrewsbury Diocesan School Association is next (in the bound volumes of Pastorals) to the Resolutions of the Catholic Bishops of England on Education, dated 31st October, 1885, and followed by another letter of Bishop Knight to the clergy of 11th Sept, 1885.

54. To the Clergy, 15th Feb. 1893.

> In view of the recent Instruction issued to Her Majesty's Inspectors by the Education Department, relative to increased requirements in School Buildings, Apparatus, etc., and of the dangers with which some of our Schools are threatened in consequence, the Catholic School Committee has offered to take note of any case in which such dangers are apprehended, and will endeavour to protect the Managers from unreasonable demands or undue pressure.

55. Pope Pius X. *On the Teaching of Christian Doctrine,* 15th. April 1905. This is bound in the Cathedral collection after a Bishop's letter concerning parish debts of 20th. Feb.1905.

56. The figures are tabulated in Marjoire Cruickshank, *Church and State in English Education* (1965) pp.191-3.

57 The year by year reports by the bishops of Shrewsbury on the Diocesan Fund, usually issued just before Lent list both school building, and in seven or eight pages the subscribers to the fund. Some information is also to be found in parish histories.

58. Again the pastoral letters often give an indication of the sort of building, and parish histories help to identify some of the school-chapels. An old print of one from St Joseph's, Sale is to be found among the illustrations in this Millennium publication.

59. St Edmund's orphanage was given some regular coverage in the pastorals. There is also a large broadsheet *Rules and Regulations of the*

Bishop Brown Memorial Certified Industrial School at Stockport, dated
Whitehall 4th Sept. 1885.
60. Cruickshank op.cit. p.88.
61. A.C.F. Beales in Beck (ed.), *The English Catholics 1850-1950* (1950)
p.385.
62. The Nantwich school deserves a separate study, and for a record of
the work of the Brothers in this field see Essay on the Christian
Brothers by N.D. O'Halloran in this volume.
63. The log books for St Hugh's are in the Archives; again see Essay by
O'Halloran mentioned in note 62 above.
64. In his preface to the *Diocesan Year Book*, 1937.
65. His pastorals and communications with the clergy indicate the
continuing problem of the schools.
66. Preface to the *Official Directory for the Diocese of Shrewsbury*, 1939.

> Last year, when sending out a word of preface to the Directory, I was happy
> to report a year of steady progress in the Diocese, and particularly I felt
> able to assure the faithful that the negotiations with the Local Education
> Authorities on the question of providing extra accommodation for our
> children in Senior Schools, were proceeding satisfactorily in an atmosphere
> of kindly co-operation. I am afraid I was over-sanguine. That hope has
> only been partially realised. In the large Boroughs we have met with
> sympathy and generosity, and agreements will, I hope, be signed in the
> immediate future.   Unfortunately the Education Committee of the
> Cheshire County Council which is the Authority for some of our larger
> towns in Cheshire and of the smaller towns where we have Catholic
> Schools, have repeatedly refused co-operation with us, unless we concede
> 25% of the class teachers in the Senior Schools. That would mean that for
> one building grant of 75% of the cost of the School we should sacrifice for
> the future having all our teachers Catholics where all the scholars are
> Catholics. This demand is clearly not in accordance with the spirit of the
> Act of 1936, but as the application of the Act is permissive an Authority
> can by its power over the purse strings refuse to enter into an agreement
> except on its own conditions Such action was not contemplated when the
> Bill was being prepared, and the Bishops were given assurances that no
> opposition need be feared from Local education Authorities in the
> application of the proposed Act.

67. Cruickshank, op.cit., pp.141ff and the tables, p.191.
68. Brian Plumb, *Arundel to Zabi — A Biographical Dictionary of the
Catholic Bishops of England and Wales (Deceased) 1623-1987*, (1987).
69. The information is from printed Minutes of the Meetings in the
Archives.
70. Terence Quirk, *Education Act 1944 and The Voluntary Schools*, (1946
?).
71. *Diocesan Year Book*, 1952.
72. Circular 245 in 1952. Its implications for the Diocese are
considered in a study by Peter Hilton, *The Catholic School-building*

Programme in the Diocese of Shrewsbury (1949-62). This manuscript is in the Archives.

73. The schools are listed in the Year Book of the Diocese, and by Peter Hilton, as above.

74. Hilton ms pp.15-16.

75. There were also to be serious problems of outstanding grants. Catholic Education Council for England and Wales, Report for the Year 1975. p.12. And a letter from R.F.Cunningham at the Catholic Education Council of the 6th Dec., 1976. Outstanding Cases of Displaced Pupils grant. With an enclosure of a letter from the DES of 24 Nov. 1976 on this subject.

76. Hilton ms p.18.

77. CEC *Report for the Year 1957*. Together with this see the CEC *Memorandum on the Present Problems of Voluntary Schools* Jan.1959. p.16 gives the net cost to the Diocese of present building and an estimated cost of future projects. Bishop Murphy was writing about school costs in his Pastoral for Lent in 1958.

78. When I was co-opted onto the Diocesan Schools Commission, I asked Mgr Rees for a briefing and was told I would learn all about it by doing the work and that finance was no concern of the Commission.

79. DES *Launching Middle Schools*. Education Survey 8 HMSO (1970)

80. From some of Canon Stratton's papers in the Archives.

81. CEC *Report for the Year 1959* p.12

82. CEC *Report for the Year 1967* p.12

83. Beck (ed.), *The English Catholics 1850-1950*, W.J.Battersby on "Secondary Education for Boys" and on "Educational Work of the Religious Orders of Women, 1850-1950".

84. St Hugh's was described as RC Central School (for boys), founded in 1921; celebrated its Silver Jubilee in Jan 1947 and flourished until July 1982. The log books are in the Archives. St Anslem's College has its archives in the Brothers' House. See Essay on the Christian Brothers by N.D. O'Halloran in this volume and cf notes 62 & 63 above.

85. See the thesis by Colin Humphries *The Development of Catholic Education in Wallasey during the Nineteenth and Twentieth Centuries*. Med Liverpool University 1972. A copy in the Diocesan Archives.

86. There are some papers from the local and regional diocesan schools commissions in the Archives.

87. c.f. The Archives' box on Blessed Thomas Holford. The head, G.Smith, managed to keep the school running smoothly while major work was carried out for a year underpining all the concrete beams.

88. When St Nicholas, Hartford, formerly a Secondary Modern school, opened as Comprehensive it achieved the full support of the parents,

and there was a total take up from all the contributory primaries in spite of grammar schools in the vicinity. Likewise St Alban's school in Macclesfield was well supported by parents, and achieved a quick transition to a full comprehensive intake. The contrast is to be found in the Birkenhead situation.

89. The details are from Provost Burgon, who worked in the area at the time, and there are plenty of papers in the Archives.

90. The Manchester re-organisation produced much paper work, and most of Canon Cahill's are in the Archives.

91. Permission was readily granted by the Governors of St Nicholas's school: Cheshire LEA were helpful, and the Governors of Aquinas delighted.

92. The Birkenhead re-organisation included in the discussion Upton Hall, Holt Hill, St Winefride's, Ladycross, all girls schools; Our Lady's which was mixed; and Blessed Campion, St Hugh's and St Anselm's which were for boys. These resolved into two Girls schools, Marian High (1976) and Healthley High (1970); and two boys, Corpus Christi and St Hugh (1970); with Upton and St Anselm's remaining independent. Then Corpus Christi and St Hugh's merged to form Bishop Challoner (1982). Finally, Marian High and Bishop Challoner joined to form the new St Benedict's in 1987.

93. Errwood Hall was the home of the Grimshawe family. Miss Dolores de Bregrin ran a school there. The family died out in 1930 and the valley eventually was developed as a resevoir.

94. St Columba's was the first of the large Catholic secondary schools in the Wythenshawe estate, to be followed by All Hallows, St Augustine's, a grammar school, and St Paul's. Columba's, All Hallows and Augustine's are now all demolished.

95. Very little of the documentation of the Diocesan Religious Education Team seems to have passed into the Archives. As it changes its role, it would be a good time to gather the papers and take some note of its history.

96. The Diocesan Education Service has a director in Canon Peter Morgan: diocesan schools manager, Michael Clarke: adviser for primary schools, Sister Catherine Darby SND: adviser for secondary schools and colleges, Ms Rita Price; advisers for parish and adult formation, Miss Paddy Rylands & Fr David Roberts: and co-ordinator for the CCRS course, Fr.Nicholas Kern.

97. Many years ago the Norwood Committee thinking about integration commented that

> . . . if anything is to be integrated it is not the curriculum that must be integrated, but the personality of the child; and this can be brought about not by adjustment of subjects as such, but by the realisation of his purpose as a human being, which in turn can be brought about only by contact with

minds conscious of a purpose for him. Only the teacher can make a unity of a child's education by promoting the unity of his personality in terms of purpose.

How this is to be considered in a Catholic school is the subject of studies like *Christian Religious Education, Sharing our Story and Vision,* by Thomas H. Groome (1980).

98. Marjorie Cruickshank, writing in 1963, thought that the 1944 Education Act was the reasonable solution to the schools question in English history. She looked at the fifteen years after the Act, but concluded on a note of warning that 'native empiricism may in the end find a permanent 'English solution' to reconcile the claims of Church and State'. op.cit. p.178.

99. The long history of European development in education is the subject of reflection by Padraig Hogan in *The Custody and Courtship of Experience: Western Education in Philosophical Perspective* (1995). Sir Alister Hardy (a marine biologist) established a research centre in Oxford to investigate the spiritual experiences of children, which has now become an established discipline in some universities. David Hay and Rebecca Nye write of *The Spirit of the Child* (1998). David Fontana and Ingrid Slack on *Teaching Meditation to Children* (1997). The days when Piaget ruled in the primary school now gives way to Kolberg on moral training and James W Fowler, *Stages of Faith: The Psychology of Human Development and the Quest for Meaning.* (1981). The Church in America had looked at its schools in Andrew Greeley & Peter H.Rossi's work, *The Education of Catholic Americans,* in 1966. There was a resumé in the *Diocesan Year Book* of 1972. After a decade there was doubt in America whether the conclusions were still valid and Andrew Greeley, William C McCready and Kathleen McCourt repeated the study and published *Catholic Schools in a Declining Church* (1976) with the conclusion that the schools were even more important. I did a summary for *The Clergy Review,* July 1977 LXII,7. The question of children's spiritual development is now enriched by a number of disciplines, and presents many opportunities.

100. From Beales's article in Beck, op.cit. p.368.

Sr Mary Campion McCarren — is the Archivist for the Faithful Companions of Jesus and was for a number of years the Chairman of the Catholic Archives Society.

Dr Peter Phillips — a priest of the Diocese of Shrewsbury, lectures in theology at Ushaw College and writes on both history and theology.

Canon E. Maurice Abbott — was the first Archivist of the Shrewsbury Diocese and is author of *Diocese of Shrewsbury 1851 - 1951, Centenary Record,* (1951); *A History of the Diocese of Shrewsbury, 1850 - 1986,* (1987); and *To Preserve Their Memory: Shrewsbury Diocesan Priests (Deceased) 1850 - 1995,* (1996).

Phil Jeffrey — when he retired, developed an interest in Local History and studied the subject for two years at Liverpool University. On joining the parish of St Mary of the Angels, Hooton, some time later, he helped prepare a parish history display and this led him to study further links between St Mary's and the Stanley family.

Dom Aidan Bellenger — is a monk of Downside Abbey and a former Head Master of Downside School. His numerous publications include *The French Exiled Clergy in the British Isles,* (1986) and he is editor of *South West Catholic History.*

Fr Michael Morton — a priest of the Shrewsbury Diocese, is a philosopher by training and is a former National Chaplain to the Y.C.W.

Dr Chris Boyle — taught history at St Anselm's College, Birkenhead and, after early retirement, has successfully presented a doctoral thesis at Salford University on the Irish in Birkenhead, 1800 - 1860.

Br N.D. O'Halloran — has spent most of his life teaching in various colleges of the Christian Brothers. He has a special interest in history and has made extensive use of the Congregation's archives.

Canon John P. Marmion — editor of this volume, is currently the Shrewsbury Diocesan Archivist and has been writing over the years on both history and education.